Why Religion Is Natural
and Science Is Not

Why Religion Is Natural and Science Is Not

ROBERT N. McCAULEY

OXFORD
UNIVERSITY PRESS

OXFORD
UNIVERSITY PRESS

Oxford University Press, Inc., publishes works that further
Oxford University's objective of excellence
in research, scholarship, and education.

Oxford New York
Auckland   Cape Town   Dar es Salaam   Hong Kong   Karachi
Kuala Lumpur   Madrid   Melbourne   Mexico City   Nairobi
New Delhi   Shanghai   Taipei   Toronto

With offices in
Argentina   Austria   Brazil   Chile   Czech Republic   France   Greece
Guatemala   Hungary   Italy   Japan   Poland   Portugal   Singapore
South Korea   Switzerland   Thailand   Turkey   Ukraine   Vietnam

Published by Oxford University Press, Inc.
198 Madison Avenue, New York, New York 10016
www.oup.com

Oxford is a registered trademark of Oxford University Press

Library of Congress Cataloging-in-Publication Data

McCauley, Robert N.
  Why religion is natural and science is not / Robert N. McCauley.
    p. cm.
  Includes bibliographical references (p.) and index.
  ISBN 978-0-19-982726-8 (hardcover : alk. paper)
  1. Religion and science. 2. Psychology, Religious. 3. Cognition and culture. I. Title.
  BL240.3.M43 2011
  201'.65—dc22   2011009751

1 3 5 7 9 8 6 4 2

Printed in the United States of America on acid-free paper

This book is dedicated to three friends

Tom Lawson, Dick Neisser, and Marshall Gregory
for their unfailing support and encouragement.

CONTENTS

LIST OF FIGURES

ACKNOWLEDGMENTS

I thank the American Council of Learned Societies, the Emory College of Arts and Sciences at Emory University, and Dean Robert Paul for research leaves during which I produced most of this book's first four chapters. Without the generosity and support of these institutions, this project would have taken much longer to complete.

This book develops and expands a position that I defended in a paper that I published ten years ago (McCauley 2000b). Just as I completed this book, I read a critical discussion of this paper in Barbara Hernstein Smith's *Natural Reflections* (2009). Here I offer extended discussions that take up virtually all of the perfectly legitimate questions that Smith raises, such as what my take is on theological enterprises and how they stand with regard to science and with regard to popular religion. I see no need, however, to respond to baseless or careless charges, such as, respectively, that I appeal to "innate intuitions" or that I include Neanderthal burial practices among religious phenomena. (With regard to the latter, it seems that Smith misunderstands what was in that paper—and what is in this book—a deliberately crafted *conditional* statement.[1]) In the third chapter I do address some of Smith's complaints about my distinction between technology and science. I do not, however, address in detail her various misrepresentations of my position, such as that I hold that "science is automatically, dependably, or even somewhat miraculously 'self-correcting,'" that "technology ... [is] an incidental byproduct of pure science," that there is "a radical difference in ... epistemic value between science and every other intellectual pursuit," and that scientific knowledge is "the only kind of knowledge there is or the only kind worth seeking."[2] It is clear in my original paper, in this book (especially in its third chapter), and in my other work in the philosophy of science that I do not subscribe to these views.

Parts of the following papers have been adapted for use in this book. I am grateful to the various publishers for permission to use them.

McCauley, R. N. (2003). "Is Religion a Rube Goldberg Device? Or, Oh, What a Difference a Theory Makes!" *Religion as a Human Capacity: A Festschrift in Honor of E. Thomas Lawson*, edited by B. Wilson and T. Light, 45–64. Leiden: Brill.

McCauley, R. N. (2010). "How Science and Religion Are More Like Theology and Commonsense Explanations Than They Are Like Each Other: A Cognitive Account." In *Chasing Down Religion: In the Sights of History and Cognitive Science: A Festschrift in Honor of Luther Martin*, edited by D. Wiebe and P. Pachis, 242–65. Thessaloniki: Barbounakis.

McCauley, R. N. (forthcoming). "The Importance of Being 'Ernest.'" In *Integrating Sciences and the Humanities: Interdisciplinary Approaches*, edited by E. Slingerland and M. Collard. New York: Oxford University Press.

I have been thinking about the ideas that I present in this book for quite some time. Consequently, the list of people who have helped me over the years is long. Lewis Wolpert, the renowned British biologist, published *The Unnatural Nature of Science: Why Science Does Not Make (Common) Sense* in 1992. Although I worked out my views on the cognitive unnaturalness of science before I discovered and read Wolpert's fine book, it has had a direct influence on both the organization and the content of this book's third chapter. Pascal Boyer published *The Naturalness of Religious Ideas: A Cognitive Theory of Religion* in 1994. We had begun what has, by now, been our nearly twenty years of conversation a few years before that. Pascal has influenced this book for the better in more ways than I can count. I also owe a debt of gratitude to Annette Karmiloff-Smith, whose 1992 book, *Beyond Modularity: A Developmental Perspective on Cognitive Science*, has influenced my presentation of some of the materials in chapter two in ways that will be obvious to anyone who knows her stimulating and suggestive book.

I hope that none of these three people will be dismayed by the ways that I have employed their ideas.

I have benefited from comments and questions from audiences in religion, cognitive science, philosophy, psychology, anthropology, and neuroscience, who have heard overviews or parts of this project in a variety of presentations at Emory University, Butler University, Villanova University, the University of Oregon, the University of Texas at Arlington, the University of Vermont, Kent State University, the Georgia Institute of Technology, Washington University, Princeton University, the University of California at San Diego, the Ohio State University, Queen's University Belfast, Queens' College of the University of Cambridge, and the Ian Ramsey Institute at the University of Oxford. Early versions of the overall position were also presented to the Deutsche Vereinigung für Religionsgeschichte at Johannes Gutenberg-Universität and in my presidential address to the Society for Philosophy and Psychology.

I am especially grateful to the School of Anthropology and Museum Ethnography and the Centre for Anthropology and Mind at the University of Oxford and to Harvey Whitehouse, who so graciously hosted me for three months in 2007 and who invited me to deliver a series of public lectures on the topics this book addresses. I thank the members of the audience at those lectures for their attentiveness, their penetrating questions, and their steadfastness. Special thanks go to Justin Barrett and Emma Cohen, with whom I shared the suite of offices at the Centre for Anthropology and Mind during those months. Their friendship and intellectual exchange produced for me the kind of visiting arrangements that every academic dreams of as they contemplate upcoming leaves.

I am grateful to Shiela Shinholster for her production of the figures in this book. She transformed my primitive renderings into clear, straightforward figures. I am also deeply grateful to the fine people with whom I have worked at Oxford University Press. Theo Calderara has been a patient, conscientious, and insightful editor, whose counsel has been incredibly helpful time after time. I also wish to thank Lisbeth Redfield at OUP for her assistance with dozens of matters of detail concerning the book's production.

Various people have read and commented on drafts of one or more of the chapters in this book, and I am deeply grateful for their comments and criticisms. They include Adele Abrahamsen, Charlotte Blease, Pascal Boyer, Emma Cohen, Marshall Gregory, Jim Gustafson, Joe Henrich, Tom Lawson, Robert Louden, Brian Malley, Dorinda McCauley, Charles Nussbaum, Paul Thagard, and Ryan Tweney. I am particularly indebted to Justin Barrett, who provided me with useful comments on the entire book. These friends' comments have helped me to improve this book in dozens of ways. The book has also benefited from the comments of anonymous referees, who approached their tasks honestly and fairly, determined to disclose any of the book's weaknesses yet helpful in proposing ways to eliminate them.

Conversations with Dan Sperber during one of his visits to Emory University were valuable in framing the ideas in this book's first two chapters. I am grateful too to Paul Bloom for his encouragement at an early stage in the process of writing this book. David Rubin furnished helpful advice about research on flashbulb memory since September 11, 2001. Whitney Taylor and Ali Madani helped me with scores of the details that inevitably accompany any research project, and Dorinda McCauley aided me in the production of some of the book's figures and the compilation of the references. To each of them, I offer my sincere thanks. I am also grateful to John Sitter and Kate Ravin, to Jack and Martha Fitzmier, to Tom Jenkins, and to Jerome and Melissa Walker, who have graciously listened to my ideas and encouraged my endeavors on numerous outings and over many memorable meals and cups of coffee.

Over the years, I have discussed various ideas in this book on repeated occasions with Adele Abrahamsen, Justin Barrett, Larry Barsalou, Bill Bechtel, Pascal Boyer, Emma Cohen, Bryon Cunningham, Robyn Fivush, Roberto Franzosi, Jim Gustafson, Joe Henrich, Tim Jackson, Mark Johnson, Tom Kasulis, Gary Laderman, Luther Martin, Dorinda McCauley, Laura Namy, Charles Nussbaum, Ilkka Pyysiäinen, Mark Risjord, Philippe Rochat, Jared Rothstein, Ted Slingerland, Dan Sperber, Paul Thagard, Ryan Tweney, Harvey Whitehouse, Don Wiebe, and Gene Winograd. Although none of them agree with everything I have to say, these friends and colleagues have helped me through dozens of intellectual thickets and provided encouragement along the way.

Tom Lawson, Dick Neisser, and Marshall Gregory, to whom this book is dedicated, have exhibited their friendship and concern for my ideas in this book and on countless other occasions for decades. Their unfailing kindness, encouragement, and support have enriched my life beyond measure. No acknowledgment that I can write will do justice to their liberality. I will be forever grateful to all three.

Finally, I wish to express my profound gratitude to my wife, Dorinda McCauley, who in the face of daunting challenges has never once looked back or complained about the time I have devoted to the production of this book. I am humbled by her courage and touched (yet again) by her generosity.

Why Religion Is Natural
and Science Is Not

Introduction

After more than a hundred years of books comparing religion and science, an author owes readers some justification for adding one more to the heap. Here is mine. This book compares science and religion in a way that has never been done before. And it has a surprise ending. Actually, there are many surprises in the final chapter.

I will offer a comparison of the *cognitive* foundations of religion and science, as opposed to their metaphysical or epistemological foundations. Some books comparing religion and science touch on cognitive themes, but, at least so far as I know, none makes cognition the focus of its comparisons.

My thesis, in short, is that religion is cognitively natural and that science is not. After clarifying both what I mean by cognitive naturalness and the type of cognitive naturalness that I have in mind, I will make the case for the cognitive unnaturalness of science and the cognitive naturalness of (popular) religion. Then I will draw out some of the far-reaching implications of this argument.

I use the term *cognitive* (and its cognates) in the sense that it is employed in the contemporary cognitive sciences. The focus is on *how human mind/brains represent and process information in perception, thought, and action.*

That sentence disguises in seventeen words hundreds of careers' worth of philosophical problems. What are minds? What are mind/brains? Why have scholars produced such an awkward neologism? How do minds and brains differ (so that we so readily use these two different words in everyday talk)? How are they related or alike (such that scholars have created that awkward term)? What is information?

What is the representation of information? What is the processing of information? What are perception, thought, and action? How should they be distinguished from one another? How are they connected with one another? Generating that collection of questions is only picking *some* of the lowest hanging fruit.

The word *thought* in that italicized sentence deserves some attention. Undoubtedly, *perception* and *action* deserve attention too. Because thought smudges into both perception and action, much of what I say about cognition holds for both of them, too. But, since most of the time thought mediates between perception and behavior, while I do say a few things about action and a few more things than that about perception, I have more that I can say with some confidence about thought. So the focus of the book will be on *thought*.

Cognitive scientists have advanced plenty of proposals about what thought is and what it is like. More to the point, nearly everyone working in the cognitive sciences presumes that thought comes in at least two varieties. I will capture the relevant distinction by contrasting what I describe as "natural" cognition over against the sort of slower, conscious, controlled, effortful, reflective thought that I will call "unnatural" cognition (largely by default). Natural cognition concerns the subterranean parts of our mental lives that constitute our fast, (mostly) unconscious, automatic, effortless, intuitive thought—the contents and origins of which can, not infrequently, prove a struggle for us to articulate.

I should stress that making such a distinction is neither new nor exotic. For example, dual process theories of cognition in psychology track this distinction fairly closely.[1] Plenty of people whose work predates cognitive science and plenty of contemporaries whose work stands outside of cognitive science concur. Deploying the language of the *naturalness* of cognition is not the typical way that scholars mark this distinction, but it is not without precedent.[2]

After introducing the notion of natural cognition, the principal burden of chapter one is to distinguish between two forms of it. The contrast I am drawing in this book about the cognitive foundations of science and religion concerns, respectively, unnatural, laborious, reflective cognition on the one hand and *only one* of the two forms of natural, effortless, intuitive cognition on the other. I will argue that the kinds of instantaneous, automatic intuitions about some matter or other that distinguish natural cognition can arise from either of two sources.

One source, what I call "*practiced*" naturalness, comes from having extensive experience in dealing with some domain. The most obvious illustrations are the sorts of good judgments that experts in any field can make in a snap, whether it is an engineer knowing what building material to use in a structure, a chess master knowing what move to make in order to avoid his or her opponent's trap, or a long-term commuter knowing how the fares work on his or her local transit system. Expertise in some domains is not at all rare. Hundreds of thousands of people in a particular locale may possess expert knowledge about the fare arrangements of their local transit system.

The second source is what I call "*maturationally*" natural cognition, and it is this form of natural cognition on which I will concentrate throughout the remainder of this book. Maturationally natural cognition concerns humans having (similar) immediate, intuitive views that pop into mind in domains where they may have had little or no experience and no instruction. Examples of maturationally natural cognition include speakers knowing how to say something in their native language that they neither have said themselves nor heard anyone else say before, people knowing what someone is feeling or thinking on the basis of observing his or her facial expressions, and even school-age children knowing that the slightest contact with some contaminant might be enough to contaminate them fully.

After distinguishing between these two forms of natural cognition, I go on to explore maturationally natural cognition in greater depth. I examine the fallibility of such domain specific "knowledge," the connections between maturationally natural cognitive systems and various conceptions of mental modules that have been advanced in cognitive science, and the fraught question of the origins of such cognition. I then discuss one particularly important maturationally natural cognitive system, namely, what cognitive scientists call "theory of mind."

Distinguishing maturational from practiced naturalness does quadruple duty in this book. First, it permits a comparison of the cognitive foundations of science and religion without having to settle whether all of the relevant systems are properly considered modular or not on one conception or another of modularity. The modularity of mind is the thesis that human mind/brains are made up of some number of comparatively isolated mental systems (modules) that each deal rapidly, automatically, and, thus, for the most part, unconsciously with some salient problems that all members of our species must solve in the normal course of life. Mental modules are domain specific. The tasks they are taken to address (depending upon the theorist) range from the analysis of inputs to our various sensory systems to such things as using language, recognizing individual faces, dealing with a nearby contaminant, comprehending others' emotional states from their facial expressions or, their tone of voice or their bodily comportment, and so on. I argue that maturationally natural systems certainly do not need to be modular in what has probably been the strictest sense proposed to date, namely, Jerry Fodor's account of mental modules.[3] Since it is a more inclusive category, however, *maturational naturalness* probably encompasses most, if not all, of the systems that have been proposed as candidates for cognitive modules.

Second, it follows that maturational naturalness also enables a comparison of the cognitive foundations of religions and science to proceed without having to settle those fraught questions about modules' origins. This is largely due to the fact that the emphasis in this comparison will be on the cognitive equipment that is typically up and running in human minds by the time children reach school age, rather than on how they are outfitted at birth.

Third, the notion of maturational naturalness provides more suitable grounds for comparing the cognitive foundations of science and religion than does the dual process tradition's distinction between intuitive and reflective cognition. Dual process theories differentiate between two sorts of cognitive systems or, alternatively, two sorts of inferences, between what I am calling "natural" intuitive cognition as opposed to "unnatural" reflective cognition.[4] The crucial point, however, is that further differentiating between the two types of natural cognition—practiced versus maturational—supplies the pivotal analytical tool for comprehending the important differences between the cognitive foundations of science and popular religion. Those differences can only be discerned by focusing on maturational naturalness, as opposed to naturalness more broadly.

Fourth, maturational naturalness also clarifies a technical matter in the literature of the cognitive science of religion. It is violations of the intuitions that our maturationally natural capacities deliver that inspire the notion of counterintuitiveness cognitive theorists employ in their theoretical treatments of religious representations.[5] It is also this notion of counterintuitiveness that I have in mind when I contrast the modestly as opposed to the radically counterintuitive products and processes of popular religion and science, respectively.

Having clarified what I mean by cognitive *naturalness*, I take up the issue at hand: the comparison of science and religion. Chapter three lays out my case for the cognitive unnaturalness of science. I want to confess at the outset that I commit the philosopher's sin of putting two clarifications up front. It may not be the most direct route into a topic, but it can forestall a lot of questions and confusions. The first clarification is that science and technology are not the same things. The second is that a couple of features of science *are* cognitively natural. The plainness of these two clarifications and what may seem like their obvious truth conceal the controversy that surrounds them, especially the first. I do not pretend to resolve these matters. Concerning the first, however, I do give a number of independent, cognitively significant reasons for distinguishing science from technology. Concerning the second, I emphasize that *all* of the cognitive differences between science and religion that I explore in this book are differences of degree. Some researchers have stressed, in effect, how natural some dimensions of scientific cognition seem by showing how infants' behavior manifests them.[6] I do not disagree. It does not follow, however, that *all* dimensions of scientific cognition are natural or that even all *important* dimensions of scientific cognition are natural or that science is remotely as natural from a cognitive standpoint as religion is.

After those clarifications, I take up the features of scientific cognition that do not come at all naturally to human beings. I examine the cognitively unnatural products of science, especially its radically counterintuitive theories, and, then, its cognitively unnatural processes. The latter concern the intellectual disciplines that science requires, the difficulties in acquiring and mastering them, and humans', even scientists', susceptibilities to error. The third chapter ends by introducing a subthesis, whose larger importance will only become clear later, that it is the special *social* arrangements of modern science that compensate (fairly successfully) for the limitations, prejudices, and mistakes to which individual researchers are prone.

I then take up the cognitive naturalness of popular religion (as opposed, for example, to some forms of theological thought). I discuss how much we know about religious matters (that we typically fail to realize that we know), considerations from natural history that point to religion's cognitive naturalness, and a theoretical framework about important cognitive foundations of recurring features of religions. That theoretical framework proposes that religions have evolved to cue a variety of maturationally natural dispositions that develop in human minds on the basis of very different considerations, both from one another and from anything having to do with the roles they might play in religions. I compare religions, from a cognitive point of view, with the wonderful devices that the great Pulitzer Prize–winning cartoonist Rube Goldberg drew. Goldberg's devices used a diverse collection of common items, frequently in ways not connected with any standard functions that they might have, to carry out some mundane task in some spectacularly unnecessary and complicated fashion.

Following the same outline I use to analyze science, I examine, in order, the cognitively natural products of popular religion before turning to its cognitively natural processes. I maintain that popular religions' cognitive products involve only *modestly* counterintuitive representations, *at most*, that are mainly the results of *normal* variations in the operations of garden-variety, domain-specific, maturationally natural, cognitive equipment. I hold that maturationally natural systems may not start out being domain specific, but that is certainly what they look like in their maturity. If that is true, then the cognitive processes that religions recruit will prove every bit as diverse as the various maturationally natural systems they engage—different systems, different processes. Consequently, I review two examples: language and the management of contaminants. I then explore theory of mind and its contributions to the cognitive processes surrounding myth, ritual, and doctrines.

So what if religion is natural and science is not? What are the implications for religion, for science, and for society as a whole? The seven conclusions that I draw from this unprecedented cognitive comparison of science and religion may not match the surprise endings of O. Henry's short stories, but they do aim to shatter some conventional wisdom. Perhaps not all seven will astonish every reader, but I am confident that most readers will find some to be surprising. At the risk of undoing the suspense, here are those seven conclusions, unadorned and unelaborated:

- Traditional comparisons of science and religion are cognitively misbegotten.
- Theological incorrectness is inevitable.
- Science poses no threat to the persistence of religion.
- Relevant disabilities will render religion baffling.
- Science is inherently social.
- Science depends more fundamentally on institutional support than religion does.
- Science's continued existence is fragile.

Nothing in this book is intended to provide an exhaustive theory either of religion or of science or of cognition. On the latter front, for example, I discuss important approaches in cognitive science concerning the embodied (thus, among other things, the emotion-laden) and the (physically and culturally) embedded character of human perception, thought, and action. Because I do not take either approach up systematically or at length, it does not follow that I am either uninterested or unfriendly to these approaches. (Careful reading will disclose more than one place in this book where I do take up findings such approaches inspire.) I have no doubt that current and future discoveries from those quarters will only enrich our understanding of the issues this book addresses. It does follow directly that nothing I say in this book is intended to provide an exhaustive account even of the cognitive dimensions of religion or of science. Over our species' history, the division of labor has mostly worked to our advantage.

Since the comparison is unprecedented, this is only a beginning.

Natural Cognition

Knowing It All at Once

People know more than they realize. Anthony Trollope exquisitely illustrates the truth of this claim in the twenty-fourth chapter of *Barchester Towers*, where he shows, in an exchange between two characters, Mr. Quiverful and Mr. Slope, how we can, sometimes, come to understand exceedingly complicated matters in a flash, as when lightning suddenly illuminates everything around us at night. The circumstances of this exchange are complicated. Bear with me, though, since spelling them out will reveal both how much Mr. Quiverful knows on the slimmest of evidence and how astonishing it is that he can know it all so fast.

Mr. Quiverful, the vicar of Puddingdale, is the struggling father of fourteen children.[1] Mr. Slope is the conniving chaplain of a feckless bishop, on whose behalf he offers Quiverful a position that would substantially improve his circumstances. Despite its obvious benefits, Quiverful is only willing to accept the position if it has already been offered to another character, Mr. Harding. When Slope assures him that Harding has declined the position, Quiverful accepts and begins planning his move.

Unfortunately, in the meantime, Slope discovers that if he can maneuver Harding to take the position he can turn the situation to his own advantage. So he pays a second visit to Quiverful—this time to convince him to decline the appointment.

What Slope wants to accomplish is tactically difficult, for it is thoroughly contrary to Mr. Quiverful's interests. Quiverful can barely manage presentable clothes to take his fourteen children to his own church's services. In anticipation of his improved circumstances, Quiverful has already agreed with an auctioneer to sell his farm, requested a curate to replace him at Puddingdale, and ordered new outfits for his wife and three eldest daughters.

Slope's task is also rhetorically difficult. Not only is he acting without the bishop's knowledge, but also he is acting contrary to his wishes and to those of his formidable wife, who has been Slope's patroness. *She* is the one who had suggested Quiverful for the position. Slope must ensure that this conversation *not* result in Quiverful thinking that either the bishop or his wife desires that he surrender the appointment. To attain his various ends, the bishop's chaplain not only is but also must be one of the slipperiest of Slopes.

If anyone is up to these challenges, it is he. Slope has schemed and maneuvered and easily talked his way into plenty of good situations and out of some bad ones. For my purposes, what is significant is Trollope's description of what and how much Mr. Quiverful knows, and of how and how fast he knows it. Trollope says of their second conversation that as Slope began to speak, Mr. Quiverful "saw at a glance that his brilliant hopes were to be dashed to the ground and that his visitor was now there for the purpose of unsaying what on his former visit he had said. There was something in the tone of voice, something in the glance of the eye, which told the tale. Mr. Quiverful knew it all at once."[2]

Slope had hardly begun to speak before Quiverful "saw at a glance" that his appointment was not to be. Quiverful had not consciously searched for evidence to this effect. He had *sensed* his fate from Slope's tone of voice and the look in his eye, long before he might have explicitly inferred it from any statements the bishop's wily chaplain would make. Slope's consummate tactical and rhetorical skills notwithstanding, he had hardly spoken a word before Quiverful had ascertained his aim, appreciated its consequences, recognized his own powerlessness, and, thus, had begun, already, to realize the prudence in comporting himself humbly, even in the face of Slope's mendacity and injustice. Quiverful knew *all at once* that his hopes and plans were crushed.

The intuitive recognition Quiverful displays—certain, detailed, and instantaneous—serves as a useful benchmark when thinking about what I am referring to as the *naturalness* of cognition. The more transparent a thought's (presumed) soundness, the more elaborated the judgment, and the faster it dawns, the more natural is the cognition involved. By contrast, conjectures that we approve only after we have spent some time reflecting on them and carefully weighing the evidence for and against them are comparatively unnatural. Natural cognition is what comes to all of us easily.[3] It takes little, if any, work.

These preliminary comments should already signal why *all* of the assessments of the naturalness or unnaturalness of cognition in this book presume the qualifier "comparatively" (even if they do not always explicitly include it). This brief gloss on the naturalness of Mr. Quiverful's insight appeals to three different dimensions, each of which varies continuously. Our cognition can come (1) with more or less obviousness or transparency, (2) in more or less detail, and (3) more or less quickly. So, not only are these evaluations *not* all or nothing, they also do not turn on some precise metric by which we can measure cognitive naturalness. Claims about the naturalness of various elements of cognition are only estimates, sometimes rough estimates, that arise from weighing numerous considerations simultaneously.

Dealing methodically with such complex problems of multiple constraint satisfaction often involves balancing many more dimensions than we can readily keep in mind. Still, in familiar realms humans usually do not find such problems too hard, especially when they are posed comparatively and especially when the comparisons are stark. So, for example, the success of numerous car manufacturers worldwide testifies to the fact that although considerations of price, size, design, comfort, handling, mileage, reliability, available features, the ease and cost of maintenance, and more can figure in people's decisions about what car to buy, most people manage to make such decisions without too much trouble.[4] While all of my assessments of the naturalness or unnaturalness of cognition are either explicitly or implicitly comparative, not all of those comparisons are stark. For example, both scientific cognition and religious cognition explain and predict. Such overlap, however, is the exception, not the rule. Even where there is overlap, we can often ascertain differences that are systematic and incline toward cognitive naturalness in the case of religion and toward cognitive unnaturalness in the case of science.

So far, then, I have suggested that natural cognition occurs when, straightaway and without reflection, human beings seem to grasp something complex about their environment. They immediately possess intuitions about some matter that are far more elaborate and refined than the readily accessible evidence supports. To say that these intuitions are insufficiently supported by the available evidence isn't the half of it. Often it is not obvious what evidence suggested them. (Trollope's account intimates that the one thing Mr. Quiverful is not completely sure about is what exactly it was about Slope's demeanor that enabled him to infer what he did so readily.) Such *intuition* is the principal manifestation of natural cognition in our mental lives.

Transparent Knowledge

As a first pass, then, beliefs and actions that are intuitive, familiar, and held or done without reflection qualify as cognitively natural. Typically, such beliefs and the actions associated with them are unremarkable and seem part of the normal course of events. Expecting a salesperson on the other end of the line might be a "natural" thing to think when the telephone rings during dinner. Closing the window is the "natural" thing to do when you feel a cold draft. Often, without hearing either what people have to say or the tone of voice in which they speak, mere glimpses of their postures and faces will elicit intuitions about their emotional states.[5] That this is generally true even when people have not met before and even when they are from different cultures only provides further grounds for deeming such perceptual capacities natural.

What I referred to earlier as the "soundness" of cognitively natural beliefs is often only apparent. Although judgments deemed natural in this sense do not require reflection, they do not preclude it either. For example, people might reflect at length on the principles that inform their systems of etiquette. Subsequent inquiry may show that intuitive beliefs about etiquette fail to square with other principles to which we subscribe. Thus, we might detect the tension between preferring that males hold doors for females and affirming the equality of the sexes. Participants in psychological experiments are sometimes startled by their inability to formulate persuasive arguments for moral convictions that they have previously found intuitively and emotionally compelling.[6] In other domains reflection may simply reveal that our intuitive beliefs are false. People's intuitions about basic mechanics, concerning such things as predicting the paths of projectiles, are frequently mistaken.[7]

The opening sections of the next chapter will further scrutinize the apparent soundness of perceptual judgments and intuitive beliefs. For now, though, it is the respect in which their (presumed) soundness is not apparent that will concern us. Often *what* we seem to know and *that* we seem to know it are *so* transparent that we take no notice of either. It is as a result of a cognitive accomplishment, although not a conscious one, that we immediately grab for the glass rolling toward the edge of the table, yet it involves neither summoning what we can articulate about the law of gravity and about the comparative brittleness of glass nor explicitly drawing the requisite inferences. Such intuitive knowledge is transparent in the related sense that it is often not only what we know the world with but what we perceive the world through. The operative assumptions in each case constitute our general background knowledge, which both frames and enables our transactions within our physical and social environments.[8] Frequently, knowledge this transparent becomes, in effect, invisible.

People fail to see just how much they know, because they know it so effortlessly and instantly. (It feels to them like they have known it all along.) They also fail to realize how much they know, because, generally, they are aware of such knowledge only when circumstances violate their expectations. Thankfully, such events are infrequent; otherwise, we would have great difficulty getting by. Glasses do fall to the floor when they roll off of tables. We almost always recognize our family members and old friends. Violations of our expectations probably arise most frequently in linguistic exchanges. Sometimes people's comments simply "do not compute," and we must request clarification. We know the language our conversational partners speak, how it sounds, what constitutes a sensible response to the last thing that we said, and sometimes we even know exactly what they will say next. Largely unconscious expectations structure how we understand the world. Transgressions of those expectations stick out.

Humans also tend to overlook the fact that they know things that they have known for a long time. People seldom think about the fact that they know that rigid objects retain their shapes when they are moved, that the offspring of two creatures of the same type is also a creature of that type, or that one way of asking an English speaker how far it is to the moon is to utter the question, "How far is it to the moon?" That such things are true seems obvious. What is not obvious most of the time, though, is that it is also perfectly appropriate to say that we *know* all of these things—certainly in the nontechnical ways we ordinarily talk about knowledge and certainly if we have been made aware of the fact that we do know these things.

What is also not obvious is just how many of these transparent things we know. One way to glimpse the extent of such knowledge is to begin to compile a list of arrangements that would violate our expectations. The easiest way to do this is to start itemizing our "negative" knowledge. We know that water does not flow uphill, that hammers do not breathe, that we do not eat through our ears, that giraffes have no opinions about the World Trade Organization, that newborns do not write novels, that for me to get three pieces of candy when you get only one is neither an equal division of the candy nor, all else being equal, is it fair—and on and on and on. The possibilities seem endless.

But even this is not all. People also tend to forget that they know the things that they never forget. People know that they have two legs and feet, that their shoes go on their feet, and that they should not step on strangers' feet. People just as readily forget that they know the things that they never forget how to do, even when those actions are quite complicated. For example, they know how to put their shoes on and tie them, they know how to walk across variable terrain, and most children (of a certain age, at least) know that if they step on strangers' feet, they have committed a mistake that calls for some form of redress—whether they can say much about it or not, let alone whether they have mastered the social skill of apology.

Cognition as Embodied and Embedded

Developing such skills and carrying out such actions as putting on our shoes and tying them, walking across variable terrain, and, especially, recognizing our lapses in etiquette and using social skills to remedy them depend on extensive and sophisticated cognitive processing. When actions become automatic, the underlying cognitive operations and, arguably, the actions themselves also qualify as cognitively natural. Patricia Churchland argues that the theory of evolution counsels that more sophisticated forms of animal cognition, including that of humans, have their roots in the systems and processes that enable animals to move through irregular and often dangerous environments.[9]

Theorists from the cognitive sciences have extended Churchland's insight in two related directions. First, they argue that understanding how the mind works requires acknowledging that every type of mentality that we can study, including our own, is embodied in material systems and that our bodily experiences shape our ideas.[10] One kind of evidence that supports the latter is the pervasiveness of metaphors that appeal to the physical, spatial, and bodily when we talk about abstractions. We speak readily (and transparently) about "the *force* of an argument" and "the *weight* of considerations," about "the *spread* of liberty" and a comment's "*containing* some truth," and about how marriage can be "a *balancing* act," "a *tug of war*," or "a *journey*."[11] Neuroscientists and cognitive psychologists cite clinical and experimental evidence suggesting, first, that virtually all of our cognitive operations at the conscious level involve intimate links to emotional states and, second, that unconscious features of cognition are closely connected to our perceptual and motor capacities.[12] In short, they stress that cognition is embodied.

The second extension focuses on the fact that cognition is also embedded. The bodies in which minds reside always operate in one or another context. Humans' physical and social environments often play a pivotal role in their cognitive successes. This can occur without human artifice, as when a hiker selects a naturally occurring feature, perhaps a pair of particularly large boulders, as a landmark. Far more often, though, humans enhance their cognitive powers by exercising their technical intelligence to alter their physical environments (for example, by installing periodic markers along a trail) or by exercising some combination of their technical and social intelligence to organize their social environments (for example, by constructing buildings for particular purposes, such as libraries, factories, and homes).

Structuring physical and social environments are not uniquely human accomplishments. Chimpanzees fabricate tools and cooperate (modestly) in hunts. Human toolmaking and environment-structuring, however, so exceed these capacities in other species that their study necessitates specialized sciences such as anthropology, sociology, economics, and political science.

Cognitive accomplishments are not confined to what transpires in people's heads. Human beings regularly construct artifacts to help them think. Try, for example, multiplying two four-digit numbers without the aid of a pencil and paper or a calculator. Among the vast array of humans' tools it was the development of writing and associated technologies (around five thousand years ago) that drove the most profound changes in humans' cognitive abilities. By imposing coded, symbolic structures on things in the environment, we accord them roles in our cognitive processing and thus transform these items into enduring cognitive accessories. Our writings usually last far longer than our thoughts. Our writings can certainly contain far more detail than we can recall. For some kinds of problems such external cognitive prostheses—from marks on a stick to pencil and paper to the newest supercomputers—are not optional equipment but *integral* components of the requisite cognitive machinery.[13] As Matthew Day has noted, the solutions to some problems may, quite literally, be *unthinkable* without them.[14]

Humans also structure their environments to support their cognitive ends. Such active structuring might be said to constitute an extension of our mentality into the external environment—both physical and social.[15] Environments ordered *by* or *as* tools that we have crafted to help us think provide scaffolding for cognitive exploits that would otherwise be not just unattainable but even unimaginable. Perhaps the best illustrations are the ways humans off-load information into their environments in order to avoid having to remember so much. Prior to the invention of writing, this was usually an irregular and haphazard process. For the past few thousand years, though, once we got smart enough to write out receipts, "to-do" lists, and directions—not to mention our best stories, ideas, and speculations—we have come to rely overwhelmingly on the technology of writing. Organizing the contents of our basement shelves may be a far more mundane way of unburdening our memories, but it is no less effective. To appreciate how cognitively valuable such arrangements can be, consider the problems that changing residences can present, especially for the elderly. Leaving their homes, for which they have well-developed spatial memories that they use to get through a day, for new quarters for which they do not possess such knowledge is disruptive at best and can appear to have induced dementia virtually overnight.

Or take grocery shopping. Keeping a grocery list stores information externally. Positioning a pad and pencil for that list prominently in the kitchen increases the probability that the list is both accurate and current. Situating it close to the door improves the chances that people doing the grocery shopping will remember to take the list along. When the entire system works, the shoppers' mnemonic skills rely on structures outside of their craniums.

We also manipulate our social environment. The grocery list not only absolves everyone from recalling what needs to be purchased, but, posted as it is, it also distributes at least some of the responsibility for keeping the list. Instead of individuals making separate lists that the shoppers must compile, household members construct the list collaboratively.

Humans not only live in a world of artifacts and architecture; they also participate in a variety of social arrangements. They are intimates with families and friends, members of corporations and clubs, and citizens of neighborhoods and nations. These social arrangements enable people to manage a host of cognitive challenges collectively, from households producing grocery lists to insurance companies aiding customers to crews sailing vessels across the seas.[16] Many systems in the modern world are so vast and so complex that their effectiveness depends on distributing the requisite knowledge across armies (sometimes literally) of individuals acting in coordination.

Active coordination, however, is not always necessary. Sometimes, as with well-run markets, the knowledge (for example, of the value of some good or service) emerges over time from local, noncoordinated actions of numerous individuals, none of whom possess that knowledge beforehand. Social divisions of cognitive labor—scribes, craftsmen, physicians, priests, and so on—existed for thousands of years before manufacturers in the Industrial Revolution began to apply similar principles to the production of material artifacts. The birth of agriculture and cities presented human beings with cognitive challenges the solutions to which depend fundamentally upon social organizations that ensure the distribution of problem solving, knowledge, and responsibility. The resulting networks structure people's physical and social environments and build complex dynamic systems that provide solutions to cognitive problems larger than any individual or even a group of individuals can comprehend or manage.[17] Surely, one of the verdicts of the history of the twentieth-century is that for all of their imperfections and susceptibilities to abuse, decentralized markets, if properly regulated, are for most goods and services much better mechanisms for obtaining such things as equilibria between supply and demand (and, thereby, stable prices) than are systems of central planning.[18]

Two Types of Natural Actions

Given how embedded in complex social and physical systems our perceptions, thoughts, and actions are, it is all the more remarkable how natural most of them seem. I argued earlier that neither the continuousness nor the multiplicity of the variables that make for the naturalness of cognition prevent us from distinguishing between thoughts and actions that are more or less natural. Nor do they prevent us from understanding the different kinds of naturalness associated with perception, cognition, and action. Before taking up cognition more directly, it will help to look at divergent kinds of human action in order to appreciate the motive for drawing such distinctions.

Some familiar, unreflective actions we undertake, like chewing or walking, seem perennial. We literally cannot remember when we were unable to do these things, but, in fact, each of us learned them in the first year or so of life. Other actions that seem comparably natural, such as writing or riding a bicycle, are also skills that we had to learn. The actions in this second group feel every bit as ingrained (it is often noted, for example, that people never forget how to ride a bike) and automatic (try writing cursive at normal speed while simultaneously concentrating on the formation of each letter) as chewing or walking. Riding and writing, however, differ from chewing and walking. First, the acquisition of riding and writing skills is not lost in the fog of childhood amnesia. We not only know that we had to learn these skills but most of us remember learning them. The distinction between the two groups of actions in question, however, concerns much more than memory.

Many activities of the second sort involve artifacts—but not all. Dancing, for example, does not. But many do. Writing and riding use writing instruments and bicycles that were created at specific points in human history. Thus, unlike us, sufficiently distant ancestors would have found neither riding nor writing familiar, let alone unreflective or automatic.

Most people learn how to write and how to ride a bicycle during the early school years—sometimes later than that, occasionally much later than that, but usually not much before. Learning such skills almost always involves some consciously structured and targeted assistance and, often, explicit instruction from older people, who have already mastered them.[19] We may offer pointers to beginners such as "be careful not to ride over large stones." Instructors seem convinced that imparting such propositional information helps. They offer it even when the goal is the acquisition of a bodily skill, which—regardless of what anyone *says*—they know from experience is mainly acquired through practice. (Some cultures have structured the process of learning to ride a bicycle in a way that cuts down on the perceived need to offer advice and explicit instruction. They do so by dividing the overall task into separate steps. For example, in much of Europe, learning to balance and steer a bicycle begins before school age with younger children learning to ride two-wheelers that have no pedals. They learn to balance and steer long before they graduate to learning how to pedal.) Still, coaching frequently seems to count, and the relative levels of expertise people manifest with skills like riding and writing vary much more within a population than is the case with more basic skills like chewing and walking. At least initially, the *practice* necessary to acquire these skills includes cognitive processing that is as conscious, deliberate, and focused as cognitive processing can be. Unlike chewing and walking, writing and riding a bicycle are not skills that all normal members of the species, across its entire history, exhibit on the basis of merely being human.

The distinction implicit here will help clarify the subset of natural cognition that I wish to concentrate on in the remainder of this book. Adults competent in all four of the skills in question find them habitual, unreflective, and automatic. In short, they find these actions *natural*. As I suggested earlier, though, that broad use of the term obscures some important differences. Chewing and walking—as opposed to writing and riding—are skills whose acquisition typically:

(1) occurs in early childhood and is not recalled,
(2) is not associated with particular artifacts,
(3) does not require older humans, who already possess these skills, to consciously structure the learning environment or any assistance or instruction they may offer, and
(4) does not turn either on inputs that are particular to a culture or (even) on inputs that are culturally distinctive.

Regarding the third point, teachers of early elementary grades use an assortment of models, drills, and special techniques to aid children in developing the fine motor skills necessary for writing. Whether the tips that we offer children about riding bicycles also merit the term "instruction," we certainly do not say just anything that comes to mind when we are helping a six-year-old learn how to stay upright without his or her training wheels. In addition, we search out appropriate places to conduct lessons, and we purposely employ different techniques for steadying their bicycles as our students progress. (As students attain better balance, bicycle-riding-instructors usually stop holding the handlebars and clasp parts of the bicycle further aft, where they are mostly out of sight.) By contrast, caretakers do not teach infants how to chew or walk. Typically, they do not consciously model these activities for them either. While adults constantly engage in these actions around infants, they almost never do so with the intention of illustrating how they should be done. Research in developmental psychology indicates that before their first birthdays infants are sensitive to the differences in adults' behaviors on these fronts. On the basis of cues such as eye contact, prosodic patterns, direct address by name, and contingent reactivity, preverbal infants can differentiate and respond to what they take to be "pedagogical" intentions.[20]

Nothing hinges on the specific examples of chewing and walking. Developmental psychologists have highlighted other behaviors that adults manifest around infants that model more sophisticated actions than infants can perform. Nevertheless, adults do not consciously model these behaviors. For example, parents and relatives tend to set up repeated and highly structured "face-to-face exchanges" with infants, in which they make eye contact, mirror the infant's emotions back to them, and, especially later on, vocalize to them in patterns that mimic the turn-taking rhythms of conversations.[21] Reciprocally, by two months of age human infants begin to give faces more detailed attention than previously, when they looked mostly at faces' external contours.[22]

Humans' nearest relatives in the animal kingdom, apes and monkeys, do not do this.[23] Their concern for their young notwithstanding, they do not repeatedly engage in such structured face-to-face encounters with their infants. Among most of these species, prolonged direct eye contact is not a means for establishing the basic skills of social cooperation; it is a means of expressing a threat.[24] Although prolonged eye contact is a peculiarly human form of interaction with infants, again it is not a behavior that adults consciously plan or model. These are activities that adults generally carry out spontaneously and without reflection.

Point four emphasizes not only the universal emergence of skills like chewing and walking among human beings but also, especially, the imperviousness of that emergence to differences in cultural practices. (What seems true here about the emergence of motor skills seems even more obviously true about the development of our perceptual capacities.) Cultures do vary with respect to when caretakers introduce solid foods to infants, what foods they introduce, and how they introduce them, but those differences do not matter. Infants in all cultures quickly discover how to chew. The same goes for walking. Different cultures approve or disapprove of diverse speeds and gaits for various persons in various circumstances, resulting in distinctive styles both within and between cultures even for something as commonplace as walking. These cultural divergences are tellingly portrayed in a scene in the 1999 film *Topsy Turvy* (about the writing and initial production of Gilbert and Sullivan's comic operetta, *The Mikado*). Desiring his actors to exhibit cultural accuracy in their walking, William Schwenk Gilbert (played by Jim Broadbent) recruits three young Japanese women, who are visiting London in connection with a cultural exhibition, to demonstrate how they walk. They illustrate for the actors and the choreographer the walk appropriate in nineteenth-century Japan for "three little maids from school."[25] Gilbert recognizes that how people walk can vary from one culture to the next. His insight notwithstanding, the point here is that none of these differences prevents infants from learning how to walk.[26]

To summarize, then, actions that humans find natural, in the broad sense that I have employed up to now, are of two types. The second of those types issues from skills such as writing and riding bikes that are activities invented at some particular point in human history and that spread from culture to culture. Acquiring these skills usually turns on experienced instructors modeling them and providing detailed, targeted tutelage in specially designed or consciously selected environments that novices will typically recall something about. A host of factors beyond their mere availability within a culture determine whether individuals obtain these skills and become adept at these actions. Those factors include access to the requisite artifacts, teachers, and environments as well as time for all of the practicing that is required. Initially, beginners (who are, typically, at least school age, that is, five to seven years old) must devote considerable concentration to these endeavors, but eventually these skills become familiar, automatic, and unconscious. With extensive practice these thoroughly *cultural* activities eventually begin to feel natural. They become *second nature*. (Often it is not easy for adults to recall what challenges writing and riding once seemed.) However natural they may come to feel, though, their cultural origins should, by now, be evident. Theirs is a *practiced* naturalness.

These practiced, cultural skills contrast with *maturational* skills, such as chewing and walking. Maturational actions are activities that in suitable circumstances human infants in every culture undertake on their own.[27] No one devised these activities, nor does their emergence rest on connections with artifacts. They serve functions and, at least in the case of chewing, include a general form that is as applicable to some other species as they are to humans. Acquiring maturational skills does not hang on instructors modeling these actions or structuring learning environments or devising verbal representations or targeting such representations at novices. No doubt, their mastery demands the exercise of these skills, and babies' initial efforts do involve concentration, but it is clearly not the kind of concentration associated with practicing cultural skills. Certainly, it does not aim at productively integrating knowledge of kinesthetic experiences with the knowledge gleaned from teachers' instructions.

It is the naturalness of actions in this maturational sense that will help clarify the notion of cognitive naturalness that I will concentrate on in this book. The category of maturational naturalness goes beyond the rough and ready criteria of intuition, familiarity, and the absence of reflection that I offered earlier. By now it should be clear that actions can seem natural for different reasons. Unlike the practiced naturalness of cultural skills, maturational skills are so fundamental to human life that their appearance helps to define what counts as "normal." Humans acquire many maturational skills not only in the first year or two of life, before they go to school, but in some cases before they even seem to comprehend much language and certainly before they have begun to produce it. The actions to which maturational skills give birth are justifiably described as natural in a more fundamental sense than are those associated with cultural skills, and it is this maturational naturalness on which I shall focus in this book to compare science and religion. Action and thought (and, of course, perception) that we find transparent, intuitive, and familiar can arise on the basis of either maturation or practice, but because of their spontaneity, their early onset, their ubiquity, and their independence both from explicit instruction and from other forms of culturally distinctive support, maturational naturalness trumps practiced naturalness. But assertions about forms of thought and perceptions are a bit premature, since I have, so far, only discussed in detail the applicability of the distinction between maturational and practiced naturalness with regard to action.

Two (Parallel) Types of Natural Cognition

Gilbert rightly spotlighted culturally appropriate styles of walking for his cast, but the *cultural infiltration* of maturational skills has little, if any, bearing on their simple emergence in normal human beings. The distinction between two types of actions that feel natural does not challenge the claim that all cognition is embodied, but it does suggest that it may sometimes be possible to overplay how much some forms of cognition may be culturally embedded or, more precisely, how much their being culturally embedded pertains either to their simple acquisition or to their overall shapes. Culture unquestionably tunes maturational capacities. It gives them culturally specific features. But culturally specific dimensions play little, if any, role in either the timing of those maturational capacities' emergence, their bare acquisition, or their general architectures.

Language, of course, is the most obvious example of cultural infiltration of a maturational skill. Children who grow up where everyone speaks Turkish themselves speak Turkish, whereas others who grow up where everyone else speaks Norwegian end up speaking Norwegian. Culture, no doubt, infiltrates every form of maturational naturalness at some level or other. (Consider the variety of foods on which infants around the world learn to chew.) Which language a child learns to speak, however, is readily distinguishable from the more general readiness of children in the first few years of life to acquire natural language. This logical point ushers in a causal one. Divergent features of cultures do not seem to have any significant role in determining common patterns of maturational actions that arise in every culture.[28]

The distinction between practiced naturalness and maturational naturalness applies no less readily to intuitions, thoughts, and beliefs.

Cognition too can seem natural simply because it is well-practiced and because it is culturally well-supported or, on the other hand, because it emerges, independently of any culturally distinctive influences, in the course of human development. (See figure 1-1.)

Like practiced, culturally informed actions, some intuitions result (i) from schooling and the study of some culturally articulated domain, (ii) from conscious, laborious, and extensive exercise with routine problems and tasks in that domain, and, eventually, (iii) from experience in independently traversing the domain's associated cognitive pathways. Examples include the intuitions that arise from learning everything from scansion, musical notation, and small motor repair to geometry, pedagogy, and tactics in chess. The breadth and amount of people's intuitions in such areas correlate fairly well with the extent of their preparation and experience. Experts are people who have had solid preparation and extensive experience in some domain, including many of its remotest corners. Experimental psychologists have found that in addition to possessing numerous, developed intuitions, experts also enjoy enhanced powers of perception, speed in making inferences, and memory for pertinent materials.[29]

Some areas of culture are so difficult to understand that few people are able to acquire expertise in those domains. Consequently, many people will not share experts' intuitions in those areas. I will argue later

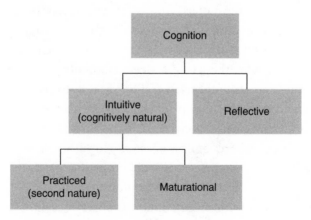

Figure 1-1. Two types of cognitive naturalness in perception, thought, and action

that science is a parade case for such arrangements, but virtually any of the traditional, educationally certified professions would qualify. Litigators have strong intuitions about which kinds of arguments to use with juries and which kinds to use with judges. Librarians immediately know good ways and places to look for various kinds of information in libraries. Engineers automatically recognize which materials will meet particular structural demands.

By contrast, other cultural accomplishments become so critical to human thriving that nearly everyone gains the necessary experience to be able to carry them out unreflectively most of the time. The skill and the knowledge that we all need in order to manage indispensable pieces of technology leap to mind (for example, in most of America, knowing how to drive a car as well as knowing the rules of the road). But cases that do not involve the command of any elaborate technology are plentiful too. For example, most citizens in developed countries have constructed representations of how their nations' postal systems work. They grasp the relationships between the major variables affecting the cost of sending a piece of mail and the efficiency with which it is delivered. Correspondingly, they have at least rough intuitions about how, when, and where to post items to ensure that they will arrive safely and on time.

In comparison with knowledge about cultural domains such as science, engineering, and law, knowledge about complex systems like the postal service is widespread. The familiarity that experts enjoy with the former and that most of us enjoy with the latter supports bodies of knowledge that become so commonplace (in the relevant populations) that they seem natural in many of the same ways that writing and riding a bicycle do. Parallel, then, to practiced, culturally supported *actions*, which become so well rehearsed and habitual as to seem natural, are *perceptual* and *intellectual* competencies that people acquire within various culturally articulated domains. Different people master different precincts with the thoroughness necessary to sustain large collections of instant percepts, apposite intuitions, automatic inferences, and deft actions. Some areas attract wider attention than others. For example, the distribution of knowledge about postal services almost certainly surpasses that associated with classical music. So, many of us would be able to infer automatically that the customary first-class postage (for a letter weighing less than one ounce) would not suffice for mailing a large envelope containing a sixty-page document, but far fewer would immediately conclude from listening to the final movement of Franz Schubert's ninth symphony that he was, among other things, paying homage to Beethoven. Both, though, are examples of culturally supported knowledge that various numbers of humans, depending upon the topic, know so well that they regularly forget that they know it.

For the comparative assessment of the cognitive naturalness of science and religion, however, it is the forms of cognition and perception that are analogous to maturational skills that matter. With cognition and perception as with skilled actions, cultural materials can come to feel natural after repeated practice or intensive study, but the maturational naturalness (of action, cognition, and perception) is the more fundamental form, because maturational knowledge arises in human minds regardless of the peculiarities of cultures. Maturational cognition, like chewing and walking, concerns not only things that humans know well but things that they have known *so long* that they have forgotten that they know them. The considerations I have outlined that differentiate the maturational from the practiced naturalness of actions are the following:

- No one invented them.
- Their emergence never depends upon artifacts (though some cultures have developed artifacts to facilitate their acquisition).
- Humans undertake them spontaneously.
- A few have general forms that we share with other species.
- Their acquisition does not depend upon explicit instruction or specially structured learning environments, and it does not turn either on inputs that are particular to a culture or (even) on inputs that are culturally distinctive.

These also apply without a hitch for discriminating the maturational from the practiced naturalness of knowledge and cognition. That this is so offers indirect support for Churchland's thesis that the architectural and operational principles governing the systems and processes in the brain that manage bodily movement also anchor humans' cognitive achievements. This suggests (i) that most of humans' maturationally natural forms of knowledge will arise comparatively early, (ii) that they will address some of the most basic problems that humans face (like those that are solved by chewing and walking), and (iii) that they will prove to be so ubiquitous that their emergence counts as normal development. In contrast to capacities that possess a practiced naturalness and are second nature to us, perception, cognition, and action that possess maturational naturalness are first nature to us.

|| 2 ||

Maturational Naturalness

Stick Close to Your Desks

In Gilbert and Sullivan's "patter" song in *H.M.S. Pinafore*, Sir Joseph Porter, their fictional First Lord of the Admiralty, reviews the secrets to his success.[1] Sir Joseph, who always travels with an entourage of his sisters, cousins, and aunts and who succumbs to seasickness the moment "breezes blow," recounts his professional history and lists his (dubious) qualifications for his position, illustrating how someone so woefully ignorant of all things nautical could have ended up as "the Ruler of the Queen's Navee." In the last verse this inept beneficiary of party patronage offers a final piece of advice. He counsels aspirants to high positions in the British Admiralty to

> Be careful to be guided by this golden rule—
> Stick close to your desks and never go to sea,
> And you all may be Rulers of the Queen's Navee!

Sir Joseph's advice has always seemed sound for landlubbers (regardless of our career goals). So it was with some hesitation that I agreed to my wife's suggestion that we take an Alaskan cruise (our first) on the occasion of our thirtieth wedding anniversary. On balance, my reservations were unjustified, as the voyage was smooth and the scenery spectacular. To my surprise, however, I discovered a further reason for not dismissing Sir Joseph's admonition out-of-hand, for I learned that in at least one important respect, humans are not at all suited to life aboard a modern ship.

I learned this lesson because I prefer walking in the fresh air to walking on treadmills in fitness centers. Given the ship's length, I calculated that three laps around it would nearly equal a mile, so that if I walked ten or eleven laps, I would be able to log the three or so miles that I put in most days at home. Descending to the Promenade deck, I exited the doors on the starboard side and started walking toward the front of the ship (the bow). As the ship's television channel had reported, the sea was calm, the sky was bright, and the temperature was on the cool side of pleasant, which is ideal for a three-mile walk. At the front of the ship the Promenade deck was sheltered, and I crossed to the port side, where I started the roughly eight-hundred-foot walk back toward the stern.

What I was not prepared for, after emerging from the sheltered area, was the *immediate* impression that the ship had accelerated dramatically in the fifteen seconds or so that it had taken me to walk across the sheltered bow. It appeared that the ship was moving nearly twice as fast through the water as it had been but fifteen seconds earlier when I was walking up the starboard side, yet I had not felt any surge in the ship's forward motion nor did the ship's motion suddenly *feel* precarious. But it did suddenly *look* precarious—so much so that I stopped dead, alarmed momentarily that I might lose my balance on this gigantic ocean-going ship that now seemed to be speeding along. Once I had stopped, I noticed that the ship had seemed to slow a bit and to slow even more as I turned to my right to look out to sea. When I turned another ninety degrees to look toward the bow I noticed in another second that the ship had seemed to slow to its previous speed. Unclear about the source of my initial confusion when I had emerged from the covered area but realizing after a few more seconds' pause that things were fine, I turned to continue my walk toward the stern and was, I must confess, after just a few steps disconcerted to find that the ship again appeared to be moving through the water rapidly.

Over the next few minutes the passengers nearby were probably convinced that I was, at best, very confused. I first walked a few steps aft, then stopped while continuing to look toward the stern, then I turned and looked toward the bow, then I walked toward the bow, then while continuing to walk toward the bow I turned my head to look behind me toward the stern, then I stopped again, turned and (when the deck was clear) trotted toward the stern. Then I walked backward both fore and aft. Then I carried out most of these maneuvers again with one eye open (the one nearer the water). Since neither I nor any of the other passengers was lurching about the deck, I was finally convinced that the ship's speed only appeared to be changing abruptly. It was a readily reproducible illusion.

I felt like a five year old with a new toy, as changes in my direction and speed on deck could produce apparent changes in this huge ship's speed. Illusions beget intellectual thrills too. It is even better than watching a magician and trying to figure out his tricks, because in the case of such naturally occurring illusions, the magician and the tricks seem to be hiding inside our own heads, unbeknownst to us!

Clearly, these were *visual* illusions. Something was tricking my visual perception. After all, one of the reasons the illusion was so readily detectable was that the proprioceptive information did not square with the visual information. I did not *feel* the ship changing speeds, even though it appeared to do so. How to explain that?

Realizing just how strange these illusory effects were put this explanatory question into sharper focus. It was not merely that I perceived changes in the ship's speed that had not occurred. A few simple calculations showed that there was more to it than that. The direction of the illusory effects was exactly the opposite of what the facts about the situation would suggest. (Sir Joseph's advice about sticking close to our desks was looking less and less comic.) After all, when I was walking toward the bow, I was moving in that direction *faster* than the ship relative to the water. The ship was moving about twenty-three miles per hour, so at my usual three-and-a-half-mile-per-hour pace I was moving at about twenty-six and a half miles per hour:

McCauley's speed relative to the water =
the ship's speed +the speed of McCauley's normal pace
26.5 = 23 + 3.5

By contrast, when I was walking toward the ship's stern, I was moving *slower* than the ship relative to the water. The ship was still moving at twenty-three miles per hour, whereas since I was now walking *toward the back* of the ship, I was moving at only nineteen and a half miles per hour:

$$\text{McCauley's speed relative to the water} =$$
$$\text{the ship's speed} - \text{the speed of McCauley's normal pace}$$
$$19.5 = 23 - 3.5$$

What is so odd about this is that it was in this second condition, when I was moving *slower* relative to the water, that the ship seemed to be moving faster. When I was walking toward the back of the ship, instead of my forward motion seeming as if it were only about three-fourths of the speed ($19.5 / 26.5 = 73.6\%$) that it was when I was walking toward the front of the ship, I seemed to be moving forward nearly twice as fast!

After using much of my walk over the next forty-five minutes to rule out alternatives, I settled on a hypothesis that hearkened to the work of ecological psychologists such as James J. Gibson on the role of optical flow in visual perception.[2] When we walk, things out ahead of us seem to flow progressively from nearer the center of our visual field (which specifies the direction in which we are walking) to out beyond its periphery as we approach them and eventually pass them by. How quickly that happens is an indicator of our speed.

My problem on the cruise ship was that this optical flow was exactly what the scene does *not* supply for someone who is moving toward the stern of a ship at a considerably slower speed than the ship is moving forward. Instead of the waves and the ship's wake moving toward and then past me, it receded away from me in the direction that I was walking faster than I could walk (or trot or even sprint) toward it. That gave the impression, presumably via some unconscious inference, that the ship must be moving forward through the water very fast. Simply stopping, turning 180 degrees, and walking back toward the bow dispelled this illusion straightaway. The ocean now moved steadily out of my visual field at its periphery, specifying my forward movement through the environment at a speed that is decidedly faster than when I walk down the street ordinarily but not nearly as fast as when I drive my car on an open road.

Earlier I referred to these illusory effects as "naturally occurring." Ecological psychologists would disavow that characterization. They would argue that I experienced illusions on the cruise ship precisely because my environment was unnatural. It involved (a) another local motion besides my just moving around on my own two feet, (b) an aquatic environment, and (c) things (e.g., the ship), some of which were not solid (e.g., the ship's wake), that were substantially larger than even the big things (e.g., trees) that populate my everyday terrestrial surroundings. According to the ecological psychologists, it is when we face such unusual stimuli that we can experience illusions.

Ecological psychologists emphasize that humans can often eradicate visual illusions by doing nothing more than moving around a bit, changing their perspective.[3] Consider the Triple Poggendorf illusion in figure 2-1. When looking at the figure directly, the more heavily striped, thinner line segments, which extend from the upper left to the lower

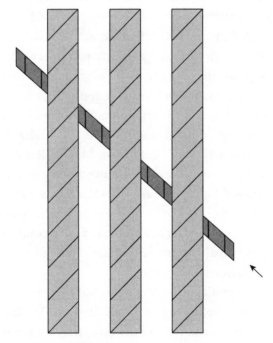

Figure 2-1. The Triple Poggendorf illusion

right of the figure, appear aligned with one another as the visible parts of a single, straight rod, which is occluded by the three wider, vertical bars. Changing perspective and looking at the figure from the direction of the arrow in the lower right reveals that, in fact, they are not aligned. (If you have any doubt about which of these two views gives the correct verdict, superimpose a straight edge on the segments.)

Ecological psychologists, therefore, argue that we should reject strong conclusions about the limitations of human perceptual systems drawn from laboratory experiments that require participants, for example, to view some stimulus from a single fixed position. The human visual system evolved to serve creatures who move around in their environments with the sorts of bodies that humans have. Over time these movements afford them multiple perspectives on the things that they see. It should not come as too big of a surprise that humans may make systematic errors about some stimuli, if experiments are designed in ways that prevent or, at least, discourage them from obtaining these additional sources of visual information. In effect, ecological psychologists vouch for the general reliability of our perceptual machinery when it is operating in what they refer to as "ecologically valid" circumstances. Those, in short, are circumstances that are similar to those in which the perceptual system evolved. Our prehistoric ancestors walked around in terrestrial environments, mostly dealing with medium-sized, solid objects, including comparatively humble tools. That acute perceptual systems for managing in such environments evolved in our species makes sense. Ecological psychologists hold that under such circumstances, our perceptual systems get the world right. It is only in the last two centuries that humans have devised technologies (such as large, fast ships, electronic lights, and airplanes) and have penetrated environments (such as the sky) or created environments (such as movie theaters) that have enabled large numbers of us to confront situations in which our perceptual systems can regularly mislead us even when we have considerable freedom to move.

The film industry relies on technologies that are specifically designed to exploit our susceptibility to perceptual illusions. Think about seeing movies on the big screen. Most of the time, they do not disorient us. We *know* that the changing patterns of light on the screen before us are not, for example, conversations between people whose heads are really nine feet tall. Sometimes, though, regardless of what we know, the deliverances of our perceptual systems overwhelm everything else. Ask anyone who has experienced motion sickness at the movies or on video "rides" at amusement parks. To escape the grip of such illusions, you need only close your eyes, which cuts off the disorienting information. In my one experience on such a ride closing my eyes brought an instant improvement in my condition even though the seat into which I was strapped continued to jerk and shake every few seconds for another minute or so as our virtual starship changed course or was battered by the aliens' weaponry. (Even my experience with a virtual starship corroborated Sir Joseph's advice!)

Persisting Illusions

Why does this matter? Because many illusions arise from the operations of maturationally natural perceptual systems. These experiences manifest all of the typical marks of maturational naturalness that I surveyed and suggest some additional ones. First, like all cognitively natural systems, those responsible here operate unconsciously, and their signals arrive to consciousness *automatically and unreflectively*. Second, characteristic of many (but not all!) maturationally natural systems, those deliverances begin arriving *early* in life. They do not all exist from birth, though. Such dimensions as visual acuity, sensitivity to contrast, and color discrimination improve markedly over the first year of life.[4] Third, the problems in play here, namely, making sense of the world around us on the basis of sensory inputs, are probably the most *fundamental cognitive challenges* that we or any other organisms face. This comports with the suggestion that maturationally natural capacities address problems that are elemental in human survival, whether it is our perceptual recognition of faces, or our cognitive discrimination of syntactic distinctions in language, or our action capacities when we think that a contaminant is nearby. Finally, their operations *do not depend on anything that is culturally distinctive*—not on instruction, or on structured preparations, or on artifacts.

That final point should not be confused with the fact, noted previously, that some structured environments (such as those in some psychological experiments and in movie theaters) and artifacts (such as stereoscopic viewers) can produce inputs that cause these systems to volunteer erroneous judgments about the world.[5] (Although I have concentrated on the human visual system, similar illusions occur with other perceptual systems as well—from auditory illusions, such as hearing orchestras between our ears when we listen to stereo headphones, to haptic ones, such as the celebrated cutaneous rabbit. Everyday experience provides plenty of illustrations of these systems' fallibility.)[6]

Ecological psychologists would likely rise in defense of our perceptual systems' reliability. How to answer their objections? First and most important, ecological psychologists *themselves* cite conditions in which our perceptual systems are not reliable, such as perceiving things in the sky and in water. These are situations in which humans' maturationally natural perceptual systems can fail to deliver sound verdicts about the way the world is. Second, although the ship, the ocean-going conditions, and the speeds involved never arose in the prehistoric environments in which the human visual system evolved, the illusion is still fairly described as "naturally occurring." It is, after all, both spontaneous and unforced (so much so that, like the Triple Poggendorf illusion, some people apparently do not notice it!). Given ecological psychologists' emphasis on the need for observers to move in order to see the world accurately, it is somewhat ironic that this visual illusion is most striking *when walking* toward the stern. Instead of resolving the illusion, some (perfectly normal) movements intensify it.

This is not to deny, however, that, as with the Triple Poggendorf illusion, my freedom to move around alerted me to the illusion and provided valuable information about making sense of it. More generally, I could not only move about as I pleased, but I could also configure my body in particular ways (walking forward with my head turned back, walking with one eye closed, and so on) as I pondered and tested various hypotheses. That I could do so suggests four additional reasons for holding that my visual system is maturationally natural or, if not my entire visual system, then at a minimum that the glitch in that system that is responsible for the illusion is.

First, as I mentioned before, the illusion is readily reproducible. Second, anyone with normal vision can experience it. Third and most notably, under the eliciting conditions, the perceptual illusion persists. (Note that this is even true of the Triple Poggendorf illusion in figure 2-1.) When I was walking toward the stern, nothing I *did* (short of closing my eyes) eradicated it. Nothing I *saw* eliminated it, nor did anything I *surmise*. I could not think the illusion away. Neither entertaining and testing various hypotheses, nor recalling Gibson's account of optical flow, nor thinking through its implications for this visual experience had any effect on the illusion. This susceptibility, at least under some conditions, to *persisting* illusions only arises in maturationally natural systems. This third consideration merits elaboration, since many contemporary accounts of perception seem to exclude the very possibility of a persisting illusion.

Some philosophers, such as Paul Churchland, highlight the role that our theories and conscious knowledge play in shaping our perception.[7] In many circumstances without such knowledge, we are nearly at a total loss about what we are seeing. This has happened to me when physicians have invited me to peruse sonograms, X-rays, or MRI scans— even when I have known what they were sonograms, X-rays, and MRI scans of! It was usually not until they gave me overt instruction about what I was looking at, which I had to consider consciously, that I began to make sense of what I was seeing.

Churchland argues that experiments with inverting lenses demonstrate how conscious knowledge influences human perception.[8] Donning these lenses literally makes the world look upside down. Most people find it surprising to learn that after an initial period of disorientation participants wearing inverting lenses adjust readily within a couple of weeks and, for the most part, experience the visible world normally. For example, they quickly cease to have problems moving about in the environment. Churchland contends, plausibly enough, that participants' knowledge that they are wearing the lenses and their knowledge of how the lenses change what they see influence how and what they see. What humans think, he argues, shapes what they perceive. Churchland holds that this is true whether people are managing inverting lenses or deploying their commonsense theories or even the most esoteric theories of science.

I do not disagree with this, so far as it goes. As the foregoing discussion of my shipboard illusion suggests, however, I do disagree with him about just how far it probably does go. Churchland foresees no limit on how thoroughly the knowledge we consciously acquire can reshape our perception.[9] By contrast, persisting illusions indicate both that some limits exist and where those limits originate.

One of Churchland's books includes a marvelous exercise about how, with the naked eye, to observe the early night sky and the visible planets as a genuine Copernican. Churchland offers suitable warnings about the vertigo this can induce.[10] (See figure 2-2.) It may be hard to imagine that by simply tilting your head (perpendicular to the plane of the planets' revolutions around the sun) and *thinking* about the things that you are seeing in a particular way, you can feel like you will fall down, but it is true. Hold on; this *does* demand that the observer keep many things in mind at once. What it takes is simultaneously to construe the earth on which we stand as a large, rotating globe that, on the same plane as the visible planets, is circling the sun, which has just disappeared beyond the western horizon (as a function of the earth's rotation) but which, nonetheless, is in a position to illuminate one-half of the moon (where we can only see some fraction of that illuminated area), which, in turn, we know circles the earth at a distance that is much less than the distances between the earth and either the sun or the visible planets. Get all of that in mind while looking at the relevant objects in a clear night sky and you will experience moments when you feel as if you are about to take a tumble because you are (impossibly!) sticking out from the side of a massive structure (the earth) without any support.

Churchland underscores that this requires considerable intellectual work, including the command of a sophisticated theory and the imaginative projection of some of its consequences for how we see the night sky. Our general familiarity with the sky may mislead us into thinking that looking at it as Churchland would have us do is not like looking at those images from sonograms, X-rays, and MRI scanners, but in at least one crucial respect they *are* similar. Neither the products of those imaging technologies nor things in the sky, as the ecological psychologists have noted, are the sorts of things that the human visual system evolved

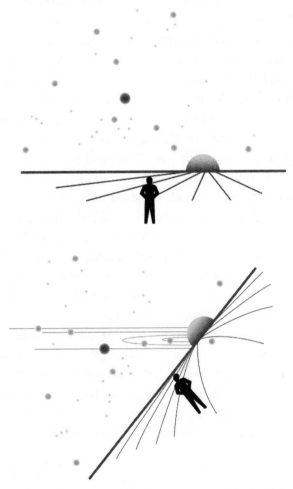

Figure 2-2. Two views of the sky at dusk (after P. M. Churchland 1979)

to handle. Even when we carefully concentrate on seeing the night sky as Copernicans, the effect is fleeting and easily dissolved by simply attending to the medium-sized objects (roughly, things between the sizes of toadstools and trees) that are nearby rather than to the distant, visible planets. The fact that so much intellectual work is required for so temporary an effect inspires reservations about how pervasively cognition can influence perception.

A second consideration is more decisive. Unlike both the Copernican case and the case of the inverting lenses, possessing some understanding of the relevant variables and deploying the relevant concepts do not erase the illusions I have been discussing. Under the appropriate eliciting conditions, these illusions persist, regardless of what we are thinking or what we know. Moreover, other visual illusions persist regardless not only of what we think or know but of what the viewing conditions are like and of any movements that we can make. For example, our conscious knowledge that the two horizontal lines in the Müller-Lyer illusion are the same length (measure them!) has no impact on our perception that they are not. (See figure 2-3.) If persisting illusions are possible with all and only maturationally natural systems, then the more malleable aspects of perception, on which Churchland focuses, pertain to phenomena of other sorts. Perhaps our knowledge penetrates perception only where any cognitive naturalness that might arise is *practiced* naturalness rather than maturational.

I should immediately point out that this would not rule out obtaining knowledge that improves upon the outputs of maturationally natural systems. That is exactly what measuring the horizontal lines in the Müller-Lyer illusion amounts to. But, as David Papineau, Todd Tremlin, and others maintain, in those cases, instead of this new information superseding our visual perception, we end up with *two* incompatible verdicts.[11] We simultaneously *perceive* one line as longer than the other

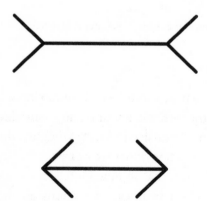

Figure 2-3. The Müller-Lyer illusion

while we *know*, because we measured them, that they are, in fact, the same length. This is what it means for an illusion to persist, and it is a different state of affairs from the ones that Churchland describes where we consciously deploy theories we possess in order to learn to perceive the world *differently*.

These remarks expose a fourth reason for suspecting that that glitch that rendered me susceptible to the shipboard illusion is due to maturationally natural features of my visual system. Regardless of what ideas we consciously entertain when experiencing these illusions, *automatic, unconscious inferences* prevail. Those unconscious expectations, rather than anything I thought or knew consciously, determined how things seemed to me. This is yet another way of saying that the illusion persisted, but the point here is that how the world appeared was a function of inferential processes about those visual stimuli over which I had no conscious control. We only *notice* the influence of those unconscious, maturationally natural expectations when they lead us into making perceptual errors that, as with illusions, we can detect. So, for example, viewing the Triple Poggendorf stimulus from the direction in which the arrow points reveals that the more heavily striped, thinner line segments are not aligned, even though they look like parts of a single straight rod when viewing the overall stimulus straight on. Illusions violate our expectations and help us to recognize that these unconscious inferential processes shape our experience.

We can sometimes experience motion sickness in movie theaters, because what we perceive overwhelms what we know about the world and what we can infer from what we know about the world. When maturationally natural perceptual and cognitive systems kick into gear, at least at that moment, they overtake our knowledge, our general intelligence, and our rational capacities.

Their influences are potent, but, as Churchland would stress, they do not supplant our knowledge or our general intelligence or our rational capacities either forever or altogether. Often, almost as soon as we experience illusions, we are aware of it, which is to say that discordant information we are receiving from different perceptual systems does not preclude our ability to reason about it. Once we recognize illusions, we are capable of thinking through them, even while we are experiencing them.

When I first emerged from the covered area of the Promenade deck at the cruise ship's bow, I quickly realized that I had not felt the ship rapidly accelerate, even if it suddenly looked as if it had. Even more telling, I was able to test a variety of explanatory hypotheses while experiencing the illusion.

This analysis suggests that illusions are ruptures that mark cognitively natural systems that typically operate just below the surface of consciousness. What it also suggests is that persisting illusions are indicators of unconscious, inferential systems that are *maturationally* natural. It is here that the notion of the maturational naturalness of a cognitive system connects with some long-standing debates in the cognitive sciences about the modularity of mind.

Mental Modules

A widespread assumption in early cognitive science was that the human mind is like a powerful, general-purpose computer. A minority view then that has become increasingly popular contends that some of our perceptual and cognitive accomplishments appear so early and so regularly and appear to be so sophisticated that we must possess more specialized machinery for handling some problems.

Jerry Fodor's *The Modularity of Mind* was the first book-length discussion of these topics.[12] Mental modules, in Fodor's view, are special-purpose mechanisms ("input systems") that are situated at the front end of our various perceptual systems: visual, auditory, olfactory, and so on. These modular input systems conspicuously contrast with more central cognitive processes, which handle such jobs as reasoning, analogy, and even more full-blown, conceptually rich, perceptual judgment (of the sort that Churchland is concerned about).[13] Fodor argues these downstream, general-purpose central systems fail to influence the operations of the specialized input systems back upstream. This "informational encapsulation" of these modules contributes to the relative rigidity of their functioning and to their stereotypical deliverances—to the central systems—about how the world appears. Special-purpose modules come equipped with hypotheses (presumably, by way of natural selection) that make sense of the stimuli in each of those modules' proprietary domains by sorting through the "observable properties of things."[14]

One of the principal types of empirical evidence Fodor cites in support of informationally encapsulated modules is the persistence of perceptual illusions. His point (which, by now, should sound familiar) is not about the mere existence of illusions but rather about our inability to shake some of them. Fodor emphasizes that no matter how much we may know about them and about their illusory effects, some, like the Müller-Lyer illusion, simply will not go away.[15] What we know neither affects the module's operations nor informs its outputs.

The mental modules Fodor describes qualify as maturationally natural systems. I shall discuss briefly and selectively in this and the next section some of the positions and quarrels that have emerged over the past two decades concerning the modularity of mind. The most controversial matter about modules is whether the systems in question are innate and what that amounts to. Whether some cognitive accomplishment is maturationally natural does not turn on whether it depends exclusively or even directly on some genetically determined capacity. Any genetically determined capacities, if any there be, will qualify as maturationally natural.[16] But maturationally natural systems need not be innate, let alone genetically determined. The notion of maturational naturalness pertains to patterns in human cognition and development that have engendered far less dispute, certainly among modularity theorists, but also among those who look beyond modularity, and even among many who have fashioned themselves as foes of modular analyses.[17]

Besides the battles over modules' origins, the other two significant clashes concern how many modules human minds have and how those modules work. Fodor advances the most restrictive views about those matters. He highlights nine characteristics of modular input systems.[18] As a result, he holds that modules operate in but six domains: the five senses, plus language. (See figure 2-4.) The nine features vary in their importance. Fodor is clear that his notion of modularity permits differences of degree.[19]

First, Fodorian modules are *domain-specific*. They are specialized mechanisms for handling particular, common (but complex) problems

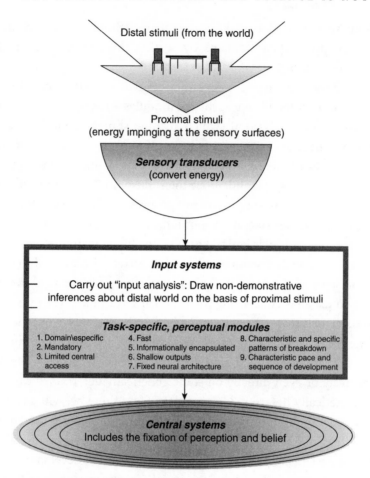

Figure 2-4. Fodorian input systems in human cognitive architecture

that humans face in making sense of the world, and they are triggered by stimuli that are characteristic of the domains they manage (the visual module by visual stimuli and so on). While Fodor construes these domains broadly—vision, olfaction, language, and so on— subsequent theorists envision many more modules, both within and outside of the broad domains Fodor outlines. These more liberal views analyze aspects of cognition and action, in addition to perception, as modular. (Fodor also allows that various motor systems may be modularized, but he does not discuss that possibility in any detail.)

Second, modules' operations, according to Fodor, are *mandatory*.[20] These input systems function like reflexes. Fodor notes that these input systems are "inflexibly insensitive to the character of one's utilities. You can't hear speech as noise *even if you would prefer to*."[21] You cannot avoid processing speech as speech.

Third, humans' central cognitive systems have extremely *limited access* to the representations that these input systems compute (unless the perceiver's conscious priority is on recalling some particular features). Even a second or two after we have viewed a conventional clock we are extremely unlikely to remember what the numerals on the face of the clock look like—unless *that* was an explicit focus of our centrally controlled attention from the start.

Fourth, modules are *fast*. The price of input systems' rapid, unthinking, automatic responses, though, is that they confine themselves to a "stereotyped subset" of the vast range of possible interpretations their inputs might support.[22] Their limited options ensure their swiftness.

Their speed is also a function of their *informational encapsulation*, the fifth feature, which I mentioned earlier. What we know about the world (for example, that the cruise ship did not double its speed in the short time it took me to walk across the bow) has little, if any, influence on how we perceive some of the world's features (it looked as if it had). That is because knowledge available in our central cognitive systems cannot penetrate these mental modules.

The sixth feature of modules is that they have *shallow outputs*. They can only make basic distinctions about items' forms. So, the linguistic module recognizes syntactic structure but not meaning. The visual module can identify medium-sized, basic-level objects, which are conceived at the most general level at which objects can be identified by their shapes. (Tables and chairs, for example, are basic-level objects within the superordinate category of furniture. Among people familiar with tables and chairs, few have any problem with conjuring up a mental image of either, as opposed to conjuring a mental image for *furniture*.)[23]

The seventh characteristic of Fodorian modules is that they are associated with *fixed neural architectures*. Fodor, writing before the widespread use of new imaging technologies, held that all of the (then) known examples of "massive neural structuring to which content-specific cognitive function can confidently be assigned appear to be associated with input analysis."[24] By contrast, these days it seems as if all functions have been confidently assigned to some area of the brain or other. Still, the hundreds of neuroimaging studies that have been done have not seriously jeopardized Fodor's claims about the *relative* localization of input analysis in the brains of most adults.

The eighth characteristic of modules is that they show *particular, detailed patterns of breakdown.* If the neural systems that subserve these modules' activities are comparatively isolated functionally and structurally, then at least some injuries or maladies (for example, strokes) will yield domain-specific deficits. Agnosias and aphasias seem to fit the bill. Agnosias are modality-specific perceptual disabilities that are often content-specific too. Forms of visual agnosia include patients who, for example, are unable to see anything in one-half of their visual fields (even though there is nothing wrong with their eyes). Prosopagnosics are persons who are unable to identify individual human faces. Aphasias are disorders that affect patients' linguistic abilities. One type, Broca's aphasics, are patients who readily comprehend the speech of others, who otherwise seem to possess normal motor control of their lips, mouths, and larynxes (who can, for example, chew, suck on straws, and, sometimes, even sing), but who are, nonetheless, completely incapable of producing fluent speech and struggle mightily to produce anything approaching coherent utterances. Significantly, with many agnosics and aphasics, these patients' other cognitive capacities seem mostly unimpaired, which partisans of modularity take as evidence of the pertinent systems' domain-specificity.[25]

Fodor's ninth feature of modules is that their development "exhibits a *characteristic pace and sequencing.*"[26] I have already mentioned the differences between the visual capacities of newborns as opposed to one-year-olds. In many areas even the most casual observations of children's activities disclose conspicuous changes as they develop. Probably the clearest example of a "characteristic pace and sequencing" is with gross motor control. Newborns have neither the muscle development nor the coordination to carry out many directed activities, but, typically, within weeks they are rolling over, within months they are sitting up and crawling, and within a year or so they stand and begin to walk. Both friends and foes of modularity have made tremendous strides in delineating the order and temporal patterns that mark children's acquisition of natural language. Although they do not concur about many of the details,[27] all agree that the acquisition of natural language does not occur all at once or in utterly haphazard ways and largely has occurred by the time children have reached six or seven years of age. These, of course, are just some of the properties that I have argued maturationally natural systems display.

These nine features are not equals. Fodor maintains that the fifth, namely, informational encapsulation, is "at the heart of modularity."[28] Modules come equipped only with information about their proprietary domains. This amounts to an architectural constraint on their operations. Ideally, they generate their outputs to central cognitive systems on the basis of nothing more than current stimuli that trigger their operation and the built-in information they possess. Their operations are not delayed by issues of recollection or conceptual nuance or by concerns with coherence or integration with the rest of our knowledge. This contributes to their speed, as do their restrictions on the amount of information that needs to be confirmed to identify items from their forms. Fodor underscores how useful this can be, citing Ogden Nash's sage advice that "if you are called by a panther / don't anther." Panther identification is something that, at least in the wild, humans always want accomplished with tremendous efficiency and do not wish to have encumbered by numerous requirements for confirming panther properties before we take action.

This characterization of the informational encapsulation of mental modules, however, is an *ideal* that Fodor qualifies. He says that it is only "in certain respects" that the operations of input systems are uninfluenced by feedback from cognitive activity further downstream.[29] He makes a pair of observations.

First, he does not insist that *perceptual judgment overall* is cognitively impenetrable, only that the workings and products of input systems at the front end of perception are. So, Fodor presumes that the visual input system enables humans to identify large dangerous cats, as such, efficiently and unthinkingly. It does not, however, enable someone to automatically identify an endangered, male Florida panther trying to obtain relief from the summer sun as such without sufficient time to consult painstakingly acquired, conscious knowledge about the signs that this large cat is a Florida panther and a male, about the conditions that have led to the scarcity of Florida panthers generally, and about the usual ways Florida panthers try to beat the heat. Even for experts that kind of detailed identification requires some time and the deployment of consciously acquired knowledge stored in central cognitive systems.

Second, Fodor concedes that experimental psychology seems to have discovered some counterexamples to the informational encapsulation of input systems.[30] He suggests, however, that the information affecting the shape of their outputs in such cases may come from *within* the module itself. Their fast, mandatory operations and their limited range of shallow, stereotypical deliverances notwithstanding, Fodorian modules will either need to include or have access to a great deal of information about the materials they deal with, if they are to encompass all of the relevant empirical findings.[31]

Subsequent theorizing about these matters indicates that these two qualifications (as well as others) have left room for skepticism about whether or not thorough-going informational encapsulation is at the heart of modularity after all. In the face of Fodor's insistence both that "the involvement of certain sorts of feedback in the operation of input systems would be incompatible with their modularity" and that "[o]ne or the other . . . will have to go,"[32] most scholars have opted to discard the strict Fodorian conception of modularity. Mostly, that has meant that they have opted to relax Fodor's conception of modules' strict informational encapsulation and to countenance the possibility of modularized areas in central cognition.[33] The consequence of loosening Fodor's criteria for mental modules has been a proliferation of proposals about cognitive provinces in which the knowledge we possess by six or seven years of age is fruitfully construed as domain-specific.

Clark Barrett and Robert Kurzban maintain that given Fodor's list of nine conditions and his insistence on informational encapsulation, in particular, it is no surprise either that he only finds input systems to be modular, that he finds so few of them, and that he thinks a cognitive science of centralized cognitive systems is hopeless.[34] Barrett and Kurzban, by contrast, defend a far more liberal conception of modularity, holding that the key insight is that our varied cognitive activities "arise from the operation of multiple distinct processes rather than a single undifferentiated one."[35] Barrett and Kurzban endorse a conception of modularity grounded in *functional specialization,* for which distinctive inputs and domain-specificity are concomitant features. On their more liberal construal of modularity, reflection on human evolution furnishes hypotheses about functionally specialized cognitive systems that might manage particular materials (faces, kinship, social contracts, contaminants, sexual jealousy, and so on) and that can be investigated empirically.

While various sorts of central cognition fall short of many of Fodor's criteria it does not follow that they will not submit to a somewhat less exacting but no less systematic theoretical characterization. Barrett and Kurzban follow Dan Sperber's contention that what can be said systematically about domain-specific forms of central cognition remains an open, empirical question.[36] None of them want to squabble with Fodor about definitions, but neither do they want to foreclose on the possibility of domain-specific, central cognitive systems or their scientific investigation merely on Fodor's say-so.

Barrett and Kurzban underscore that their more liberal version of modularity does not turn on automaticity or on informational encapsulation or on fixed neural architectures or on detailed patterns of breakdown or on innateness. The modules they envision might manifest all of those properties, but it is not necessary that they display any of them. Instead, they stress functionally specialized systems that deal with problems that all humans face and whose dedicated operations turn on limited forms of input as evidence. Such systems' domain specificity does not result from innate specification. Instead, these functionally specialized systems, characteristic recurrent problems, and distinctive inputs as evidence jointly produce domain specificity.[37] Barrett and Kurzban (correctly) *reject* assumptions: (1) that proximate explanations about the development of some modularized central system and ultimate explanations about the role that natural selection might have played in its form are competitors and (2) that the proximate

explanations must include some strong claim about the innate specification of the system in question. By contrast, they endorse an "interac-
tionist position that includes as causal factors, genes, environment,
interactions with the environment, and self-organizing processes . . ."
that jointly generate what they refer to as "reliable development."[38]
Reliable development of a modularized central system, then, does not
require that it be innately specified, spatially localized, or identical
across individuals with regard to its physical structure. All that matters is
that it "will exhibit specialization to process certain kinds of information
in certain kinds of ways," that is, that it will be functionally specialized in
the relevant way.[39]

As Barrett and Kurzban note, such a liberal conception yields massive modularity.

Massive Modularity

Several theorists contend that the human mind contains many more
modules than Fodor allows. Among these theorists, the evolutionary
psychologists have proven the most vocal advocates of massive modularity.[40] They hold that the human mind is composed of dozens, perhaps hundreds, of specialized mental modules each of which evolved
to handle some distinct challenge to our ancestors' survival. They
maintain that these mechanisms operate, for the most part, independently of one another and of general intelligence, and, thus, they offer
their—simultaneously celebrated and notorious—comparison of the
human mind to a Swiss Army knife. They contend that the mind, like a
Swiss Army knife, contains an assortment of special purpose tools,
which work relatively independently of one another and, in a pinch,
can be enlisted for dealing with problems for which they were not
designed.[41]

According to the evolutionary psychologists, the mind contains
scores of cognitive mechanisms for managing everything from mate
selection, to tool use, to recognizing emotions from facial expressions.
These modules are specially adapted machinery for coping with the
scores of problems our prehistoric predecessors needed to solve in

order for them to be fruitful and multiply. For example, an evolution-ary imperative to assist kin, since kin share copies of the same genes, presumes the ability to detect kin. Evolutionary psychologists theorize about mechanisms that would go some way toward meeting the requi-site cognitive demands.[42] Candidate models should produce adaptive behaviors and avoid maladaptive ones. From an evolutionary stand-point, the machinery underlying kin detection is maladaptive, if, for example, it generates too many false positives. That would lead the organism to give, on balance, too much aid and comfort to non-kin and not enough to genuine kin, including not only offspring but even sisters, cousins, and aunts.

Evolutionary psychologists plausibly conjecture that these special-ized cognitive modules will employ different computational principles, since the problems and relevant inputs can differ substantially from one domain to the next. What it takes to recognize a fair distribution of resources does not overlap much with what it takes to deal with a nearby contaminant. They also hold that for some problems of great evolutionary importance (for example, mate selection) individual life-times offer insufficient opportunities to arrive at fitness enhancing judgments inductively. Undirected trial and error in such cases is not such a great option. It seems a reasonable strategy to inquire whether natural selection has come to instill some preferences in us that nudge members of our species toward better prospects in the mating game.

Whether any particular mental module is adaptive is a function of the environment in which it operates. Natural selection operates on behavioral outputs, not on the cognitive systems responsible for those behaviors. Especially in atypical environments, these systems can make mistakes. That they generally do their jobs well but that they do not do them perfectly is fully consonant with the theory of evolution. Evolution by natural selection does not guarantee perfect design (where perfect design in a perceptual system might, for example, entail always perceiv-ing the world aright). It only ensures a design of organisms *overall* that is good enough to produce another generation in the environment in which the species evolved. The accompanying cognitive and percep-tual systems are not optimal solutions to the problems they address. They have, instead, only been good enough solutions.

Perhaps the most striking illustrations of evolved modular systems that may no longer contribute to human fitness are those responsible for our penchant for consuming sugars and fat. When both were considerably harder to procure, this predilection led our ancestors to consume ample quantities of foods containing them whenever they were available. The advantages for our ancestors of ingesting these foods probably determined why we find these foods so appealing. The problem, though, is that in an environment where such foods are readily available, people tend to overconsume them. This has led in our time to what some experts are now describing as an obesity pandemic as well as to rapidly increasing rates of diabetes. The World Health Organization now estimates that the obese (calculated to number around one billion) exceeds the malnourished of the world by about four hundred million.[43] Artificial sweeteners and fat substitutes are like the movies. They work by creating illusions that provide enough cues to trigger these systems' operations. We experience the attendant positive emotions, that is, the pleasures associated with the consumption of sugars and fats, without facing the concomitant risks.

Evolutionary psychologists advance hypotheses about likely selection pressures that have shaped the human mind over the very long term, and they explore those hypotheses' implications for the minds of *modern* human beings. They wish to reorient cognitive psychology so that it focuses not just on what human minds may be able to learn about current circumstances but also on what natural selection designed them to do in the past. Cultural evolution speeds along compared to biological evolution. The cultural changes of the past five thousand years, especially, have arisen so swiftly that any evolved cognitive dispositions would have changed little, if at all. Thus, evolutionary psychologists maintain that humans operate today with most of the same cognitive equipment that prehistoric hunter-gatherers possessed. We continue to do so amidst all of the cultural upheaval and change, for which that equipment is at least partially responsible. Consequently, evolutionary psychologists hold that: (1) contrary to sociobiology, which appeals directly to biological evolution, exclusively evolutionary explanations of human conduct at the biological level will not suffice and (2) contrary to social scientists, who appeal only to some broad conception of learning or socialization or enculturation, explanations of cultural transmission that fail to recognize how specialized psychological mechanisms contribute to that process are unsatisfactory. Champions of socialization ignore what Leda Cosmides and John Tooby call "evoked culture," recurrent patterns across cultures whose forms substantially depend upon evolved dispositions of the human mind. Cosmides and Tooby propose, for example, that we should have modular capacities overseeing foraging and food sharing, which are sensitive to variance in the productivity of foraging for diverse items. Such sensitivity, they argue, would lead people to prefer one approach to the sharing of high variance resources and another with respect to low variance resources. Their suggestion, in short, is that such preferences may depend at least as much upon evolved psychological dispositions about such matters as they do on any particular body of cultural learning.[44]

Evolutionary psychologists' account of the human mind implies that *contemporary* human behavior and mental life should yield evidence for their hypotheses. If the modern human mind has evolved as they suppose, then that should be reflected in its structure and organization, in features of human performance, and in those recurrent, evoked patterns across cultures. Social scientists' field observations and systematic studies as well as the findings from psychological experimentation should provide means for testing these hypotheses empirically. For example, among Cosmides and Tooby's proposals about the massive modularity of the mind is the supposition that human beings have inherited dedicated cognitive machinery for reasoning about social contracts, understandings bearing on the distribution of benefits and costs within a group. Thus, Cosmides and Tooby looked at human reasoning about such social problems in contrast to how humans reason about other types of materials.[45]

In dozens of previous studies of a familiar reasoning problem in the psychological literature (namely, the Wason selection task) experimenters had found that people generally do not do well in carrying out some basic logical inferences when they involve statements about conditional relations between propositions.[46] The original version of the task concerned a set of cards and rules about them such as "if a card has

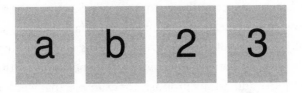

If a card has a vowel on one side,
then it has an even number on the other side.

Assuming that each of these cards has a letter on
one side and a number on the other, indicate only
those card(s) that you definitely need to turn over
in order to ascertain in this conditional rule is true.

Figure 2-5. Wason selection task

a vowel on one side, then it has an even number on the other side."
Most participants (usually around 70 to 80 percent) were unable to
identify all and only the cards in a set of four that they would need to
turn over in order to test the truth of the rule on the basis of information that they had about what was on the side of each of the four cards
that they could see. See figure 2-5. For this version of the problem, the
correct answer is to turn over the cards with the "a" and the "3" and
only these. For more than a decade, experimental psychologists, with
no definitive success, investigated various conjectures about what
feature of the Wason selection task was making the comparatively elementary problems of logic underlying it so difficult for participants to
solve.[47]

Notably, Cosmides and Tooby demonstrated participants' vastly
improved performance on the Wason selection task when the abstract
logical problem at stake was reformulated as a problem about the detection of cheaters in some socially regulated setting, that is, when the
problem was formulated in terms of a social contract. For an example,
see figure 2-6. In this version of the problem, the correct answer is to
turn over the cards with the words "drinking beer" and "16 years old"
and only these. Cosmides and Tooby's prediction is that solving this
problem should not be nearly so difficult as solving the problem in
figure 2-5, and that has been the finding with most participants.

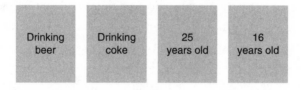

Assuming that each of these cards has information
about what a person is drinking on one side and
about his or her age on the other, indicate only those
card(s) that you definitely need to turn over in order
to ascertain if any of these people are breaking this law.

Figure 2-6. Wason selection task as a problem about a social contract

As Cosmides and Tooby predict, far fewer participants (20 percent–30 percent) err on versions of the Wason selection task formulated in terms of social contracts. They take this as evidence that humans possess evolved dispositions of mind for maneuvering in the social world and, in particular, for detecting those who break social rules pertaining to the allocation of benefits. They cite additional experimental evidence from clinical psychology about schizophrenics and from clinical neuropsychology about victims of brain lesions that also seems to support their view about dissociation between social contract reasoning and generic logical reasoning.[48]

By briefly sketching this parade case, I do not mean to indicate either that Cosmides and Tooby's view of it is unanimously endorsed or that intriguing alternative accounts of the findings do not exist. What it does show, though, is that reflection about long-term evolutionary processes can inspire provocative, new models about the modern human mind that have consequences that are experimentally testable and that connect directly with long-standing work in cognitive psychology.[49]

Whenever human cognitive accomplishments that seem critical to our ancestors' fitness also seem woefully underspecified by anything that might be gleaned from experience, evolutionary psychologists suspect the intervention of evolved, task-specific modules. For example, long before they have witnessed (if they ever do), studied, or even discussed any of the relevant biological processes, early school-age children know that piglets do not have parents who are ponies and that no matter how well he might imitate a duck, a swan is not a duck (even if, as the story goes, he inadvertently found himself among ducks and even if, as the popular saying goes, he quacks like one!). Other examples include such capacities as our visual recognition of medium-sized objects and of individual human faces, our comparatively rapid mastery of natural language, our presumptions about and interest in avoiding invisible contaminants, our sense of what constitutes a fair distribution of resources, our understanding of what other people are thinking, and many, many more.[50]

These are domains in which, first, children seem to know more about how to deal with problems than it would appear that their experience has prepared them to know and, second, at least some of the inferential principles involved seem to be peculiarly suited to the domains in question. Children do not need to be told that medium-sized organisms have parents and that medium-sized artifacts do not. Concerning these domains, Steven Pinker claims that "*the brain supplies the missing information*, information about the world . . ." in which our species evolved.[51] It follows that not just human brains, but other animals' brains also come with evolved dispositions that pertain to the ways that various parts of the world work, namely, those parts of the world that have been vital to *their* ancestors' survival. Evolutionary psychologists presume that natural selection has shaped animals' cognitive systems to cope with a variety of problems of this sort, and they hold, as William James did, that humans have more, not fewer, instincts than other animals.[52]

This account of the organization and the contents of human knowledge has gained wider support over the past two decades, but what have been perceived (Barrett and Kurzban's efforts to the contrary notwithstanding) as many modularists' claims about the *innate* origins of cognitive adaptations remain no less controversial than they have ever been.[53] What exactly claims about innateness amount to is not obvious, and slashing my way through that entire thicket would take another book. Moreover, what makes a system maturationally natural does not hang on this question. Thus my observations about these matters in what follows will be selective and spare.

Plato initiated a long tradition of theorists making assumptions about what, today, would be called the *innate* contents of babies' minds. Discussions of human knowledge in Western philosophy have largely concerned categorizing the kinds of knowledge that humans suspect they have, formulating arguments about which, if any, of those suspicions are correct, and (though philosophers have rarely framed their discussions this way explicitly) debating what things babies must know at birth in order for them to be able to obtain the knowledge that they do. Speculations have varied considerably about how much of human knowledge should be treated as standard equipment. Presumably, to claim that something is innate is at least to say that components of the human genome have some definitive role to play in the shape that item takes. The difficulties associated with pinning down exactly what that claim amounts to, though, are notorious. Most of that notoriety attaches to the challenges associated with (a) explicating which causal roles should count as "definitive" and (b) surveying which details the metaphor about an item's "shape" cover. Moreover, even so bland an observation as this points up a telling feature of the often acrimonious debates that have swirled around the putative innateness of mental modules, and that is how little evidence any of the parties to these quarrels have offered from research on human genetics. So far, these conflicts have mostly been played out in psychology and the social sciences.

The analysis of the cognitive foundations of science and religion that follows in this book looks to the notion of their maturational naturalness and *not* to whether the forms of cognition, perception, and action in question can be described, in some sense or other, as innate. If features of cognitive systems are usefully understood as innate in some sense, they will almost certainly qualify as maturationally natural, but maturational naturalness includes other patterns of cognitive activity, regardless of their origins, that exemplify the features I have outlined. Maturationally natural cognitive, perceptual, and motor operations are those that are effortless, automatic, unreflective, (mostly) unconscious, subject to persisting illusions in certain circumstances (that may not yet be known), and (usually) up and running before children can remember that they are, and, although culture frequently tunes these systems, they do not rely on instruction, structured preparations, artifacts, or anything else that is culturally distinctive.

By examining the maturational naturalness of cognition rather than nativist conceptions of mental modules, I aim to capitalize on points of growing agreement about the organization and the contents of our knowledge and to avoid the continuing controversies about modules' genesis, which, if Barrett and Kurzban are right, are mostly misguided anyway.[54] There seems to be fairly broad agreement about what many aspects of the minds of early school-age children are like. The parties to these disputes may not see eye to eye about the origins of these patterns or about the operating principles of the systems that realize them, but they do concur that by school age children the world over possess a surprisingly large amount of similar knowledge that pertains to a variety of the same domains across individuals and across cultures.

Developmental research over the past three decades also keeps showing that infants understand things in some domains at far earlier ages than anyone suspected. That includes the suspicions of Jean Piaget, whose work launched modern developmental psychology. Piaget's constructivist theory of cognitive development pictured a series of stages through which individuals proceed in the course of attaining mature cognitive capacities.[55] According to Piaget's constructivism, procession through those stages relied upon domain-general learning mechanisms. The problem is that subsequent work in developmental psychology includes squadrons of empirical studies demonstrating that children have these capacities long *before* Piaget contended and without having gone through the stages his theory described. The general direction of these studies has been to provide evidence for infants' possession of these capacities at ever earlier ages. As a result at least some developmentalists argue that *nativist* hypotheses are the most plausible way to explain such evidence arising from early infancy.[56] Babies as young as four months of age possess many of the same expectations in some domains that adults do. It looks as though in some areas, infants may need little experience, practice, or training.

That infants possess conceptions in the first year of life about how some things are settles few disputes either about which cognitive dispositions have lineages that stretch unswervingly back to what is coded in the genome or about the character of the neural machinery and its operations. That babies possess such conceptions does, however, impose additional demands on what will qualify as satisfactory accounts of their capacities.

The progressive development, the complex operations, and the intricate interactions with their variable environments, which very young children's structured neural networks (and which any genetic mechanisms that might play a key role in those networks' generation) exhibit, point to a pair of related questions at the psychological level. Those questions, vaguely reminiscent of (in)famous questions that arose in the U.S. Senate's Watergate hearings more than three decades ago, are "what particular things do babies know and when do they know them?" (The senators' concerns, of course, focused on what President Richard M. Nixon knew about the break-in at Democratic party offices in the Watergate Hotel in Washington, D.C., during the 1972 presidential campaign and when he knew it.) To answer the Watergate questions for babies, scientists have had to figure out how to read babies' minds. (Philosophers have gotten away with advancing so many divergent proposals about these matters over the centuries because no one, until the last few decades, had devised any convincing means for determining the contents of infants' minds.[57])

The Watergate Questions for Babies

It is not just that preverbal infants cannot say anything about what they know or about what they are thinking. By definition, they cannot yet say anything at all. They also have profoundly limited repertoires of emotions, postures, movements, facial expressions, tones of voice, and more. To say this, however, is not to claim either that they have nothing to communicate or that they cannot communicate—ask any new parent who has gone weeks without sleeping more than a couple of hours at a time. Such expressions notwithstanding, infants furnish few clues from which we can draw inferences regarding their expectations about the world. Babies do not offer scientists much to go on.

Consequently, scientists must construct special environments that will elicit leads about the conceptions infants use to make sense of the world. The assumption is that when scientists present babies with arrangements that violate their expectations, their reactions will resemble those of adults when their expectations are overturned. For example, when I began walking toward the cruise ship's stern, I was startled initially and interested for hours. That some of these arrangements will pique babies' interest shows that they have prior expectations that can be upended. Developmental psychologists have invented a variety of selective looking tasks by means of which they can both ascertain whether some condition violates infants' expectations and obtain measures of how interesting infants find that new situation.

One of the available techniques, known as "preferential looking," involves tasks that are directly comparative. Researchers present two stimuli to infants simultaneously and see which of the two the infants prefer to look at. When the stimuli do not involve the kinds of items to which infants are particularly attracted (for instance, human faces), the operative assumption is that infants will spend more time looking at the display that (more grievously) violates their expectations.[58]

Another technique explores infants' recovery from habituation, which developmental psychologists take as evidence of what infants notice and of their offended expectations and as a measure of their interest. Such experiments begin by repeatedly presenting some unproblematic event to infants until they become habituated to it, that is, until they become so familiar with it that it no longer holds their attention beyond some very short amount of time. Once infants have habituated to this stimulus, the experimenters present them with either of two new stimuli *both of which include some additional feature in common*. In the first experimental condition ("experimental condition A" hereafter), that addition to the original display results in a new event with a perfectly natural outcome, but *an outcome that is different* from that to which the infant had become habituated. The point about this new stimulus is that, although it differs from the habituated stimulus, it too is *unproblematic* (at least by the experimenter's lights) given what has been added to the display. By contrast, the new stimulus in the second experimental condition ("experimental condition B" hereafter) preserves more of the surface appearances of the habituated stimulus and, hence, it has the *same outcome*. The point, however, is that in this second new display the addition recasts the original outcome as something that would, presumably, count as an *unusual or impossible* event.

The critical dependent measure is how long the babies look at these new stimuli. Do they look longer at the first new stimulus in experimental condition A that is less similar visually to the habituated stimulus but unproblematic? Or do they look longer at the second new stimulus in experimental condition B that is more similar visually to the habituated stimulus but apparently anomalous? Or do they look at neither any longer than they would look at the original habituated stimulus? Scientists reason that the third outcome would signal that the infants have not even discriminated the new stimuli from the habituated stimulus. By contrast, either or both of the first two outcomes would imply that the infants do detect differences, and scientists construe the length of time the infants look at some new stimulus as a measure of how much it surprises them and of the level of their (resulting) interest in it. The assumption is that stimuli that disrupt babies' deepest and longest-held expectations will produce longer looking times from these young participants.

Elizabeth Spelke and her colleagues employ this approach in many experiments.[59] For example, in one they repeatedly present four-month-old infants with a stimulus in which a ball above a screen is dropped behind it and comes to rest on the floor of the display. Two seconds later the screen is lifted so that the infants can see the ball resting on the floor. After the infants habituate to this, the researchers present the babies with either of two novel stimuli, both of which include a tabletop that intervenes between the point from which the ball falls and the point where it lands on the display's floor in the habituated stimulus. In the new stimulus that is unproblematic, experimental condition A, the ball comes to rest on the table instead of on the floor. In the second anomalous situation, experimental condition B, the ball comes to rest on the floor of the display (as it did in the original display to which the infant was habituated). See figure 2-7. Notably, in this anomalous second condition, though, the ball appears to the infant as if it has fallen right *through* the table.

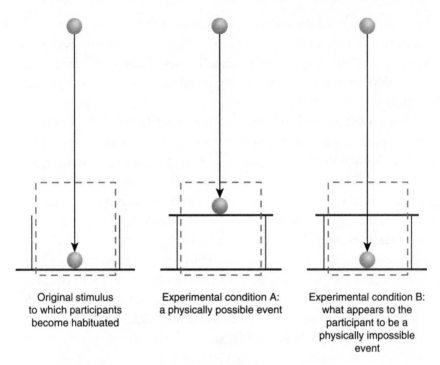

| Original stimulus to which participants become habituated | Experimental condition A: a physically possible event | Experimental condition B: what appears to the participant to be a physically impossible event |

Figure 2-7. First experiment (after Spelke et al. 1992)

That the infants spent significantly longer time looking at the display in experimental condition B than at the one in experimental condition A is evidence that they find it surprising. These babies are not as interested in the new stimulus in experimental condition A that diverges more from the habituated stimulus as they are in the one in experimental condition B that diverges less but appears to involve a physically *impossible* event. An obvious hypothesis is that babies at four months of age are already aware that solid objects do not pass through one another, and, thus, they are intrigued when they view a stimulus that seems to violate that physical principle. More generally, the infants seem more concerned with the physical principle at stake than they are with the superficial, visually accessible differences in the displays.

Another of Spelke's experiments discloses the power of such experimental designs.[60] In this experiment the initial stimulus to which the four-month-old babies become habituated is identical to the novel stimulus in experimental condition A of the previous experiment (in figure 2-7) in which a ball, dropped behind a screen, comes to rest on a table, instead of on the floor below it, as they can observe when the screen is lifted a couple of seconds later. Once habituated, the infants are then presented with either one or the other of the following new stimuli, both of which involve the removal of the tabletop from this experiment's original display. In the unproblematic experimental condition A in this experiment the ball falls to the floor of the display. In the anomalous experimental condition B, the ball's path is identical to the path of the ball in the display to which the babies have become habituated. (See figure 2-8.) Thus, in this experimental condition B, the ball drops only to the height of the tabletop, but, now, the tabletop is no longer there. Therefore, from the standpoint of the observing infant the ball appears to have stopped in midair without any supporting surface.

The findings from this experiment are particularly revelatory, because the new stimulus in experimental condition B does *not* elicit significantly longer looking times from the four-month-old infants than the new stimulus in experimental condition A does. These four-month-old babies are indifferent about whether the ball falls all the way to the floor or stops, apparently suspended, in midair. From this study these developmental psychologists conclude that four-month-old children do not yet appreciate some of the most ordinary consequences of the principles of gravity and inertia.

So, part of the answer to the first Watergate question for babies, namely, "what particular things do babies know?" is that although the available evidence indicates that four-month-old infants know that different solid objects cannot occupy the same space at the same time, there are some very basic things they do not know about gravitational effects, for example. Scientists can also use experiments of this sort to obtain evidence about *when* babies subsequently acquire such knowledge, that is, they can also use these experiments to answer the second Watergate question for babies. For example, Spelke and her colleagues carried out the second experiment concerning expectations about gravity with six-month-old babies too. They found that, unlike the four-month-old infants, the six-month-old babies look significantly longer

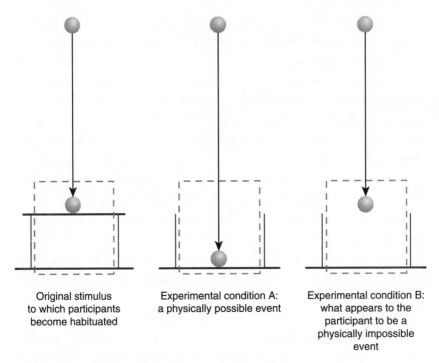

| Original stimulus to which participants become habituated | Experimental condition A: a physically possible event | Experimental condition B: what appears to the participant to be a physically impossible event |

Figure 2-8. Second experiment (after Spelke et al. 1992)

at the ball suspended in midair (experimental condition B), even though, again, it is superficially more similar to the habituated stimulus than is the stimulus in experimental condition A, in which the ball falls to the floor. It looks as though in the two months between four and six months of age, young children acquire some new expectations about gravitational constraints on physical events.

On the basis of these and a wealth of additional studies, Spelke and her colleagues have formulated physical principles (concerning cohesion, contact, and continuity) and constraints (concerning continuity and solidity) that they argue are innate.[61] Various experiments show that these principles guiding human perception and reasoning about physical objects apply across perceptual modalities and that the principles concerned with objects' motions supersede Gestalt considerations.[62] That they are in place at such early stages of development and that they play such a fundamental role in humans' understanding of

physical objects and their relations make these principles and constraints plausible entries on the list of items that come standard in a
human cognitive system.

Saying even roughly when children come to know something, however, is often not so straightforward. That young children often exhibit
U-shaped learning curves can sometimes make answering the second
Watergate question even more challenging. For tasks as varied as using
arbitrary gestures as symbols, producing the past tense forms of irregular English verbs, and balancing blocks, the available evidence reveals
that, first, young children are (at some point) able to do the task, then
at some later point they prove *unable* to complete the task reliably, and
then, finally, at yet a later time and thereafter they are again able to carry
out the task successfully.[63] Such patterns result in what is literally a
U-shaped function. (See figure 2-9.)

For example, four- and eight-year-old children are reliable block
balancers, but six-year-old children perform significantly less well.

Annette Karmiloff-Smith argues that such U-shaped findings result
from a series of systematic changes in children's mental representations, regardless of the domain. She provides a theory about the underlying general process that involves what she calls "representational
redescription" and that characterizes children's mental representations

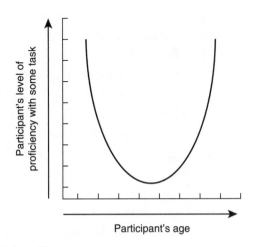

Figure 2-9. A U-shaped learning curve

in each phase and the transitions between them. Representational redescription is, in effect, a *meta*-representational capacity, that is, the capacity to construct representations of representations.[64]

Karmiloff-Smith argues that children begin by striving for behavioral mastery, which results in them formulating *implicit* representations to which they have no conscious access. The process is driven by the available inputs. In block balancing, four-year-old children approach each block to be balanced as a new task (even when some blocks are identical). They rely on feedback about the direction in which a block falls on particular trials for eventually figuring out how to get it to balance.

Of course, this particular example of block balancing no longer involves reading babies' minds. It does, however, involve ways in which developmental psychologists obtain information about things children know at a point in their cognitive development when they are unaware that they know them and (therefore) incapable of saying anything about what they know. Karmiloff-Smith's theory supplies a framework for comprehending humans' cognitive transitions (ultimately, regardless of whether the learners are children or adults).

During the second phase of representational redescription children move to *general* representations. This second phase is marked by children forming new meta-representations that are grounded in the collection of implicit representations that they acquired in the initial phase. In this second phase, children still have no conscious access to these new general representations, but the children's behaviors betray their influence. In the block balancing case, six-year-old children arrive—on the basis of a broadly reliable, but imperfect, induction—at a general representation for balancing blocks, which is equivalent to something like "center each block on the fulcrum." This general principle works fine, so long as the blocks are symmetrical. As a result, unlike four-year-old children, who rely on trial and error to balance blocks, six-year-old children no longer balance asymmetrical blocks. They presume that the problem resides not with their general principle but with them or with the troublesome blocks. So, instead of experimentally shifting the position of a block that will not balance, they center it on the fulcrum ever so much more *carefully* on subsequent attempts.

After many such unsuccessful attempts, they reject the block as one that is impossible to balance.[65] Children confront new predicaments, if the generalization with which they are operating is clearly inadequate (as is the case in the block balancing example). They must now contend with a group of anomalous instances—namely, blocks that will not balance—that they did not face before, and, therefore, they must also cope with operating on the basis of a generalization that does *not* apply to what had looked earlier like a single set of materials.[66] The joint force of these considerations (no doubt, along with other factors) can eventually lift these matters to the level of conscious reflection.

In the third phase of representational redescription, children adopt *explicit theories*, which are consciously accessible.[67] Simultaneously, children can sometimes even articulate what they can now consciously represent—in what Karmiloff-Smith treats as a closely related fourth phase of representational redescription. In other cases they reach this fourth level later, and sometimes they never reach it at all. In the latter situation people possess skills and intuitive knowledge over which they have a thorough-going command but about which, nonetheless, they find it difficult, if not impossible, to report on in much detail. This can be true of cognitively natural actions regardless of whether their origins are maturational or practiced, but achieving the ability to talk in a sophisticated way about either is nearly always a function of studied cognition that itself attains a practiced naturalness in experts only. This inability to articulate some things we know well is why even some of the greatest athletes cannot coach and why some of the greatest artists cannot teach. George Bernard Shaw commented that "he who can does. He who cannot, teaches."[68] What he overlooked, however, was that those who teach can *say*.

The theories that children embrace in the third phase may improve upon less satisfactory generalizations to which they had previously clung. They may offer new unified accounts of the domains that encompass what had in the second phase come to seem anomalous. So, in the block balancing case, eight-year-old children understand that the centering strategy of the six-year-old children works only for symmetrical blocks, and they have developed at least a qualitative appreciation of the more general law of torque in order to balance the asymmetrical blocks. Like the four-year-olds, they can once again balance all of the blocks.

Experimental research of this sort procures some empirical leverage with the difficult chore of sorting out how clean or how cluttered the slates are that babies are born with. Various findings indicate that young infants know enough to be able to reproduce facial gestures but cast doubt on the presumption that they know about gravitational effects.[69] Yet even findings such as these, which appear to provide fairly compelling evidence, ultimately, occasion further questions. For example, although the finding that young infants will reproduce facial gestures is, by now, uncontroversial, disagreements persist about how best to describe the knowledge that enables them to do so. By the same token, Spelke and her colleagues' findings do not establish whether the acquisition of expectations about gravitational effects is simply an induction (after roughly six, as opposed to four, months' experience) or whether it is something more like the eruption of teeth, which is initiated by specifications in the human genome and emerges—under most circumstances—during a particular period in human development. We need more information about, among other things, the range of stimuli to which newborns are differentially sensitive to begin to address the first option, and we need *much* more information about how and when the genome directly influences humans' cognitive achievements to begin to address the second.

Maturational Naturalness Redux

The second Watergate question inquires about *when* babies know things (and, therefore, about when they do not). Answering that question can help to clarify (a) the timing and progression of any endogenous capacities and (b) the prior cognitive accomplishments and the types and amounts of experience that are typically involved to obtain particular kinds of knowledge.

The emergence of the cognitive sciences and of the scientific study of cognitive development, in particular, has introduced the possibility of providing more precise answers to the Watergate questions. The earlier discussion of preferential looking and recovery from habituation as techniques for exploring what babies are thinking furnishes a glimpse of the exciting progress scientists have already made. The brief sketch of the obstacles that U-shaped learning curves can present for answering the second Watergate question hints at how complicated these matters may prove. (Who knows? Some learning curves may prove even more exotic.) And that sketch only touched on a bit of the prominent *psychological* evidence of the past few decades. Generally, as developmental psychology progresses, the complexity of the patterns to be explained has increased.

Karmiloff-Smith's treatment of U-shaped learning curves in terms of representational redescription argues that some patterns of cognitive development defy simple proposals, whether they focus on innateness or on learning. Neither routine nativist accounts, including those about innate capacities whose functioning particular environmental cues putatively elicit, weeks, months, or even years after birth, nor traditional inductive accounts of learning, will suffice to explain such patterns. On the one hand, popular nativist proposals have generally had little to say about U-shaped learning curves. On the other hand, learning theorists' standard conceptions of humans' inductive capacities have not contemplated the sort of meta-representational operations that Karmiloff-Smith's representational redescription requires.[70]

How Karmiloff-Smith's specific theory of representational redescription will fare in the long run as an account of the patterns in cognitive development is not the issue.[71] What matters are the patterns themselves and the complications that they introduce for answering the Watergate questions. The transformations in our understandings of what babies know and of when they know it have arisen from:

- deploying the new experimental methods that developmental psychologists have invented for examining young children's expectations,
- attending to the resulting findings about humans' successes, failures, and difficulties (and to *their* underlying temporal patterns) in any domain, and

- entertaining eclectic approaches (like Karmiloff-Smith's) to explaining those findings that incorporate promising insights (regardless of their origins or orientations)

These findings provide a potent rationale for deploying the notions of practiced and maturational naturalness. On many fronts the distinction between practiced and maturational naturalness tracks Lev Vygotsky's distinction between the cultural and the natural (or what Michael Tomasello calls the "individual") lines of ontogenetic development.[72] The distinction permits scientists, on the basis of evidence from the social, cognitive, and neurosciences, to inquire about the relative contributions of natural and cultural variables to both human development and cultural forms.

Crucially, *none* of the conflicts about innateness undo the relevant capacities' maturational naturalness. Cardinal capacities such as recognizing faces, uttering comprehensible sentences, and walking, like all cognitively natural systems, operate automatically, unreflectively, and (mostly) unconsciously. In addition, they possess other features peculiar to maturationally natural systems.

(i)   They prevail in the human cognitive economy before humans can remember that they do.
(ii) They concern problems that are so basic to human survival that
(iii) possessing these maturational skills and knowledge qualifies as normal development for members of our species and in some especially fundamental cases (for example, locomotion), what counts as normal development for members of other species as well.[73]
(iv) Their appearance does not rely on either schooling or instruction or artifacts.

Typically, they also do not seem to depend on others' structured preparations, though research on infant-directed language certainly suggests that such practices can sometimes assist their development.

Adopting parsimonious views about what is in babies' minds naturally encourages greater attention to what I referred to earlier as the socially and culturally embedded character of cognition. For example, some recent accounts of language learning emphasize the roles (1) of the sustained cooperation of competent speakers (especially infants' caregivers) and (2) of the infant's developing social skills. As an example of the first, adults in some cultures, however unconsciously, structure their linguistic inputs to infants by speaking to them in special ways to which infants are demonstrably more responsive.[74] When talking to babies, people utter grammatically simplified forms slowly and melodically, in higher than normal pitch, with elongated and exaggerated vowel and consonant sounds. Baby talk, which occurs throughout the world,[75] has earned the more honorific name "motherese" among developmental psychologists because of its contribution to enabling infants to acquire their native languages. Some have alternatively suggested "parentese" or "caretakerese," since others, including males, usually adopt this form of speech with infants too.[76]

Attention to such patterns in language learning has inspired a wave of experimentation in developmental psycholinguistics, looking at many aspects of young children's language acquisition in detail. The findings signal that infants' language acquisition[77] rests on, among other things, their procuring accumulating layers of interpersonal and social skills, described collectively in the literature as "theory of mind." Minimally, they distinguish human faces, make eye contact, follow another's gaze in order to attend jointly to things and events in the world, and recognize that other human beings have both communicative intentions and mental states (more generally) that can be *about* such things and events (and, hence, can be said to *represent* those things and events). This collection of activities underlies the young child's growing understanding that others are agents with mental representations about things in the external world and that those representations "may be followed into, directed, and shared."[78]

Tomasello argues that children must also engage in "role-reversal imitation,"[79] meaning that they must learn to use symbols with the aim of directing their interlocutors' attentions to some thing or event in the same way that their interlocutors have with them. They must intend to direct their interlocutors' attentions to the same things in the same ways.

On this view language acquisition and the acquisition of cultural knowledge more generally arise in tandem with the emergence of this repertoire of social skills.

It is interesting that, typically, adults adopt baby talk unconsciously. Since baby talk is not universal across cultures, it clearly counts as but another way that culture can infiltrate and influence the development of maturationally natural systems. Infiltration, however, is not determination. Cultural infiltration of these systems is always possible. Sometimes, for example, in the case of natural language, it is necessary. Occasionally, cultural and physical environments even infiltrate fundamental perceptual systems.[80] What is culturally distinctive about such infiltration, however, is typically incidental. Babies born in China could just as readily learn Quechua or Swahili as Mandarin. Babies born in Christian settings could just as readily learn the beliefs and practices of Islam or the Inuit.

Nothing that is the *same* about the development or about the patterns that maturationally natural systems manifest across *all* human cultures causally depends on anything that is culturally distinctive. On the other hand, the features I have reviewed set maturational naturalness off from practiced naturalness, regardless of whether any of the phenomena are innate. So, being innate would be a sufficient condition, but it is not a necessary one for establishing some cognitive pattern's maturational naturalness. Learning more about the genetic foundations of some phenomenon is always worthwhile, but it is *not* a precondition for attributing roles to maturationally natural systems or for considering them and their connections with the cultural.

Such connections are often myriad and complex. Sometimes they also appear to be decisive for maintaining maturational accomplishments. Although what is culturally distinctive about infiltration is usually incidental to a maturationally natural system, domains do exist where (1) like language, the cultural infiltration of the maturationally natural system seems central in subsequent developments yet (2) unlike language, there are *vast* differences in competencies between both individuals and cultures. These, then, are domains in which cultural infiltration of maturationally natural capacities can be simultaneously *fundamental* to ensuing developments yet obviously *different* from one culture to the next (and from one individual to the next). For example, it is widely recognized that infants possess the capacity to count (initially, only very small numbers of things), yet the mathematical sophistication of different cultures and of different individuals within the most mathematically sophisticated cultures diverges *dramatically*.[81] It is uncontroversial that cultural support is necessary for initiating, let alone sustaining, anything beyond the most elementary achievements in the mathematical domain. Ethnographic evidence about some cultures' mathematical impoverishment, though, indicates that cultural support may be necessary for *sustaining* such basic accomplishments.[82]

Focusing on the interaction of maturationally natural systems and culture, instead of on what is innate or what should qualify as a module provides a ready means for highlighting what virtually all of the participants in these debates agree about. However much they may quarrel about the human mind's evolution, architecture, and fundamental learning principles, their views about what young school-age children know largely coincide. The research suggests that they should.[83] There is, if not unanimous, at least widespread agreement that by this age most children possess a large body of domain-specific knowledge and principles of inference that constitute much of what cuts across all cultures as (adult) *commonsense*. These are the things that even these young children know intuitively. At the perceptual level, they know both what basic-level objects and what their friends' and family members' faces look like, what sounds melodious, which tastes and smells appeal and displease, and when someone is talking.[84] Cognitively, they know that an object moves on one and only one connected path across space and time, that hawks beget hawks, that it is a waste of time to interrogate a handsaw, and what someone means when they ask in their native language how far it is to the moon. From the standpoint of action, they know how to walk and run, how to chew, and how to avoid contact with sources of contamination.[85] However complex the competencies, however complicated the developmental patterns, and however convoluted the proposed mechanisms' origins, architectures, and operations, theorists on all sides overwhelmingly accept that by the time people reach middle childhood they have in a wide variety of domains acquired, as Karmiloff-Smith puts it, "relatively modularized" cognitive capacities that exhibit the characteristic features of maturational naturalness.

Ever Mindful

The most celebrated of these domains is theory of mind. That humans should be able to appreciate vital social complexities in a flash, as Mr. Quiverful did, is revealing. Humans' intuitive knowledge about others' minds and what goes on in them and the enriched social world that that knowledge sustains explains the scope, diversity, and complexity of human social arrangements and plays a pivotal role not only in individual and collective survival but in individual and collective accomplishment.[86]

Acquiring theory of mind involves a series of attainments, and it apparently takes some years just to get the maturational basics down.[87] Its precursors, according to Philippe Rochat, reside in infants' particular interest from birth (maybe even before) in the ways other people look and in the things they do and say.[88] Andrew Meltzoff and Keith Moore and subsequent researchers have documented very young infants' interest in people's faces, which seem to stand out as appropriate for imitation. Rochat summarizes some of the other features of people that infants find interesting: "People have the special feature of reciprocating and engaging in prolonged face-to-face interactions; games with high-pitched vocal interventions, particular facial expressions, and . . . sustained eye-to-eye contact."[89] Soon thereafter infants begin to attend to the directions in which others' eyes are looking.[90] (Apes' eyes do not have the white sclera that makes the orientation of human eyes so much easier to detect.)

Infants' early knowledge about objects' motions corroborates these judgments about the special status of humans among the things in their environments. People are numbered among a restricted set of things in the world that are prominent because they are *animate*. Compared to inanimate things that move (at all), animate things, among middle-sized objects, commonly move more often and nearly always move in more ways. Like other things their motions can result from external forces, but animate things are the ones that can start and stop and move on their own as well as move in variable ways along irregular paths. Infants are attentive to these distinctions and preschoolers consciously deploy them when classifying things that they have never confronted before.[91]

People are the most conspicuous members of the subset of animate things that qualify as *agents*. Agents not only move about in these irregular ways; their movements constitute *actions* with specific *goals*. Rochat and his colleagues have provided evidence that infants are sensitive to goal-directed actions at three months of age.[92] Crucially, the displays to which the infants responded included neither humans nor animals. Employing the preferential looking paradigm, they demonstrated that three-month-old infants attend differentially to displays portraying one disk "chasing" another in contrast to an otherwise identical display, including all of the same dynamic parameters, in which the disks' movements are (otherwise) random. For infants at least as young as three months movement information seems sufficient to specify events that involve what adults recognize as a form of goal-directed action and, when it arises between humans, as an example of social causality.[93] No theorist questions the adaptiveness of such a trait. Detecting agents, their actions, and their goals is a prerequisite for managing complex social relations in human communities, but it pertains to more basic matters as well. Recall Nash's counsel about panthers.

The set of possibilities for parsing agents' motions into categories of action is indefinitely large, but a variety of experimental measures intimate that human beings, from infancy, seem naturally disposed to divide those movements up in some ways rather than others.[94] Although humans have no problem recognizing simple *gestures* (such as sliding into a booth at a restaurant) and overall *scripts* (such as going out to eat at a restaurant), they show cognitive and perceptual biases favoring analyses at the level of the *behavioral episode* of intermediate duration *involving a specific goal* (such as ordering dessert).[95] Gestures are usually insufficient to clarify an agent's goal, while scripts include many goal-directed actions. This intermediate behavioral episode to which people assign a particular goal is the level at which adults spontaneously characterize individual actions and for which they have the best recall. In addition, the borders between actions construed at this level are salient on multiple counts. They are the temporal points in these movement sequences at which the most changes occur in everything from the direction and pacing of agents' movements, to the parts of their bodies involved, to the settings and objects of their actions.

Rochat also notes important developments that appear around nine months of age. Infants at this age not only notice goal-directed actions, but they also discern when agents reverse their roles—for example, when among two moving disks in a display, the chased and the chaser change jobs.[96] This is also when infants stop looking at the extended appendages of someone who is pointing and start looking, instead, at what they are pointing at. Over the next many months infants themselves begin pointing in order to direct the attention of others, not just to benefit themselves in some way but sometimes simply to show something to someone else. Between nine months of age and their first birthdays most children have begun to exhibit the first signs that they understand that other human beings have the ability to represent the world mentally.[97] Their subsequent recognition that others not only have goals but mental states such as desires and beliefs enables toddlers to begin to envisage and engage in cooperative activities. They also understand others' communicative intentions. These are the critical ingredients for establishing joint attention and, thus, for infants beginning to appreciate the connections among mental representations (others' as well as their own), language, and the world.

It is only a beginning though. Young children seem to understand that other people perceive the world and act on what they believe as a result of what they perceive, but these children do not seem comparably adept at tracking the contents of others' beliefs.[98] By now, scores of experiments exploring various versions of the famed false belief task have established that even as late as their fifth year of life children do not seem to fully grasp that others' representations of the world can be false.[99] When children under the age of four observe both that Maxi sees where the chocolate is stored initially and that, after Maxi leaves, someone hides the chocolate in a second, new location, they indicate, when asked, that, when he returns, Maxi will look for the chocolate in that second, new location. They seem unable either to represent Maxi's false representational state or to draw warranted inferences about it. Researchers have tested a wide range of variables that might influence children's responses in false belief tasks, but beyond shifting the threshold for success at the task a month or two on average within some experimental group, none have proven particularly influential, not even formal schooling.[100]

The fact that, the world over, it is not until children are around their fifth birthday that they begin to pass verbally formulated, false belief tests seems plausible evidence that no culturally distinctive inputs play any crucial role in the development of this capacity.[101] Nativists hold that it is evidence that an innate system influences the subsequent character and direction of cognition some years after birth. (This seems just what Fodor meant by the "characteristic pace and sequencing" of the development of an innate modular capacity.)

Recent experimental findings have complicated the picture. Kristine Onishi and Renée Baillargeon have constructed a *nonverbal* form of the false belief task, where the dependent measure again was youngsters' comparative looking times.[102] Onishi and Baillargeon's experiments with fifteen-month-old infants provide striking evidence that these infants have some understanding about others' false beliefs. These youngsters looked significantly longer at displays in which those who should have had false beliefs behaved as if they had true beliefs as well as at displays in which those who should have had true beliefs behaved as if they had false beliefs.

It is possible that the verbal demands of the various forms of the false belief task that have been administered to older children constitute a special processing obstacle for them. Ironically, in light of Onishi and Baillargeon's findings, Tomasello has argued that it is precisely their developing abilities to communicate linguistically that enable older children to gain the richer appreciation of other humans as mental agents that is necessary to succeed at this task (as opposed to simply being able, finally, to articulate what they have known, at least implicitly, since not very long after their first birthdays). He notes, for example, that hearing children and deaf children of deaf parents who converse with them in sign language pass these tests considerably earlier than deaf children of hearing parents who do not use sign language.[103] But the question about where Maxi will look does not seem difficult for three- and four-year-old children to comprehend, and, in many versions of these tasks, the children need do nothing more than point to some location in response to that question. The special-linguistic-processing-obstacle hypothesis does not look particularly plausible, but neither, in light of Onishi and Baillargeon's findings, do Tomasello's claims about the role that more sophisticated linguistic communication must play in children's appreciation of other humans as mental agents (such that they can *only then* pass a false belief test).

Beginning between nine months and one year of age and certainly achieving fruition by the time they are six years old, children come to adopt what Daniel Dennett calls "the intentional stance" toward other agents, which is, in effect, to treat them as "intentional systems," that is, as if they possess not only goals but mental lives and mental representations of their own.[104] Once they reach early school age humans know about a world filled with other humans and have already acquired the basic skills and knowledge necessary for handling the problems such a world presents. Gaining social experience and ingesting the voluminous narrative materials (stories, myths, dramas, novels, and so on) that saturate cultural spaces provide humans ample bases for elaborating, extending, and embellishing their theory of mind.

The speed, facility, and sophistication with which human beings deploy the intentional stance to make sense of their social world contrast starkly, though, with their liberality and frequent lack of insight about what will reliably qualify as an intentional system. Deborah Kelemen has documented preschool-age children's "promiscuous teleology," children's penchant for overattributing functions to things as a result of their new ability and growing experience with purposeful agents pursuing goal-directed actions.[105] Unlike most adults, most children this age are willing to attribute functions to biological wholes (for instance, tigers) and to parts of natural objects (for instance, a mountain protuberance) as well as to the natural objects themselves (for instance, icebergs).

Adults as well as children are remarkably profligate in their ascriptions of agency, yet any individual who fails to take the intentional stance toward effectively structured systems of much complexity will be at a distinct disadvantage when it comes to predicting their behavior. One of the benefits of employing Dennett's technical terminology to discuss these matters is that it readily accommodates the fact that humans are so often indiscriminate in their presumptions about intentional systems. If not, upon reflection, in their assignments of minds to things in the world, then, at least, often in their *treatment* of many things, humans proceed not only as if inanimate things are agents but as if they are agents who understand what we say. This proclivity of the human mind manifests itself in everything from children's play to adults talking to, coaxing, even begging for cooperation from machines like cars and computers. The point is not so much that humans, even children, have a clear sense of how to take the intentional stance toward inanimate things (though *that* is certainly noteworthy too) as much as it is that we so often *feel compelled* to do so[106] and that we so often derive some comfort from doing so. Dennett observes that:

> The practice of overattributing intentions to moving things in the environment is called *animism*, literally giving a soul (Latin, *anima*) to the mover. People who lovingly cajole their cranky automobiles or curse at their computers are exhibiting fossil traces of animism. They probably don't take their own speech acts entirely seriously, but are just indulging in something that makes them feel better. The fact that it *does* tend to make them feel better, and is apparently indulged in by people of every culture, suggests how deeply rooted in human biology is the urge to treat things—especially frustrating things—as agents with beliefs and desires.[107]

In some ways, the adults' behaviors are more revealing than the children's. Children generally know when they are pretending, however steadfastly they may keep up the pretense for a time. By contrast, adults' own online, unreflective episodes of taking the intentional stance toward inanimate things, though, regularly seem unremarkable to them.

Evolutionary psychologists have a ready account for these extravagances.[108] So long as the costs of false-positive signals are not too high, it pays to have an agent detection system that is easily cued. In a hostile, competitive world that is red in tooth and claw, the costs of false-negative signals are *prohibitively* high. All else being equal, the creature that is inattentive to the movement in the periphery, the shadow passing overhead, or the rustling in the leaves (let alone the sound in the basement) is less prepared to protect itself from predators, competitors, and foes. A mechanism with a low activation threshold for spotting agents may leave a critter a little jumpy, but, again, so long as the costs are not exorbitant, a hypersensitive agency detection device (HADD) is also more likely to leave it alive to be cautious another day.[109]

Supplementing this basic equipment with a rich theory of mind equips an individual to manage in a complex social universe, where, among other things, people make alliances, have conflicts, cooperate, compete, joke, threaten, ameliorate, inform, trust, and deceive. Among social animals, human beings are unmatched in their appreciation of an entire social world fashioned by individual agents' actions. A HADD disposes them to look for agents and, thus, to deploy the categories of agent causality when things go bump in the night (an intruder?) or when an unexpected event occurs amidst complex social arrangements (a conspiracy?). This maturationally natural proclivity steers human minds away from inventing or investigating other causal conceptions concerning *things* going bump (at any time of day) and, especially, concerning *human* affairs, where the detection of intentional agents is as unproblematic as it can *possibly* be.[110]

The remainder of this book examines the implications for science and religion of people having minds that naturally mature in the ways that human minds do. Their maturationally natural systems equip human minds to readily generate, retain, deploy, and transmit religious representations. By contrast, the prominence of those maturationally natural systems is mostly an obstacle to the invention and the investigation of alternative causal conceptions. Broadly speaking, this is why science is so hard to learn and why it is so hard to do. The next chapter takes up this cognitive unnaturalness of science.

3

Unnatural Science

The Boxing Day Disaster

December 26, 2004, was to prove one of the most deadly days known to humankind; that was the day of the great Sumatra-Andaman earthquake and the most destructive tsunami in human history. The Boxing Day Tsunami is estimated to have killed around two hundred thousand people and wrought immeasurable personal and economic losses on the lives of millions more.

The earthquake began a few degrees north of the equator, about 290 kilometers south of Banda Aceh at the northwestern tip of Sumatra. (See figure 3-1.) Approximately thirty kilometers under the Sunda trench in the eastern Indian Ocean, the India plate (a part of the larger Indo-Australian plate) pushed to the northeast under the Burma plate (a part of the larger Eurasian plate) by as much as twenty meters. Over the first one hundred seconds this slipping motion proceeded along the fault to the northwest. After a pause of about another one hundred seconds, the slipping commenced a second time and continued as the fault proceeds more directly north—quickly for the next six minutes, much slower for the next half hour, and even more slowly over the next two hours or so. The earthquake involved both the longest-lasting rupture in recorded history in excess of eight minutes as well as the longest rupture in recorded history, almost thirteen hundred kilometers, a distance approximately equivalent to the entire length of California. At its fastest, the speed of the slippage along the fault exceeded eight thousand kilometers per hour.

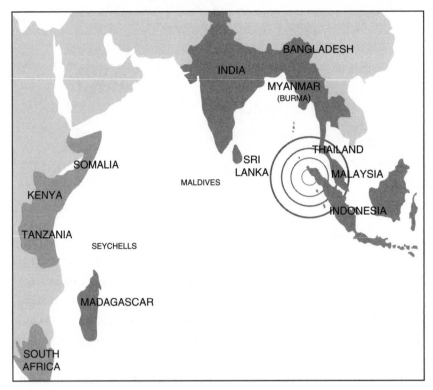

Figure 3-1. Map of the 2004 Indian Ocean earthquake (after Hammond World Atlas 2008)

This was the largest earthquake in the past forty years, since the installation around the world of digital broadband, high-dynamic-range seismometers, which capture not only the massive motions in the earth from the main shocks of earthquakes but the resulting free oscillations of the entire planet and the many smaller aftershocks as well.[1] The Sumatra-Andaman earthquake generated a shift in the earth's mass that caused the earth to speed up enough to decrease the time of its daily rotation by 2.5 microseconds.[2] It also disrupted the earth's gravitational field enough to measurably deflect the orbits of man-made satellites and generated the longest-distance earthquake triggering known.[3] In the 1990s scientists had ascertained that the shock waves from one earthquake could spawn other earthquakes in seismically active regions as far away as three thousand kilometers. After the Sumatra-Andaman quake, a train of shock waves triggered fourteen smaller earthquakes more than eleven thousand kilometers away in the Mount Wrangell region of Alaska.[4]

Without a doubt, though, the most dramatic and terrible effect of the Sumatra-Andaman earthquake was the tsunamis that it bred. The Indian plate's push against the Burma plate also caused the latter to move *vertically* between three and four meters on average and as much as eight meters in some places at its edge. This occurred at one of the earth's many subduction zones where an oceanic plate dives beneath a continental plate. It measurably tilted both the Andaman and Nicobar islands up in the west and, correspondingly, down in the east. The earthquake similarly shifted hundreds of square kilometers of the sea floor and the ocean above it, displacing hundreds of cubic kilometers of ocean water.[5] Incredibly, it is estimated that the resulting tsunamis consumed less than one-half of one percent of all of the energy expended in this geological event.[6] The tsunamis traveled perpendicularly, basically east and west, away from the entire thirteen-hundred-kilometer-long rupture along the fault. Since the slippage in the northern reaches of the earthquake zone proceeded at a much slower pace, the size of the resulting tsunamis and the damage they caused in the northern Bay of Bengal, in areas that were, in some cases, less than a thousand kilometers from the fault, were—contrary to commonsense presumptions—considerably *less* than the size and impact of the tsunamis seven hours later on the coast of Somalia in Africa nearly five thousand kilometers away.

Of course, the greatest havoc occurred on Sumatra, where at least 131,000 people lost their lives. In deep ocean waters a tsunami can move at speeds between five hundred and a thousand kilometers per hour,[7] but with wave lengths often more than one hundred kilometers long, they will not raise the surface of the water much more than thirty centimeters and rarely more than a meter.[8] Many are surprised to learn that an oceangoing vessel on the (deep) high seas will be unfazed when overtaken by a tsunami. The speed of a tsunami will slow substantially (to as little as forty kilometers per hour) as it travels over shallower waters near coastlines. As its pace slows, however, the amplitude of the wave grows. As it approaches a shoreline, a large tsunami will increase to proportions that are staggering. The evidence, including the devastation after the fact, suggested that the tsunami resulting from the Sumatra-Andaman earthquake reached heights of twenty-five meters as it hit the shore and of thirty meters as it traveled inland at various points in the vicinity of Banda Aceh.[9] People in this area had no more than fifteen minutes or so to evacuate the coastal area, even if they had been warned instantly. Moreover, the tsunami reached as far as four kilometers inland.

Geoscientists had anticipated such events. More than a year before the Boxing Day Tsunami, Phil Cummins, a scientist who works for the government agency Geoscience Australia had been making the case in scientific and government forums for constructing a tsunami warning system for Australia and other Indian Ocean nations comparable to the one that has been built in the Pacific Ocean. Just three months before the great Sumatra-Andaman earthquake, Cummins published a prescient piece. It described an 1833 earthquake that occurred farther south and east along the same fault in the Sunda trench and what contemporary computer models indicated about the pattern of tsunamis that resulted (corroborated, in part, by historical documents in Indonesia). Cummins showed that these tsunamis affected not only the northwest and western coasts of Australia (which were far more sparsely inhabited in 1833 than they are today) but also, ultimately, the "entire Indian Ocean basin."[10]

A modern tsunami warning system is an amazing and complicated scientific achievement. It involves coordinating both seismic and oceanographic information across vast stretches of the earth's surface. One that relied on seismic information only would initiate too many false positive signals, since most earthquakes, even most earthquakes under the oceans, do not displace the seafloor in any serious way. Thus, the tsunami warning system in the Pacific Ocean also includes tsunameters on the ocean floor, which can detect the changes in water pressure as a tsunami passes over them and relay that information to satellites, which convey it to scientists at the Pacific Tsunami Warning Center at Ewa Beach, Hawaii.

The seismic activity of the Sumatra-Andaman earthquake, in fact, tripped alarms at the center within minutes, and scientists there were able to determine in fairly short order that this seismic activity would not produce any massively destructive tsunamis in the Pacific. Over the next hour or so, though, further analysis of the information that was coming in enabled them to infer the possibility of a dangerous tsunami in the Indian Ocean. Their initial attempts to warn the governments of the nations most likely to be affected preceded by but a few minutes the very first news reports of the tsunamis' impact. Of course, scientists at seismographic centers in some of the affected nations had also recognized the dangers the earthquake presented. In the face of affected areas so immense, a communications infrastructure (in many of those areas) so fragmentary, appropriate lines of communication so ill defined, and a nearly total absence of evacuation plans, their efforts to warn people proved no more effective than the efforts of scientists at the Pacific Tsunami Warning Center. That people did not receive warnings was not a failure of science but a failure of public policy.

Arguably, the need for a tsunami warning system is greater in the Indian Ocean than anywhere in the world—in the light not just of the havoc and damage the Boxing Day Tsunami created, but because of the population densities along the Indian Ocean's coasts and because it is much *smaller* than the Pacific. That, of course, means that the time available to warn people of a tsunami will, on average, be less. In the aftermath of the Boxing Day disaster various governments and international bodies have made commitments to develop a tsunami warning system for the Indian Ocean, but even if those groups live up to those commitments, it will take many years to put all of the necessary components of such a system into place.

Recounting these dramatic and sad events supplies a ready means for demonstrating the ability of science to enhance our understanding, our explanations, and, even in so unlikely a case as this, our predictions of events. However important those considerations are, and they are extremely important, what matters most for my purposes is how this case exemplifies a number of the respects in which the products and practices of science profoundly diverge from the deliverances and processes of human beings' maturationally natural cognitive systems. On many critical counts science is, in this sense, profoundly unnatural from a cognitive standpoint.

Clarification Number One: Material and Abstract Tools; or, Technology Is (Still) Not Science

With talk of satellites, tsunameters, and digital broadband, high-dynamic-range seismometers in the previous section, it may seem odd to begin by insisting on the need to distinguish science from technology.[11] More accurately, I will distinguish scientific theory and methods and other abstract tools, such as mathematics and formal logic, from material technology, both artifacts and structured environments. Every culture possesses material technology, even if only clothing, shelter, and crude tools, but, as I will argue later, science is rare. Science is one of many knowledge-seeking activities that humans undertake, but as a continuing, systematic endeavor to account for the empirical world, it is unsurpassed. This is true, however, not because of what science has in common with material technology but because of what sets it apart.

Science and technology have always been connected, but since the middle of the nineteenth century, they have become inextricable. Scientific advances have regularly depended upon the invention and construction of all kinds of special machinery capable of creating rarefied environments in which scientific hypotheses might be tested—from particle accelerators in physics to computerized displays in psychology. Even more familiar, though, is how theoretical progress in science has created and improved increasingly widespread technologies. These include what has become everyday electronic gadgetry (radio, television, computers, cell phones), medicine's basic toolkit (stethoscopes, blood pressure cuffs, X-ray machines, pace makers, vaccines), and the wide range of pharmaceuticals that do everything from fight infections and regulate moods to deter the coagulation of the blood and suppress the immune system.

Teasing apart theoretical science and its methods from technology risks the appearance of underplaying the inextricable connection between science and technology. I certainly do not mean to imply that they are not deeply connected. Although I have never said that they are not and although I have said many things (and have and will say them again here) to the contrary, Barbara Hernstein Smith maintains that I (and Wolpert) hold that technology is "an incidental byproduct of pure science."[12] In fact, I fully concur with John Gribbin's observations that "technology came first, because it is possible to make machines by trial and error without fully understanding the principles on which they operate. But once science and technology got together, progress really took off." Gribbin further notes that once Western science "got started, by giving a boost to technology it ensured that it would keep on rolling, with new scientific ideas leading to improved technology, and improved technology providing the scientists with the means to test new ideas to greater and greater accuracy."[13] By drawing the distinction between science and technology that I do in this section, I intend nothing more controversial than the distinction between them that Gribbin's comments presume. Technology is a necessary condition for the pursuit of science, but it does not follow that every cognitive feature of science depends on technology.

Smith claims that I have adopted a "narrow, historically and culturally quite specific, understanding of 'science'" in order to get my treatment of science and technology off the ground and have offered a distinction between them that "can only be arbitrary and artificial."[14] For reasons that I will spell out I confess both to bolder ambitions and to skepticism that the treatment that follows applies so narrowly. But even if, in fact, she were right that my analyses of the cognitive foundations of science were to cover no more than Western science since Copernicus or Galileo or Harvey or Boyle or Newton or Dalton or Darwin (take your pick), it would not diminish those analyses' interest much, since *that* is precisely the science that most participants compare with (usually modern, Western) religion.

I am not clear what Smith means by "artificial," but to the extent that the distinction I draw between science and technology is not perceptually manifest and depends on a variety of different considerations (outlined in what follows), perhaps it is artificial. Artificiality in that sense, however, makes the distinction no less useful. Artificial distinctions— such as those between retail and wholesale, between novels and novellas, and between people who are permitted entry into an art exhibit at 12:24 as opposed to those permitted entry at 12:36—abound and are far from meaningless. In fact, I think that the distinction points to some natural (as opposed to artificial) differences concerning the cognitive foundations of science and technology, but more on that later.

That my distinction does, indeed, rely on a variety of different considerations, though, demonstrates that it is not arbitrary. In fact, examining science's *cognitive* foundations provides strong grounds for distinguishing it from technology.

The first set of grounds is *historical*. The ties that bind science and technology in their current intimate relationship make it difficult for us to envision a world in which those connections were fewer and less extensive, let alone one in which no such ties existed at all (because science did not exist at all). But nearly all of the time in nearly every place prior to the mid-nineteenth century and certainly prior to the rise of modern science, that was, in fact, the state of things. From a historical perspective, two considerations spotlight the independence (including the cognitive independence) of technology from science.

The first is the comparative scarcity of science in human history. Across history there has not been enough science to have exerted much influence on technology. Even on the most liberal conceptions of science, its ongoing pursuit has bloomed infrequently and flourished even less. If the list of instances of continuing scientific activity were to include (a) the collection of ancient cultures from the Chinese to the Babylonians to the Egyptians to the Mayans (by virtue of their astronomical observations and record keeping and their cosmological speculations), (b) the ancient Greeks, (c) some segments of Muslim societies and the Chinese during the last centuries of the first millennium through the Middle Ages, and (d) the Europeans in the sixteenth and seventeenth centuries and the subsequent emergence of modern science that their work inspired, that entire list would, in spite of everything, include but a fraction of human history in a tinier fraction of human societies. And that list, according to the reckonings of some historians and philosophers of science, is already an unjustifiably liberal one.[15] After all, on one of the most prominent views of the history of science, only the ancient Greeks and the modern science of the past four centuries should qualify. The point here, though, is that even on more lenient conceptions science has arisen rarely in human history.[16]

The second historical consideration is the obverse of the first. The rarity of science in human history contrasts starkly with the ubiquity (even the prehistoric ubiquity) of technology. Although the vast majority of cultures in the history of our species have not established continuing scientific investigation, *every* culture possesses technology. On even the most liberal conceptions of science that are plausible, prehistoric technologies would still have surfaced and progressed wholly independently of science, since they predate even the earliest of those ancient civilizations (under item (a) above) by more than one hundred thousand years among our species (and by more than a couple of million years among our earlier distant cousins). From the standpoint of the natural history of our species, science is a recent development.[17] This prehistoric pattern of technology thriving independently of science has persisted in most places at most times since. That it would take scientific inspiration to guide technological progress is a very recent notion.

Historians of science have noted how the development of science was abetted by technological developments throughout the modern era. Historians of technology, however, largely concur that the development of technology was mostly unrelated to science prior to the final decades of the nineteenth century in Europe. The synergy between science and technology over the last century and a half probably turned at least as much on technological change as it did on changes in science. Their recent closer relationship depended as much on the Industrial Revolution and mass communication by electronic means as it did on science having attained either some institutional or theoretical tipping point.

Attention to the role of technology in human prehistory raises a second ground for recognizing the independence of material technology from science. This rationale is rooted in two facts about *natural history*.

First, archaeological research has disclosed, in addition to modern *Homo sapiens*, a half dozen other prehistoric species that produced and used technology. Among others, that list includes our close relative, *Homo neanderthalensis*, who, according to the fossil record, only disappeared about thirty thousand years ago. Aiming to square the archaeological evidence from all of these species with the psychological evidence about modern humans, Steven Mithen has advanced a theory of the evolution of the modern human mind that construes our basic technical intelligence in terms of a collection of domain-specific mental modules. Mithen sides with the more liberal modular thinkers (rather than with Fodor) on two crucial fronts. First, the modular capacities that he envisions both in us and in our species' predecessors are not confined to input systems, and, second, *our* modular capacities are not informationally encapsulated. Mithen argues that the crucial evolutionary change that provoked the explosion of culture over the last forty thousand years among *Homo sapiens sapiens* is a significant breach of many modules' informational encapsulation during the course of cognitive development. As they mature, modern human minds benefit from what becomes a nearly pervasive "cognitive fluidity" among many of their mental modules, which permits a ready exchange of information between them and, thereby, our abilities to produce metaphors and to reason analogically.

According to Mithen, this cognitive fluidity results in what Karmiloff-Smith characterizes as representational redescription.[18] It provides the mind with meta-representational capacities, including the ability, at Karmiloff-Smith's final stage of explicit representation, to produce, for example, linguistic representations of technical representations. Karmiloff-Smith's four-year-old block balancers, presumably, operate unreflectively on the basis of their modularized technical abilities. They approach the balancing of each block as a new task (even when blocks are identical), relying on feedback about the directions in which blocks fall on test trials. They generate *implicit* representations about what was required for success in each case. Six-year-olds differ. They have achieved some cognitive fluidity and are able to formulate a general theory about what is required to balance blocks that is more efficient but less reliable. It makes for far fewer trials and errors so long as the blocks are symmetrical. But it also renders six-year-olds less able to balance nonsymmetrical blocks than the four-year-olds. Instead of shifting the blocks' positions on subsequent trials as four-year-olds do, the six-year-old children try to center them with ever more care. Eight-year-old children have had more experience, possess greater cognitive fluidity, and are, therefore, able to create more kinds of representational redescriptions.

Rather than declaring nonsymmetrical blocks un-balanceable, as some six-year-old children do, they have not only acquired a more sophisticated set of meta-representations, but because of what Mithen describes as the cognitive fluidity between their technical and linguistic modules, they are now able to *talk* about what they are doing and why. Newly emerging cognitive fluidity in the course of individual development in this case would seem Mithen's choice for explaining U-shaped learning curves.

Mithen maintains that Cosmides and Tooby's Swiss Army knife model of the mind, in which the mind possesses myriad modules, most of which are cognitively impenetrable, properly describes not our minds but, rather, the minds of early modern humans before the evolution of substantial cognitive fluidity.[19] His account of relations between the archaeological record and modern humans' conduct and mental lives offers a cognitive rationale for distinguishing science from technology. That our developing technical capacities profit both from the emerging cognitive fluidity among these and other modular systems and from cultural infiltration does not obviate the fact that, on Mithen's view, these capacities start out as modular and, thus, as maturationally natural systems. Consequently, in terms of the analytical framework that I am employing in this book, the origins of human technical capacities certainly look to be cognitively natural.[20]

By contrast, Mithen proposes no primordial modular capacity whatsoever for science. He explicitly holds that developing cognitive fluidity between various modules is a prerequisite for the possibility of science.[21] The theoretical originality of science relies upon humans' abilities to discover metaphors and analogies that can issue from any corner of human knowledge. The mind can deliver items from its farthest reaches for comparison with one another because of the open avenues that cognitive fluidity establishes. It is these abilities to exploit anything we know and to ponder each thing in light of everything we know (or least in the light of everything that we can remember at a particular moment) upon which scientific creativity and judgment depend.[22] Mithen's theory points, then, to a worthwhile cognitive criterion for distinguishing science from technology.

The second fact about natural history relevant to the distinction between science and technology is that not even the members of our genus (*Homo*) have a monopoly on the manufacture and use of tools. Over the last few decades, researchers have discovered that more and more animals not only use tools but also fabricate them—from Jane Goodall's finding in 1960 of standard chimpanzees stripping leaves from sticks that are broken to appropriate lengths for extracting termites from their mounds to recent work showing New Caledonian crows demonstrating a very similar aptitude for producing tools for procuring grubs from trees.[23] In short, natural history testifies to the fact that the construction of artifacts, unlike the pursuit of science, is not a uniquely human accomplishment.

I commented earlier about the embeddedness of cognition and the important role that external cognitive prostheses, like the technology of writing, play in many of our intellectual feats. (Recall the challenge to multiply two four-digit numbers without the aid of some external device or another.) Those observations are of a piece with broad conceptions of technology, which include within its purview not just fabricating implements and structuring environments but developing *abstract* intellectual tools as well. Such broad conceptions of technology may afford a slightly different perspective on the relation of science and technology, but one that, for cognitive purposes, justifies distinguishing them nevertheless. If abstract symbol systems such as language and mathematics or, at least, their external representations in systems of writing and calculation, respectively, count as a genus within the family of products and endeavors that constitute technology, then science *would* qualify as a species of that genus. But, as we tend to think about ourselves, some species stand apart. If science is an instance of technology, it stands apart from material technology in at least two obvious ways.

First, the persistence of science, if not its birth (as well), depends upon literacy. Merlin Donald[24] maintains that the invention of writing and reading was not necessary for the initial sparks of science in human cultures, but even he thinks that, without literacy, none of those scientific sparks could have ignited a steady flame among communities of inquirers for decades at a time. Neither the beginnings nor the persistence of material technology, however, hinges on the discovery of writing.[25]

The ability to talk is not enough. Talking and writing *do* have some things in common. Both spoken and written language can convey the contents of the minds that create them. Both utterances and written documents externalize the contents of their creators' minds for people to hear or see. Written symbols, however, differ from spoken (and manually signed) symbols in some pivotal respects.[26]

Spoken symbols are short-lived. Written symbols *last*. They are persisting material things instead of fleeting acoustic events. Until Edison's invention of a sound-recording device, the existence of utterances was always momentary, lasting no longer than its echoes. The material medium utilized for written symbols, whether paper and ink or neon lights or combinations of pixels on a computer screen, is what underlies their longevity.

Because written symbols last, literate cultures do not need to rely solely on human memories to preserve knowledge. At least in the ideal, they only need to preserve written records and to teach each new generation how to read and write. For the literate, written symbols are critical aids to memory. The compiling of a household's grocery list that I discussed earlier is every bit as fitting an illustration here as the millions of volumes in the world's libraries. In both cases, human beings, who know how to read and write, can return to those documents after long delays and retrieve the knowledge they embody— readily in the case of most grocery lists, a great deal more laboriously with some of those libraries' weightier tomes.

Unlike speech, written works can be copied and transported far from where they were produced, and they can be read, considered, and criticized in times and places where no one has ever met the author. All of this is just as true for texts by unknown authors. This is the sense in which texts and the contents they embody can be said to take on lives of their own. Writings not only last, but they also acquire an existence that is independent of their creators.

Karl Popper maintained, in effect, that the innovation of writing was indispensable not just for increasing the quantity of human knowledge but for increasing its quality as well.[27] On Popper's account the combination of written symbols' externality and persistence is the key to the possibility of objective knowledge. Prior to the invention of writing, humans may have been capable of entertaining contents and reasoning about them subjectively, but they had scant means for achieving *objective* knowledge, given the ephemeral character of the spoken word. For Popper *that* epistemic achievement hangs on texts' independence from their authors, which commences as soon as authors write them. Those texts and their contents exist independently of what the author thinks about them.

According to Popper, this independent life of texts is decisive for the objectivity of rational inquiry, in general, and of science, in particular. What inquirers, including scientists, contemplate, debate, and criticize (often in further writings) are the contents of these externalized texts, rather than the contents of their creators' mental states. At least currently, the contents of those mental states are available, at most, only to themselves. What gives texts their objectivity is this independent existence both from the minds that create them and from the minds that scrutinize them. Unlike the contents of mental states, the contents of texts are available to anyone who is (sufficiently) literate. Scientists discuss theories and, most of the time, even evidence and experiments as they are objectified in texts. They do not have access to other scientists' mental representations of those items. What they do have access to, though, are symbolic descriptions of those items in texts. Consequently, they can, among other things, carry out actions that will enable them, first, to witness some things that will directly count as evidence for some hypothesis and, second, to reconstruct and re-perform experiments. Among the features that characterize science are the public availability of such texts, the freedom, indeed the obligation, of scientists to scrutinize and criticize them, and the range of tools and resources that the sciences have generated for doing so.[28]

Written symbols are not only critical aids to memory—they are also critical aids to thought. Not only can critics read and ponder texts at length; so can authors. Conventions for most kinds of writing regularly arise in literate cultures that censure the various glitches, interruptions, incompletenesses, corruptions, and more that pass without comment in most human speech. Because readers can study texts at length, they can spot vagueness, incoherence, errors, and other problems that often get by when someone is only talking. Because authors are readers of their own texts, they too can locate weaknesses and mistakes and, before they make them public, remedy them. The positive side of all of this, especially for continuing rational inquiries such as science, is that in extended presentations of complex contents written symbols permit a kind of clarity and precision that is almost nonexistent in spoken utterances (certainly when they are unguided by written aids) but is imperative for presenting and testing scientific theories.

The recognition that potential critics will have plenty of time to peruse a text can prompt considerable care about its formulation. This is because even though texts gain an independence from their authors, authors are, nonetheless, typically identified with the texts that they produce. Because of those texts' independence, though, authors have little control over the treatment that those texts receive. All of these considerations counsel greater caution about what we write than about what we say, and it is for just these reasons that although science is not only about what gets written and published, it is always finally about that.

The second way in which science differs from other types of tools is that it always includes an abstract theoretical interest in understanding nature for its own sake. In fact, this comment comprises two differences. The first is that science pursues richer accounts of the world for no more reason than their intrinsic interest. The second is that those pursuits always involve speculations that aim to elucidate some aspect of the world's workings.

Humans develop artifacts to solve problems they face in dealing with their environments. If science began with ancient societies' systematic collections of astronomical observations, then it may also have been born out of practical concerns. It was, after all, not only the priests and soothsayers who were interested in the stars. Systematic observation of the heavenly bodies was the means for obtaining a workable calendar, which is a practical problem of profound importance for farming. Clearly, such conscientious observation is a prerequisite for *empirical* science, but it is other elements that capture what is distinctive about science. Still, even on such lenient conceptions of science as Donald's, the subsequent science of the ancient Greeks differed crucially from the protoscience of those earlier astronomical observers, because, among other things, the ancient Greek scientists and philosophers had enshrined reflection about the natural world for its own sake.[29]

Wolpert provides an especially apposite instance of this view, citing Plutarch's account of the great Greek scientist Archimedes. Plutarch reports that Archimedes regarded success in mere mechanics and concerns about ideas' practical applications as "ignoble and sordid." Although he was one of the greatest applied scientists of all time, Archimedes, who invented such things as the compound pulley and the water screw, "placed his whole ambition," according to Plutarch, "in those speculations the beauty and subtlety of which are untainted by any admixture of the common needs of life."[30] Whatever practical advances scientific research may spawn, science is always about gaining a deeper understanding of the world.[31] From Aristarchus's heliocentric model of the cosmos to recent speculations about contemporary human origins exclusively in terms of an exodus of ancestral humans out of Africa, the goals have been, in each case, explanatory, not practical.

That science traffics in such abstract theories is a further reason that it sometimes has little connection with practical matters. The point is not just that scientific theories do not directly address practical problems. Rather, the point is that, regardless of the practical offshoots they may eventually engender, scientific theories are inherently speculative (and no other human endeavor proceeds with such a self-conscious recognition of that fact). They make claims that go *beyond* what is known. In that respect, they take intellectual risks and they are eminently impractical. Scientific theories discuss entities, processes, and relations that not only are removed from the practical problems we face but that are also, at least sometimes, removed from the body of human experience heretofore.

This is where the frequently complicated experimental arrangements and machinery, which researchers create, play a vital role in the life of science. These devices furnish scientists with opportunities to examine phenomena in unfamiliar environments or in what would typically be the inaccessible provinces of ordinary environments where theories' implications can be tested empirically. Sometimes the apparatus manufactures a special environment where some phenomenon becomes detectable that was, in normal environments, not so. Examples range from the construction of super-conductor-super-colliders to fixing infants' attention on two video screens in order to find the one, if any, to which they differentially attend. Other tools, from Geiger counters to microscopes to eye-trackers, allow scientists to observe or measure phenomena in everyday environments that would otherwise be undetectable by unaided human sense organs. Finally, yet other items of scientific technology, for example, the Hubble telescope, permit observations of exotic environments, without which humans would not even have had access—in this case, to remote regions of the universe.

In the light of the many considerations that I have scouted in this section, I am willing to introduce an observation that critics such as Smith might regard as a concession. Plenty of the new, more practical, and widespread technologies that science has engendered (in medicine and communications, for example), especially these "complicated experimental arrangements and machinery" that are so inextricably intertwined with developing scientific theories and research, may, themselves, qualify as cognitively unnatural. They qualify as such to the extent that laypersons either readily recognize that they are unaware of the theoretical underpinnings of those technologies' structures and operations or find those structures and operations radically counterintuitive, relative to the deliverances of their maturationally natural systems. (I will discuss the notion of radical counterintuitiveness at greater length later.) For nearly everyone other than the experts, this encompasses most experimental apparatus in the physical and biological sciences. For most of us, it also encompasses many routine forms of technology such as air conditioners, computers, and cell phones, their practical familiarity notwithstanding.

The practical benefits of the technologies for which modern science is responsible play an undeniable role in what cultural prestige science enjoys. This is particularly true with respect to the biomedical sciences. This is not just a point about popular views of science. Science's epistemic standing rests in large part on the fact that the natural sciences regularly enable us to do things that once seemed, if not impossible, then at least hardly possible. This includes matters that have become common in the modern world, such as speaking with people on the other side of the globe or flying hundreds of people there in less than a day. It also includes well-known but somewhat more exotic achievements—from finding oil thousands of meters below the earth's surface to transplanting human organs to landing humans on the moon. The significant point about such accomplishments is that it was only on the models that the sciences have made available that most of them were even envisioned, let alone realized.

Scientific speculations depict idealized worlds (of frictionless planes, classical genes, and rational consumers), which enable us to make some sense of how the world appears. They regularly use such unusual theoretical notions to explain common phenomena.[32] What makes such speculations scientific, however, is not their explanatory scope. That it organizes what had, up to then, seemed to be unrelated phenomena is a virtue of any explanatory proposal, but it does not guarantee that that proposal is scientific. What makes them scientific proposals is that they possess additional consequences that are empirically testable. What makes them *interesting* scientific proposals is that they possess at least some empirically testable consequences about which the facts of the matter are currently unknown, and what makes empirical tests of those unknown matters especially telling is when they lend themselves to controlled experimentation. These idealized worlds that scientific models and theories describe not only supply insights about the real patterns behind familiar appearances, but they also have implications for how parts of the world, which up to that point have gone unexplored, should prove to be.

To summarize, then, unlike science, which is rare, neither the contriving nor, perhaps, even most of the improvements of hand axes, harpoons, or hairpins have required the existence of literacy. Not only is technology pervasive among humans, but it also precedes both literacy's invention and our species' "invention." Furthermore, only abstract tools like science incorporate speculative contents, which people explore for the insights they may offer about the way the world works and, oftentimes, for that reason only. All of this is utterly unlike what most people most of the time do with and think about eggbeaters, elevators, and exit ramps. On these various fronts, science stands apart.

Clarification Number Two: The Cognitively Natural Dimensions of Science—A Penchant for Theorizing and Sensitivity to the Importance of Evidence

As I wrote earlier, my claims about the cognitive naturalness or unnaturalness of some capacity or activity are always intended to be *comparative*. The analyses of science and popular religion that follow imply neither that everything cognitive about religion is rooted in maturationally natural cognitive systems (systematic theologies are not) nor that nothing cognitive about science is. So, when I present a case for the cognitive unnaturalness of science, I do not mean to deny that *some* aspects, even some central aspects, of scientific thought are ones that come fairly naturally to human minds.

Without a doubt, the best illustration of what appears to be a relatively natural cognitive predilection that is integral to science is human beings' readiness to formulate speculative theories.[33] Adults, at least, do it all the time. Most prominently, we do it precisely when we confront circumstances that overthrow our expectations. Nowhere is our spontaneous theorizing more transparent than in our social dealings. If someone does or says something unexpected, we instantly begin to guess what that person intends, what he or she is thinking, what is really going on. For the first twenty-five years of our marriage my wife learned that, if at the end of an evening she found some domestic object conspicuously misplaced along one of my customary household pathways, I must want to remember something the next morning. (More recently, I have begun taking the time to write notes to myself, since I started finding a few years ago that more and more the only thing these conspicuously misplaced objects were reminding me of was that I needed to remember something.) Whether inexperienced spectators questioning their hearing, experienced social players guessing others' intentions, or a patient wife assuming that her husband's shoes in front of the refrigerator were one of his mnemonic devices, all of these situations involve hypotheses to which the mind leaps so naturally that it is easy to overlook their speculative character. Admittedly, these hypotheses are fairly low-level ones designed to deal with specific sets of circumstances. Arriving at plausible hypotheses to explain the apparent motions of the heavenly bodies or the causes of tsunamis takes a good deal more imagination and work. In the face of the unexpected, humans are spontaneous theorizers.

Talk of facing the unexpected hearkens back to earlier discussions of visual illusions and of infants' comparative interest in some anomalous stimuli as opposed to others. Both are examples of human beings confronting the unexpected. Novice mariner that I was, my first stroll on the Promenade deck provoked an hour or so of articulating and testing conjectures aimed at explaining the apparent alterations in the ship's speed. Whether young infants' prolonged attentions to certain anomalous stimuli reveals anything more than that they found them unexpected is a point of some controversy among theorists. Alison Gopnik, Andrew Meltzoff, and Patricia Kuhl have proffered an adventuresome account here, proposing that human cognitive development and scientific progress proceed in the same way—that babies are "scientists in the crib."[34] Gopnik, Meltzoff, and Kuhl claim that, just like scientists, infants are not only active theorizers but are sensitive to the importance of evidence. Arguably, the designs of the various looking tasks developmentalists have devised for figuring out what babies know presume that the latter claim is true. The variety of significant findings that these tasks (and others that these authors cite) have generated collectively provides powerful evidence that it is.

That young infants produce new theories, however, is a harder sell, certainly if we use the term "theories" to mean the elaborate linguistic constructions that philosophers of science have presumed. Gopnik, Meltzoff, and Kuhl join the philosophical dissenters (such as Churchland), advocating a more expansive notion of theories.[35] Still, on the analyses of the cognitive foundations of science and of human cognitive development that Mithen and Karmiloff-Smith favor, infants as creative theorizers (even in the liberal sense) would seem less likely. The reason is that, while still operating at the stage of *implicit* representations, young infants would not yet have achieved the capacity for the explicit redescription of representations, which would indicate that they did not yet possess the cognitive fluidity that is requisite for theorizing of the kind that scientists engage in. On the other hand, the findings about infants' understanding at six months of age, but not at four months, of what we would describe as the influence of the earth's gravity on normal medium-sized objects in their environments surely imply that *infants can and do develop new expectations* about the world.

However far along it is, exactly, when young children deserve recognition as explicit theorizers, the question remains whether the cognitive naturalness of any human proclivity to theorize is practiced or maturational.[36] Pinker suspects that it depends on the domain.

> For many domains of knowledge . . . the brain and genome show no hints of specialization, and people show no spontaneous intuitive understanding either in the crib or afterward. They include modern physics, cosmology, genetics, evolution, neuroscience, embryology, economics, and mathematics.
>
> It's not just that we have to go to school or read books to learn these subjects. It's that we have no mental tools to grasp them intuitively. We depend on analogies that press an old mental faculty into service, or on jerry-built mental contraptions that wire together bits and pieces of other faculties. Understanding in these domains is likely to be uneven, shallow, and contaminated by primitive intuitions.[37]

That humans seem so much more adept at forging theories in some domains (for example, theory of mind) than others (for instance, geology) suggests a maturational basis for hypothesis generation with regard to the former. That possibility is intriguing but hardly compelling, since humans have, as a rule, far more experience in dealing with social and psychological problems than they do with geological ones. Humans' facility for formulating theories in social and psychological domains takes the form of constructing stories about agents' actions and states of mind in order to make sense of things. These speculative proposals explain the world on the basis of appeals to agent causality. Take, for example, the idea that a volcano rumbles because the mountain wishes to communicate its displeasure. Intentional agents are the sorts of things that have wishes to communicate their displeasure. To take this approach to explaining events in the natural world is a paradigm case of cognitive fluidity. It deploys a problem-solving strategy from one domain (concerning social and psychological knowledge) to manage phenomena cognitively in another (concerning geological matters).

On this front science does not differ from religion or any other human enterprise that presumes to explain or predict. Popper holds that, like these other human enterprises, science begins in myth. Science begins with conjectures and speculations that aim to explain, are contrary to at least some of the appearances, and are not immediately testable. When they address matters of explanation, religious myths qualify as a subset of theoretical speculations. They are simply ones that focus on agent causality and take a narrative form. Myths and theories resemble one another in another way. They also both account for the world of our experience by describing alternative worlds. Myths usually describe the amazing actions of gods and goddesses and heroes and heroines. Scientific theories, as I mentioned earlier, describe idealized worlds (of point masses, neural networks, cognitive processing, and market equilibria).

Theorizing, of which myth-making counts as a species, plays a fundamental role in science, but, as the foregoing indicates, it is not unique to science.[38] The theorizing that Gopnik, Meltzoff, and Kuhl attribute to infants and young children is necessary but not sufficient for some activity to count as scientific. What decisively distinguishes science from other enterprises that include explanation and prediction is science's fixation on the obligation to criticize theories both logically and empirically. Scientific criticism should be rigorous, systematic, and fair, which is to say that, without lapsing into pervasive skepticism, scientists constantly push theories for consequences that they can test empirically and for coherence with the best theories available about closely related matters.[39] Popper identifies within science, in addition to a tradition of myth-making, this "second order tradition" of "adopting a critical attitude toward the myths," commenting that "science is one of the very few human activities—perhaps the only one—in which errors are systematically criticized and fairly often, in time, corrected."[40] It is in this light that he locates the birth of science with the ancient Greeks, rather than with earlier astronomical observers. The Greeks were the first to discuss their scientific myths critically, to marshal empirical evidence for and against them, and to advance competing theories.

In their case for babies as scientists in the crib, Gopnik, Meltzoff, and Kuhl underscore the attention even infants give to evidence. Babies heed the testimony of their senses when it challenges their expectations about the world. These authors are correct that this is one of the indispensable prerequisites for doing science. It stands at the heart of that second-order tradition of criticism.

Science calls on some cognitive processes that come to humans relatively easily. Humans are naturals at thinking up theories, and they are sensitive to some kinds of evidence that bear on those theories' truth. Gopnik, Meltzoff, and Kuhl review evidence that indicates that these proclivities are already in place and developing while babies are still in the crib, and Cristine Legare has examined how in the face of upended expectations toddlers and young children seek out evidence in their exploratory play.[41] I grant freely that not all aspects of scientific thought are cognitively unnatural. I wish merely to argue for the *comparative* unnaturalness of science. To make that case, I will begin at the end, with the strikingly unnatural *products* of science.

Science's Cognitively Unnatural Products

In his *Dialogues Concerning the Two Chief World Systems*, Galileo reserves his highest praise for Copernicus and Aristarchus, because of the fact that they, on the basis of their reasoning about the natural world, produced theories that overturned the evidence of their senses.[42] Now we are all Copernicans, but we still speak of the sun rising and setting each day. It still *appears* that the sun makes a daily circuit across the sky and that it circles a stationary earth. (The persistence of that intuitive conception is why Churchland's exercise in seeing the night sky as a Copernican can cause vertigo. See figure 2-2.) Galileo understood that an earth rotating once every twenty-four hours and revolving around the sun annually would account for those appearances and more. It would also entail predictions about hitherto unknown phenomena. One of the most historically significant of the Copernican theory's novel predictions was that the planet Venus should exhibit phases, similar to those of the moon. Galileo, in fact, observed those phases of Venus through his telescope and, thereby, corroborated this account. Embodying an imaginative new arrangement, the Copernican theory not only made sense of the known appearances but stimulated human beings to learn new things about the world that up until then had gone unobserved.

The worlds our scientific theories and models describe often diverge profoundly from the world of our unreflective experience. The greatest scientists, as Galileo declares, are able to think beyond the appearances. They do not need to be prodded by visual illusions to suspect that the world is not as it appears and to construct idealized models of it that depart from the pronouncements of their maturationally natural systems. Churchland aptly asserts that perceiving the world through the theoretical lenses that the various sciences afford demands "that we suppress certain habits of processing 'natural' to the naked eye and to the familiar world of middle-sized objects."[43] The way the world appears and what we make of those appearances unreflectively is a function of what our maturationally natural perceptual and cognitive systems serve up to us. The deepest source of science's cognitive unnaturalness is the ever-growing disparity between our maturationally natural perceptions and intuitions about things and the very different picture of the world that science discloses.[44] Pinker remarks that "as science and technology open up new and hidden worlds, our untutored intuitions may find themselves at sea."[45] In virtually every domain on which science has spoken up, the discrepancies have ended up proving as drastic as they did in the Copernican case.

Any *evolved* cognitive capacities that we might possess exist because they were adaptive in our ancestors' environments and, thus, were the objects of natural selection. Crucially, the criterion for their selection was not that they handed over the truth about the world. Rather, the test they met was that they handed over answers that enabled people to manage some problem that affected their survival and reproduction. Evolution is not extravagant. The only assurance we have about any of the machinery it outfits critters with is that that machinery has been good enough so far. The verdicts of our maturationally natural, domain-specific capacities are mere heuristics that suffice, most of the time, for getting by in the environments humans find themselves in, but not ones that render perennial accounts of the way the world is. These maturationally natural systems constitute our minds' "quick, best guesses."[46]

Our maturationally natural dispositions do not endow us with the best cognitive inclinations for explaining and predicting the world. That natural urge to know that Aristotle ascribes to human beings impels us to reflect on aspects of the world that are inaccessible to our basic sensory equipment and to imagine arrangements that depart from our maturationally natural conceptions. Aristotle is right that some of us at least some of the time seem *naturally* driven to ponder things and events that are too small (or too big), too fast (or too slow), or too distant (or too near) for us to capture by means of our unaided senses.[47] They are things and events that we have reasons to suspect play a central role in shaping the world as it appears to us. Repeatedly, science's conclusions about both those rarefied environs and more commonplace ones are that they often differ enormously from how the world *seems* to minds like ours.[48] The sciences' formulations of alternative accounts of things are where its cognitive unnaturalness begins to take shape. Every science has progressed toward theoretical accounts that fail to square, often on multiple fronts, with the pronouncements of our maturationally natural systems and that also improve upon those pronouncements—at least for the purposes of explanation and prediction. Science gets started because, as Aristotle noted, humans naturally want to know more about their world and they take delight in their discoveries. Science becomes cognitively unnatural, however, because it reliably traffics, usually sooner rather than later, in representations that are *radically counterintuitive* in this sense.

Perhaps no better evidence for the tenacity with which maturationally natural conceptions grip our minds and, simultaneously, for the radically counterintuitive character of many scientific representations is the fact that, as noted earlier, although we are now all Copernicans, it is stunningly difficult, in our everyday affairs, for us to see the world that way. The only place and time that I have found Churchland's exercise (see figure 2-2) of seeing the night sky as a Copernican *easy* to carry out is when I have been on the eastern shores of large bodies of water—in my case, Lake Huron in southern Ontario—at dusk on clear nights. Ironically, the payoff, as Churchland warns, is a sudden rush of vertigo! Galileo devotes substantial sections of his *Dialogues* to address-ing and resolving these conflicts between our ordinary perception and commonsense about these matters, on the one hand, and the Copernican account, on the other.

The passing of time and the growing acceptance of some scientific theories, learned now in the course of even the most basic formal edu-cation, can obscure how radically counterintuitive some successful theories seemed when they were first proposed. Consider what is, by now, the utterly familiar scientific claim that microscopic organisms can kill human beings. Antonie van Leeuwenhoek first discovered micro-organisms with his microscope in 1674. It took nearly two hun-dred years for a few people—most famously, Louis Pasteur—to adopt and investigate seriously what was at that time the profoundly counter-intuitive proposal that those tiny creatures might be the underlying causes of many human diseases. The proposal was counterintuitive because such causes did not seem remotely proportional to the effects. The germ theory of disease did not instantly emerge ascendant in the last decades of the nineteenth century on the basis of its early triumphs in producing effective serums and vaccines to treat and prevent some diseases. This was a scientific revolution in slow motion. So, for exam-ple, although he accepted the germ theory of disease, William Osler, in accord with the ancient theory of the bodily humours, still recom-mended venesection (bleeding) for the treatment of pneumonia in *The Principles and Practice of Medicine*, one of the most popular medical textbooks of the early *twentieth* century.[49]

The quintessential example from the biological sciences of a theory advancing radically counterintuitive representations is Darwin's theory of evolution by natural selection.[50] Since the publication of *On the Origin of Species* in 1859, the controversy that has reliably attracted the greatest attention has been the theory's incompatibilities with the bib-lical account of human beginnings. It should come as no surprise that the psychological barriers that our maturationally natural capacities erect to assimilating the theory of evolution cognitively are every bit as formidable as any that religious ideologies construct.[51] As I observed in the previous chapter, young children do not need to be taught that piglets do not have parents who are ponies. What they and all other human beings *do* need to be taught, though, is that all current organisms are, when we keep enough intervening variations, selection pressures, and generations in mind, descendants of other organisms who would not have qualified as members of their species. Darwin's theory undoes the essentialism concerning species that reigns in humans' intuitive biology. This is the most prominent front, but it is by no means the only front, on which Darwin's legacy sustains radically counterintuitive representations.[52]

The physical science of the last century is so radically counterintuitive that it has become nearly incomprehensible to most nonspecialists. Arthur Eddington's "two tables" illustrates the basic point about science's radically counterintuitive representations. The two tables in question are two, apparently conflicting, *descriptions* of the same table. What Wilfrid Sellars called our "manifest image" of the table pictures it as the everyday, solid, not easily penetrable, brown wooden object, which is supporting the breakfast dishes. This commonsense view of the table, however, contrasts markedly with the account of the table that modern physical theory provides in which it is composed of mostly empty space and clouds of colorless, dynamically related particles that are exquisitely small. What Sellars pinpointed fifty years ago as the discrepancy between our manifest and scientific images of the world (and Edmund Husserl discussed more than twenty years before Sellars in his *Crisis of European Sciences*) is one of the principal wellsprings of science's cognitive unnaturalness.[53]

String theory, anti-matter, and universes with a dozen dimensions are some of the more recent developments that most nonphysicists find tough to parse. Members of the educated public, however, still struggle mightily to swallow claims, from the first decades of the twentieth century, of relativity theory and quantum mechanics. There should be no embarrassment about this. These theories envision a world that is overwhelmingly incompatible with our commonsense conceptions of space and time and matter. According to authorities as renowned as Richard Feynman, in the case of quantum mechanics, physicists may have swallowed the theory but not even they have digested it very well. Feynman repeatedly asserted that *nobody* understands quantum mechanics.[54] The mathematics is clear enough, and, collectively, the empirical findings are convincing, but physical interpretation of the theory unfailingly boggles the mind.

Over the decades since these theories arose, those inclined to disparage such radically counterintuitive representations in the physical sciences not only find themselves swimming against a swiftly flowing current of consonant empirical findings and related technologies, but they also find themselves swimming in the same direction as, if not in synchrony with, some of the twentieth century's most loathsome figures.

Captured by the racist vision of the National Socialists and anxious to ingratiate themselves to their Nazi overlords, prominent German physical scientists and Nobel laureates Philipp Lenard and Johannes Stark bitterly attacked relativity and quantum mechanics (and their defenders) in the 1920s and 1930s. One of their two major grounds for vilifying these theories was unsurprising. Relativity theory, after all, had been invented by a Jew (Einstein), and major proponents of both theories included some scientists who also happened to be Jews. Lenard and Stark advocated a German Physics (*Die deutsche Physik*) that excoriated the formulations of Jewish physicists. Although their movement dominated physics education in most German universities during Hitler's rule, it played no role whatsoever in the German effort to build an atomic bomb, headed by Werner Heisenberg, whom Stark once labeled a "White Jew."[55]

The second ground that the Nazis' favorite physicists had propounded for condemning these theories, however, is eye opening. Nazified physics eschewed relativity and quantum mechanics in favor of a physical science that accorded with humans' intuitive understandings of the physical universe. They denounced relativity theory and quantum mechanics for *so grossly offending commonsense.* (Ironically, during the first two decades of the twentieth century French scientists and philosophers, for example, Pierre Duhem, attacked relativity theory and the emerging theory of quantum mechanics as disreputable *German* science, on precisely the same ground![56]) The "Aryan physicists" championed theories and scientific practice that were *anschaulich*, that is, science that was transparent or intuitive.[57] By contrast, deploying these radically counterintuitive theories required flights of imagination, uses of abstract mathematical representations, disciplined reflection, and standards for logical and empirical criticism that were incompatible with the Nazis' monopoly on power.

For all of these reasons, but especially because of its expectations and standards for logical and empirical criticism, science has a "liberalizing influence—as one of the greatest forces that make for human freedom."[58] Good science and good social arrangements depend upon participants' freedom to ponder and criticize ideas openly and honestly, without fear of retribution.

As a final example of the cognitive unnaturalness of many of the products of science, consider the radically counterintuitive representations involved even in the explanation of events of global scale, such as those surrounding the great Sumatran-Andaman earthquake. First, modern geological theory holds that the gigantic plates that collectively constitute the apparently stable surface of the earth, in fact, have for hundreds of millions of years been incessantly pushing into or underneath one another with motions that regularly produce events that have detectable (and sometimes calamitous) consequences. That apparently stable surface of the earth, on which humans conduct their day-to-day affairs and which they think they know so well, has other surprising properties too. It can, for example, propagate seismic waves around the entire planet for days after major geological events. Recall, further, that the Sumatran-Andaman earthquake triggered lesser earthquakes (at moments that were, at least in principle, predictable) nearly halfway around the world. That a geological event like the Sumatran-Andaman earthquake could alter the earth's gravitational field enough to deflect the paths of satellites, detectably alter the speed of the earth's rotation on its axis, and, thus, permanently decrease the length of a day are further instances of scientific findings where our intuitive understandings of the world are, as Pinker says, at sea.

Consider further the tsunamis. Without the understanding that our physical science furnishes how waves are propagated in water, people find it astonishing that tsunamis, which can move as fast as a thousand kilometers per hour over the deep ocean yet lift the ocean's surface there no more than a half meter or so (such that they can be unrecognizable to mariners sailing through them), can be transformed into mountains of water that wash ashore at speeds of only forty kilometers per hour. Along the western coast of Thailand humans' intuitions about the activity of the water failed them tragically. Recall that the earthquake tilted the Nicobar and Andaman Islands up in the west and, correspondingly, down in the east. Their eastern shores, which face the western coasts of Thailand and Burma/Myanmar (as little as five hundred kilometers away at some points), suddenly dropped and the ocean waters followed, creating massive waves with very large wave lengths. Consequently, the ocean waters *ran out* to the west *away from the coasts* of Thailand and Burma/Myanmar *initially*, constituting a substantial retreat of the water, known as a negative wave, on their shores. Many people reportedly went down to the shore to see the spectacle of the ocean going out and seized the opportunity to explore the newly exposed beach. They were, of course, lost when the rebounding tsunami swept in some minutes later.

This case abounds with counterintuitive theories and findings that baffle maturationally natural capacities. The apparently stable surface of the earth proves to be remarkably unstable at times. Movements of mountains in Alaska are not the results, primarily, of local conditions but are the effects of events that occurred hours before in Southeast Asia beyond the opposite end of the world's largest ocean. Earthquakes can permanently change the length of a day (yet another piece of counterevidence, incidentally, to any proposals about a stationary earth at the center of the cosmos). The apparently tranquil sea can unexpectedly give way to gigantic, destructive waves on the basis of events that occur not only kilometers *below* the ocean floor but, as was the case with the eastern coast of Africa, events that occurred many thousands of kilometers away. Moreover, such tsunamis sometimes follow episodes when the ocean *retreats* from the shore in an otherwise unprecedented fashion for which human intuition is unhelpful. We either possess no maturationally natural understandings about such matters or, when we do, they are woefully inadequate to make sense of what is happening. Explaining and predicting these phenomena satisfactorily and, in many cases, even recognizing these phenomena in the first place demand the radically counterintuitive representations of science.

I have illustrated the radical counterintuitiveness of science with examples from the physical and biological sciences, but the psychological and social sciences abound with examples of theories built around radically counterintuitive representations as well—from psychological hypotheses about such things as the visual icon, implicit memory, and distributed representation to hypotheses in the social sciences about relative deprivation, social conformity, and incremental compensator generation.

People easily appreciate the *speculative* character of science's radically counterintuitive concepts and theories. What may be a bit less obvious, however, is their genuine *novelty*.[59] A few scientific ideas, such as atomism, heliocentrism, and the movement of the continents, have enjoyed a second act in the history of science, but they are the exceptions. I will argue later that no matter how peculiar the representations employed in narrative forms, such as fantasy or myth, may seem, they, in fact, deviate hardly at all from our ordinary understandings of the world imposed by our maturationally natural cognitive systems. As the Nazis' favorite physicists complained, however, many scientific representations insult those maturationally natural systems at every turn. Again, there are no better cases in point than the objects of the Nazi scientists' ire, relativity theory and quantum mechanics.

Radically counterintuitive ideas not only veer from the well-worn paths of human understanding but from the well-worn paths of human speculation as well. Both of those sets of paths traverse territories where maturationally natural conceptions of the world dominate. In the history of human thought, science, mathematics, and some philosophy and science fiction are, virtually, the only human endeavors that strike out in such completely fresh directions toward unexplored conceptual spaces.

Their radical counterintuitiveness not only makes these ideas new, but it also is the source of the relevant scientific ideas' *theoretical depth*. Scientific ideas with theoretical depth are always speculative, but not all speculative ideas (whether scientific or not) possess theoretical depth. All speculations extend beyond the known, but theoretical depth concerns *how* speculative ideas do this. For theories to be accorded (and retain) theoretical depth, they must satisfy three conditions. First, they must be radically counterintuitive in the sense I have specified. Radically counterintuitive theories re-order, re-categorize, and re-group things in the world, identifying new, unobvious regularities. Importantly, though, they do so, even in psychology and the social sciences, on the basis of claims about the properties, relations, and operations of additional imperceptible things and forces (as opposed to claims about the properties, relations, and actions of *agents*— imperceptible or not). The second requirement for theoretical depth is that, as research proceeds, scientific concepts and the regularities they inspire continue to be *extendable* beyond what is currently known. This is usually in concert with other theories and findings in science. New scientific theories must square with the facts they presume to explain, but, at least eventually, they should also square with the ascendant theories in other sciences that address the same or related phenomena.[60] And finally, those additional theoretical extensions continue to have consequences that are *empirically falsifiable*. Researchers can assess these theories' possible truth by examining states of affairs in the world about which those theories speak.

Together, the second and third conditions amount to insisting that, in order to be accorded theoretical depth, radically counterintuitive theories must prove to be independently testable. Claims about those newly formulated regularities and about the imperceptible things and forces underlying them have implications for a wide variety of circumstances beyond the ones that they were designed to address. For example, Darwin's theory included claims about idealized, radically counterintuitive concepts, such as intermediate forms to be found in the fossil record, which informed unobvious regularities (in short, evolution by natural selection). By design, those regularities accounted for such things as organisms' adaptations to their environments and various species' morphological similarities. By extension, evolution by natural selection would also prove consilient with modern molecular genetics and agree with the results of such experimental findings as those from DNA-DNA hybridization. It is also advantageous, if such extensions include circumstances that have, so far, gone thoroughly unstudied. Johann Galle's discovery of Neptune in 1846 on the basis of John Adams's calculations in 1841, for example, showed Newtonian mechanics' capacity to enable scientists to foresee the existence and orbital paths of unknown planets. Their various radically counterintuitive concepts collectively enable theories to make predictions and retrodictions about an array of situations that scientists can check out empirically. As an example of retrodiction (and as a counterexample to the widespread but thoroughly erroneous view that Darwinian theory takes no such risks), consider how Darwin's theory, in effect, looking back in time, anticipated that archaeologists would eventually locate fossils that exhibited intermediate forms between those of major divisions within the natural world. In what has been, perhaps, the most notable archaeological discovery ever, a fossil of *archaeopteryx*, an organism that possessed some traits of birds and some traits of reptiles, was discovered in Germany in 1861, within two years of the publication of Darwin's theory. The continuing empirical corroboration of theories' proposed regularities in new provinces and, hence, the corroboration of the radically counterintuitive representations that inform those regularities, establish scientists' claims to supply ever more penetrating explanations of the world.

Modern geological theory explains earthquakes by appealing to such items as tectonic plates, faults, subduction zones, sea floor spreading, and seismic waves, which, if not imperceptible themselves, have causally salient features that are nearly always so, particularly to anyone unfamiliar with this theory. All of those notions were, at best, puzzling, if not radically counterintuitive, when they were first advanced. The earlier discussion scouted ways in which the theory and its regularities have been extended to contribute to explanations of tsunamis. The theory of plate tectonics has also been extended to enhance and explain what had previously been other sometimes well-known but, nonetheless, unexplained geological patterns. One example is the correlations between a collection of properties that the Hawaiian Islands exemplify. The big island of Hawaii currently sits over a "hot spot"—points on the earth where magma is spewed from the earth's mantle up through the lithospheric plates to the surface above. Unlike the lithospheric plates above them, these hot spots do not seem to move. Consequently, the magma that a hot spot transports to the surface is constantly building up, which, when the hot spot is located under an ocean, forms a volcanic island. The lithospheric plates, however, continue to move over the ages, hauling these volcanic islands along with them in the direction that the plates are moving. The motion of the Pacific plate has in this case produced the Hawaiian island chain that stretches roughly west-northwest away from Hawaii. In addition to the islands' locations and alignment, this process explains a host of the islands' features whose dimensions correlate with one another. Obvious examples include such things as the disappearance of volcanic activity as the islands are carried away from the hot spot, the comparative regularity of their coastlines, and the islands' comparative sizes and highest points. Less obvious features include the comparative ages of the islands' rocks and the string of submerged reefs and sea mounts that continues in the same direction to Midway Island and beyond.

To summarize, scientific theories that include radically counterintuitive representations introduce genuinely new ideas; those theories' initial empirical accountability and their ongoing independent testability attest to their persisting theoretical depth and to their abilities to foster more penetrating explanations and more extensive and accurate predictions.

All of this is dramatically contrary to our maturationally natural cognitive systems. Early in human history, people relied overwhelmingly on their most versatile cognitive capacity, namely, theory of mind, for the explanation of just about everything that their other maturationally natural systems did not prepare them for. Their cognitive fluidity permitted them to deploy social and psychological strategies, with which their theory of mind armed them, to manage problems in scores of other domains.[61] They appealed to agents of all sorts, their states of mind, and their actions to explain, predict, or cope with everything from the most immense natural forces to the most minor, unexpected coincidences. These cognitively natural explanations certainly included religious accounts, but they were not confined to them. The entire world was animated. The sun, sky, clouds, winds, mountains, forests, caves, oceans, and more were agents themselves or demonstrated others' agency. The ancestors' satisfaction with the sacrifices that were presented to them explains this year's fair weather and bountiful harvest, the elves hid the shoemaker's tool, and an unidentified witch made the oldest son of that family ill.

One way of characterizing the history of science is as a process that has, over time, steadily restricted the domains in which appeals to agent causality (of any sort) are any longer deemed legitimate, at least for the purposes of scientific explanation. The ancient Greek scientists did not only invent Popper's second-order tradition of the criticism of myths. As a result of that increasingly systematic criticism, they began to look beyond appeals to agent explanations to theories cast in terms of radically counterintuitive representations of impersonal things and forces (from Thales's hydraulic account of physical phenomena to Democritus's claims on behalf of atoms).

Although science's influence was only temporary in the ancient world, over the past four centuries modern science has progressively banished reliance on agent causality, first, from the explanation of physical phenomena and, subsequently, from the explanation of biological phenomena. By the beginning of the previous century, vitalism, the theory that vital impulses or vital spirits were responsible for life, had virtually vanished in the biological sciences.

Now it appears to be psychology's turn. Over the last four decades, the cognitive and psychological sciences have provided increasingly detailed accounts of cognitive operations that, as Dennett puts it, repay more of the "intelligence loans" that constitute the very foundations of the maturationally natural conception of agency.[62] In addition, machinery, such as parallel distributed processing networks, has proven capable of solving more and more of the complicated problems that, when humans solve them, we treat as intelligent accomplishments— precisely the sorts of intelligent accomplishments that we have always uniquely assigned to agents.[63] Arguably, such successes of science's radically counterintuitive theories have brought us much closer to where envisioning a world, in which appeals to agent causality for the purposes of explanation are even more restricted, is less philosophical fancy than an increasingly plausible theoretical ambition.

Science's Cognitively Unnatural Processes: Discerning, Collecting, Recording, Generating, Analyzing, and Assessing Evidence

I emphasized previously that just because, overall, science is far less cognitively natural than religion, it does *not* follow that *nothing* about scientific cognition comes naturally to human beings. If babies are not quite fully certified scientists in the crib, their conduct in their first years of life provides ample support for the importance of evidence to changes in their expectations. The process of trial and error that has largely animated the ongoing improvement of our technologies, especially over the last forty thousand years, is yet another manifestation of humans' attention to evidence. Whether designing and fabricating tools merits description as "theorizing," recognizing the superiority of one tool as opposed to another for carrying out some task is a kind of attention to evidence—one that predates the invention of science by dozens of millennia and has persisted among humans even in those cultures where science was completely unknown. So, I open this section, which highlights the *distance* of most of the cognitive processing that science involves from the workings of our maturationally natural systems, by acknowledging, first, that humans seem to recognize the importance of evidence to what they make of the world and, second, that the evidence that they discern can lead to changes in the expectations that they have about things and even spur them to entertain new theories. Both of these proclivities of the human mind contribute fundamentally to the enterprise of science, but, as I intimated before, science comprises much more.

The features that I spotlighted in the previous section, namely, the radical counterintuitiveness, speculative character, novelty, theoretical depth (and accordant independent testability), and increasingly penetrating explanatory power of scientific theories and representations, so conspicuously display their cognitive unnaturalness that, at least in retrospect, the case for that thesis may seem obvious. But a separate brief for the unnaturalness of science looks to the various cognitive *processes* scientists employ. Wolpert remarks, "If scientific ideas were natural, they would not have required the difficult and protracted techniques of science for their discovery."[64]

Our minds did not evolve to enable us to do science, nor do their maturationally natural systems prepare them for it.[65] Our maturationally natural cognitive systems outfit us with propensities for handling especially familiar parts of the world under most circumstances, but they do not endow us with foolproof cognitive inclinations for its description, explanation, and prediction. By reviewing some of the major factors that inevitably make scientific investigation "difficult and protracted," I will demonstrate the second prominent respect in which human beings are ill equipped to pursue science. Nature does not groom human minds for carrying out the *disciplined criticism of theories* that is the obligation of science.

Infants, young children, and those people who have lived in cultures in which science never flowered understand that evidence matters, but that capacity is just the beginning. First, it does not guarantee that they will be able to discern (relevant) evidence. *That* depends on their knowledge of theories, for evidence is always evidence-relative-to-a-theory. Researchers must know the ascendant theories and their implications as well as the alternative theories competing with them in order to understand what even counts as relevant evidence.[66] In addition to having to learn a whole lot of science, gaining such familiarity with theories frequently depends upon having an extensive education in mathematics, since scientists often formulate their theories in mathematical language. Mathematical forms of representation possess a clarity and a precision that are crucial for dissecting the dynamics of complex systems and for guiding the exploration and measurement of everything from the most commonplace circumstances to the most extraordinary environments.

Without knowing the theories at stake, people will fail to recognize evidence when it is right before their eyes. Most of the features that inform the correlations between islands' distance from one another in island chains and their volcanic activity, size, elevation, and more are not hard to observe, but it requires the command of an esoteric scientific theory with radically counterintuitive elements—namely, the theory of plate tectonics—to grasp their evidential status. It is not as if no one ever noticed these patterns before the triumph of the theory of plate tectonics. It is just that without that theory the role those patterns might play as evidence about how the world works and about what the world is, was, or will be like is obscure, at best.

Second, scientists must not only discern relevant evidence, but often they must systematically collect and record evidence. For some kinds of theories and models, such as those addressing the relative stability of climate, scientists must examine trends over long periods of time, in widely disparate places, with considerable precision (since, among other things, average changes in the short term can be ever so slight). A ready illustration from the history of astronomy was the *forty years* of hourly measurements of the positions of the planets and various stars that John Flamsteed, Britain's first Astronomer Royal, took with the aim of building definitive star maps.[67]

The pressure to show that a new targeted theory coheres with other theories in science is both a burden and an opportunity. The burden is that over time it impels scientists to excavate and examine every possible nugget of fresh empirical insight the targeted theory might contain. But the opportunity is that the theories with which it connects provide instruments for digging deeper and sifting more thoroughly in pursuit of additional empirical evidence bearing on that theory's truth. Scientists, for example, can extend their records about the weather to refine and test their models of the earth's climate by drilling down through the annual layers of compacted, frozen snow that have accumulated in massive ice sheets at the top and the bottom of the world. The differences in the gases trapped in these samples from the layers of ancient ice that have accumulated can reveal the meteorological conditions that prevailed when the ice was formed. Consequently, they provide scientists with a catalog of climatic variations that stretches far beyond the limits of recorded history. The burden of establishing a newer theory's consilience with dominant theories in other areas of science provides opportunities for tapping new bodies of evidence by means of which the theory may be further tested.

Third, scientists are not only adept at gathering existing evidence, but they are also experts at generating new evidence. Faced with evidence that was inconsistent with a theory they had entertained, some young children's exploratory play in Legare's experiment generated new evidence.[68] The idealized theories of science define a list of relevant variables that affect a system's behavior over which scientists seek to gain control in their experiments, when the systems under scrutiny are not so large (or so small) or so complex or so remote in space or time that they defy human interference. They do so by constructing rarefied, "unnatural" environments that hold many of those variables at bay in order to ascertain the impact, at least in the best case, of the one left in play. The outcomes of experiments that manipulate variables in this way provide information about their influences on the system. The history of science is a history of the extraordinary insight and ingenuity that researchers have brought to the planning of scientific experiments.[69] They produce conditions that differ from typical circumstances in theoretically important ways. They create situations in which humans' maturationally natural cognitive systems are uninformative and, thus, unhelpful. Just so.

Scientists must also know how to analyze and assess the evidence they amass. It is one thing to obtain evidence; it is quite another thing to know what to make of it. The inferences to be drawn about a hypothesis's viability on the basis of the evidence scientists can bring to bear on it depend upon the command of logical and mathematical tools that are quite foreign to the operations and verdicts of humans' maturationally natural cognitive systems. Historically, it was the pursuit of science that was the principal impetus for the creation of most of these tools— from Aristotle's systematization of syllogistic inference to R. A. Fisher's invention of the statistics of experimental design, of the analysis of variance, and of the significance of small samples. The various sciences' demands for the systematic treatment of data in order to ascertain their evidential import have led in the modern era to the development of a variety of mathematical tools for their analysis, of which the descriptive and inferential techniques of modern statistics are probably the most well known. These formulae underwrite inferences about properties of a population on the basis of mathematical information procured from a random sample of those items. The inferences concern two matters, *estimates* and *tests of hypotheses* about the populations' properties. Experiments aim to generate data pertaining to the roles of the variables that, under various controlled conditions, those hypotheses keep in play.

In addition to recognizing the value of evidence and possessing a readiness to entertain new hypotheses in the face of anomalies—dispositions of mind that crib-based scientists exhibit—scientists of the more mature sort must also learn a tremendous number of things and develop a multitude of additional skills. They need to acquire a facility with the numerous forms of mathematical representation in order to learn about the sciences' reigning theories and about those theories' principal competitors. Only with this theoretical knowledge in hand can they discern which data, facts, and findings constitute evidence that pertains to competitions between theories. The principle that, in general, getting both more and more diverse evidence is a good thing imposes on scientists a directive to assemble and document evidence conscientiously as well. That principle also encourages scientists to become accomplished experimentalists, since experiments not only spawn new data but data that directly addresses the points in dispute where scientific theories speculate about how the world should be. Finally, scientists must attain proficiency with the specialized analytical tools of logic and mathematics in order to assess the import of the available evidence for the theories and models under scrutiny.

Science's Cognitively Unnatural Processes (Continued): Fallible Heuristics, Persisting Deliverances, Confirmation Bias, and Motivated Perception

Perpetuating that second-order tradition of criticizing scientific theories systematically requires that scientists become proficient with those additional intellectual skills. Normally, a decade of scientific training is necessary for novices not only to gain control of these tools but to begin to appreciate the subtleties involved in their employment. That is because their acquisition and application call for forms of thought and types of practice that people find extremely challenging to master, since these intellectual skills are not ones that human beings naturally acquire.

Recall the discussion in the previous chapter of the Wason selection task. (See figure 2-5.) What I wish to focus on here is not the explanation of participants' enhanced performance when the task takes the form of applying a social contract (see figure 2-6), but rather participants' comparatively dismal performance when the task addresses virtually any other topic. Completing the task successfully requires participants to apply two of the most elementary forms of hypothetical inference, *modus ponens* and *modus tollens*, and to resist the allure of two fallacies. (See figure 3-2.) The first premise in all four argument forms advances the same conditional claim. The second premise in *modus ponens* affirms the conditional's antecedent. The second premise of *modus tollens* denies the conditional's consequent. These two forms of inference are valid, because the truth of their premises guarantees the truth of their conclusions. By contrast, the two fallacies' names describe the forms of their second premises. They are invalid because, in each case, the truth of their premises does *not* guarantee the truth of their conclusions.

Most of the errors that participants make involve one or both of either succumbing to the fallacy of affirming the consequent or ignoring *modus tollens* (that is, in figure 2-5, either turning over the card with the 2 on it or failing to turn over the card with the 3 on it). Typically, between 70 and 80 percent of participants go wrong in one way or

Valid mixed hypothetical syllogisms		Fallacious mixed hypothetical syllogisms	
Modus ponens	Modus tollens	Fallacy of denying the antecedent	Fallacy of affirming the consequent
If V, then E.	If V, then E.	If V, then E.	If V, then E.
V	It is not the case that E.	It is not the case that V.	E
E	It is not the case that V.	It is not the case that E.	V

Figure 3-2. Valid and fallacious mixed hypothetical syllogisms

another in versions of the task that do not involve social contracts (or hazard precautions).[70] Those findings suggest that, when human beings reason hypothetically about what may well prove to be every domain but two, they are frequently inept. These considerations, alone, should substantially dampen optimism about the naturalness of some of the most basic forms of scientific reasoning. For reasoning hypothetically, not only about social contracts and hazard precautions, but also about all other empirical domains, is precisely what scientists do all of the time. Exploring the implications of an idealized theory, contemplating the operation of some mechanism under varying conditions, or pondering the nexus of causal variables contributing to some phenomenon all demand such hypothetical reasoning. The research on the Wason selection task (the fascinating findings about the special cases aside) seems to show that this is reasoning that most humans do not do very well.

Basic deductive inference is not the only area of scientific thinking where human beings almost always fall short.[71] Influential work in psychology over the past three decades has revealed that humans are terrible at making judgments about probabilities, when they do not have access to all relevant information. Estimating the likelihood of events about which scientists have less than complete information is pivotal in scientific theorizing, argumentation, explanation, and decision making. Again, this seems to be work that human minds are not particularly well cut out for.

Amos Tversky, Daniel Kahneman, and their colleagues have demonstrated that humans' intuitive judgments under conditions of uncertainty routinely transgress normative principles of probabilistic inference. Scores of studies have disclosed that in their judgments about the probabilities of events humans repeatedly neglect such considerations as regression to the mean and base rate information, all-too-often fail to attend to sample sizes when weighing the significance of evidence, and persistently disregard some of the most basic principles of probability theory.[72] For example, contrary to the overwhelming majority of participants' intuitive judgments, the probability that Linda, who was a bright, outspoken philosophy major in college and who was active in a variety of causes concerned with questions of justice, is both a bank teller and a feminist cannot be greater than the probability that she is a bank teller.[73] (The probability of two claims both being true can never exceed the probability of the truth of the least probable of the two claims.)

Tversky and Kahneman argue that a small collection of cognitive shortcuts, which human minds consistently take, explains these and other failures of human judgment. For example, participants' mistaken inferences about the probabilities of Linda being a bank teller or of her being both a bank teller and a feminist display the impact of the *representativeness* heuristic. Thomas Gilovich describes the representativeness heuristic as the rough and ready principle that "like goes with like."[74] In college Linda was more like people's stereotypes of feminists than she was like people's stereotypes of bank tellers, so participants judge—again in violation of the norms for assessing the probabilities of conjunctions—that Linda is more likely to be both a bank teller and a feminist than she is to be a bank teller.

The considerations that affect humans' perceptions of similarity are critical to the application of the representativeness heuristic.[75] Humans' estimates about the probabilities of events diverge from objective probabilities when the factors that make for the perception of similarity and, thus, for judgments of representativeness do not actually bear on the probability of the events in question. Gilovich argues, for example, that the penchant of human minds to rely on representativeness impeded widespread acceptance of the germ theory of disease.[76] Given the catastrophic effects of diseases, the microscopic culprits hardly seemed sufficient to the causal task.

A further example: Tversky and Kahneman also offer numerous studies that illustrate the operation of the *availability* heuristic. "Availability" describes the inclination of humans to estimate probabilities according to the ease with which they can recall or construct relevant examples (or associated items) in the class in question. When asked to recall some species of bird, Texans will probably name familiar birds such as cardinals, instead of ostriches, because, in fact, cardinals occur more frequently than ostriches in Texas. The mistake involved with the availability heuristic, however, is that because Texans might also recall whooping cranes more readily than ostriches, they infer that whooping cranes must occur more frequently than ostriches. If people can swiftly recall or imagine some instance (or associate), they automatically infer that it is a function of its high frequency (or co-occurrence) and estimate probabilities accordingly. Physicians' judgments about the probability of bacteremia in some case correlate significantly with the number of previous cases of bacteremia that they can recall.[77]

Clearly, the availability heuristic can lead to breaches of the normative principles of probability theory. For example, though all words that end in *i-n-g* are examples of words that end in ___-*n*-___, participants estimate that the former class is larger than the latter one. To the extent that factors such as recency or emotional salience, which do not gauge frequency, affect humans' abilities to recall or construct examples, the ensuing estimates of probabilities can be seriously mistaken. Humans' abilities to form mental images of items constitute another factor that typically affects their abilities to remember them. People who have been asked to imagine what it would be like to experience the symptoms of some disease subsequently regard themselves as more likely to contract that disease than do those who have not carried out that imaginative task. Also consonant with the availability heuristic, the easier participants find that task the more likely they are to think that they might contract the disease.[78]

Representativeness and availability are two of a handful of heuristics that researchers have identified. There are many more.[79] Tversky and Kahneman maintain that these heuristics prompt the mind's "*natural* assessments" of the probabilities of events.[80] With the exception of the fact that these heuristics apply across domains, they, otherwise, meet all of the criteria that mark the maturationally natural dispositions of mind that I have been discussing.[81]

By now, this profile should sound familiar. These heuristics' intuitive appeal and persisting influence on our judgments (even in the face of verdicts that often flout the norms of probability theory) speak to just how *natural* they are. They require no conscious deliberation. They operate intuitively and automatically. They offer up solutions to common, but demanding, problems in a flash, and for most everyday, practical purposes those solutions work perfectly satisfactorily.[82]

On the other hand, even when they are satisfactory, the solutions that they supply are usually not exact. That imprecision testifies to these heuristics' inappropriateness for many scientific jobs. The sciences' standards in theoretical modeling and experimental measurement routinely call for levels of precision that appreciably exceed the abilities of these natural forms of cognitive processing.

These heuristics' second disadvantage is that the *biases* these shortcuts incorporate can lead to incorrect answers, as the examples just noted establish.[83] Biased, fallible heuristics at the cognitive level, just like heuristics at the perceptual level, work fine for most purposes. Unusual circumstances, though, like nearly all of the rarefied environments in which scientific experimentation takes place, contravene the presuppositions on which our cognitive and perceptual systems naturally operate. This is why scientists often initially have no intuitions or the wrong intuitions about the probable outcomes of their experiments. The latter case, of course, is when science surprises.

Tiny microscopic organisms differ markedly from large macroscopic ones. Consequently, the notion that the former might cause the deaths of the latter runs afoul of the representativeness heuristic. The resulting judgments about the probable causes of diseases might be deemed just as illusory as the difference I saw in the ship's speed as I walked in one direction and then the other. Walking toward a ship's stern at a speed a good deal slower than the ship itself is moving forward yields perceptual experiences that baffle a visual system that relies on the heuristic of optical flow. Those arrangements generate a perceptual illusion that can be thought through but not dispelled. Heuristics biased toward managing common situations can render us comparably susceptible to *cognitive* illusions in many of the circumstances of interest to scientists.[84] And, like the most telling of the perceptual illusions, even though these cognitive illusions can also be thought through (with the help of normative probability theory), they *also persist.* Tversky and Kahneman's experimental materials reliably elicit responses from participants that violate the norms of probabilistic reasoning. Tversky and Kahneman stress, however, that even though they know the correct answers to the problems that they pose in their experiments, the incorrect answers still *feel right* to them. The applications of our cognitive heuristics feel so normal to participants that not even providing monetary incentives to them for correct answers boosts their performance.[85]

Although these lapses in deductive and probabilistic inference concern processes that are integral to work in science, the studies that I have discussed to this point concern problems that, from the standpoint of content, are distant from most of those the contemporary sciences address. Furthermore, the participants in these studies were neither scientists nor people who were particularly well educated in science. Psychological research on expertise might seem to indicate that people who are particularly knowledgeable in some field (for example, scientists or even, perhaps, people who are comparatively well educated in science) will be immune to the influence of these heuristics in their area of expertise. Experts, for example, show far better memory than nonexperts for materials that the experts know about, and they show better memory for materials about which they are experts than they do for other sorts of materials.[86] Perhaps people with advanced training in probability and statistics, for example, will overcome these natural tendencies to ignore normative principles? Unfortunately, with respect to these cognitive heuristics, the findings are mostly negative. Tversky and Kahneman, for example, ascertained that there was "no effect of statistical sophistication" in how participants performed on tasks that asked them to rank the probabilities of (among other things) conjunctions and their conjuncts (like the example about Linda, the feminist bank teller). In their experiments more than 80 percent of "highly sophisticated respondents" provided rankings that, in conformity with the representativeness heuristic, violated the dictates of probability theory.[87] Posing problems in terms of materials from participants' areas of expertise (especially if the problems are cast in forms that are at all out of the ordinary) makes little, if any, difference in experts' not-so-impressive performance on problems such as these.[88] Note that the problem does not appear to be about gaps in experts' knowledge. Physicians, for example, who provide accurate estimates of the frequency with which some disease occurs in the population, unfortunately, prove fully capable of ignoring that base rate information when making diagnoses in individual cases.

This research on experts' susceptibility to these cognitive heuristics, even in their fields of expertise, shows just how contrived, how puzzling, how *unnatural* human beings often find many of the principles of deductive and probabilistic inference. That is of a piece with most of the work in the cognitive sciences, over the past thirty years or so, which has looked directly at these and other facets of scientific thought. These cognitive studies of science have uncovered an assortment of intellectual pitfalls connected with doing science that constantly threaten to trip its practitioners up.

The first of these hazards is simply a function of the tenacious grip of maturationally natural systems on human cognition. Learning scientific models and principles that correct maturationally natural systems' deliverances about the world does not seem to undo those deliverances. Maturationally natural cognitive systems of the most diverse sorts not only substantially resist cognitive penetration, but they regularly reassert themselves, even in the face of scientific training that contradicts them.[89] One of the important obstacles to learning and doing science is the *recurring intrusions* of such maturationally natural intuitions. During the first year of life babies either have or quickly develop many correct expectations about the basic physics of solid objects. By contrast, experimental research with older students and adults, even those who have had formal courses in physics, reveals that many of them continue to operate with numerous false assumptions about projectile motion.

Research by Michael McCloskey and his colleagues shows that people frequently misperceive, misconceive, and miscalculate objects' motions.[90] People seem to possess intuitions about objects' motions that conform to something very much like the medieval theory of impetus.[91] That theory held that the source of the force (a thrower, a cannon, and so on) moving a projectile on the earth imparts "impetus" to the projectile that is proportional to the projectile's speed and mass. That force continues to move the projectile in the same direction after it no longer is in contact with the force's source. Both the resistance of the air and, on the prevailing Aristotelian conception of objects' natural motions, the natural inclination of the projectile (toward the center of the earth) progressively reduce the impact of the impetus on the projectile's motion until its influence is completely spent. At that point, with its imparted impetus exhausted, the projectile's path is exclusively determined by its natural motion toward the center of the earth.

In various experiments many of McCloskey's participants manifested and articulated such false, pre-Newtonian assumptions that led them to numerous false conclusions about what were often thoroughly commonplace phenomena. The experiments asked participants to make judgments about the trajectories of (1) balls that people dropped while walking (but not swinging their arms) to hit a target on the floor; (2) a puck ("consisting of a ball bearing surrounded by a loose fitting, doughnut shaped plastic collar"[92]) to be rolled over each end of a 90-degree segment of a ring drawn on a tabletop without touching the ring's sides (see figure 3-3); (3) a metal ball as it emerged after being shot through a curved metal tube; and (4) balls on strings that were being spun (for example, overhead) and then released.

In the first of these conditions 80 percent of naive participants presumed that when the walker released the ball it would fall straight down from the point at which it was released. Seven percent thought that it would fall downward but laterally as well in the *opposite* direction from which the person who released it was walking. Only 13 percent of these

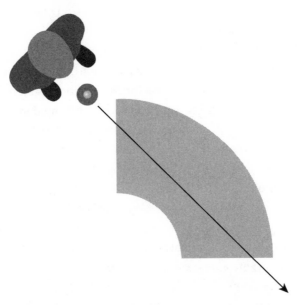

Figure 3-3. The correct trajectory for moving a puck through a 90-degree segment of a circular ring (after McCloskey and Kohl 1983)

participants correctly answered that the ball should be dropped *before* the person reached the target. McCloskey offers evidence that not only do people have incorrect intuitions about these motions, but they also suffer from a corresponding visual illusion under such circumstances. From the perspective of the person walking who drops it, the ball *appears* to fall straight down.[93]

More important for my purposes here, however, are McCloskey's findings with students who had taken at least one high school– or college-level course in elementary physics. Such training did have an impact. Nearly three-fourths of these participants answered correctly. More than one-fourth, however, did not, opting instead, as most naive participants do, for dropping the ball when the walker was directly above the target. McCloskey's comment that "students may often retain the intuitive impetus theory as a framework for interpreting course material on Newtonian mechanics and therefore distort the new material to fit the impetus theory" is just another way of saying that after extensive conscious reflection about such matters, human beings' maturationally natural assumptions in these domains can still intrude and influence not just perception, but also cognition. (McCloskey and his colleagues provide evidence that the "straight-down" assumption prevails in the guidance of action as well.)[94]

In the second experiment participants had to roll the puck over the tabletop themselves. (Again, see figure 3-3.) One-fourth of participants, including some who had completed a course in physics, demonstrated, both by the way they tried to roll the puck and by their subsequent commentaries about their attempts, their assumption that they could impart a *curvilinear* motion to it in order to get it to cross both ends of the 90-degree segment of the circular ring without it touching the ring's sides. Similarly, in the third and fourth conditions, about one-fourth of participants, again, including some who had successfully passed a high school– or college-level physics class, revealed their assumptions about the ability of the two conditions to impart a curvilinear motion to the balls. Clearly, formal education in physics helps, but it is remarkable how fragile that knowledge can be.

The various experiments furnished evidence that their false intuitive assumptions influenced participants' perception, cognition, and action.

Among McCloskey's participants who had no formal training in physics, most made incorrect observations and predictions about a variety of different motions, and many (in some cases nearly half) attempted actions with objects that were aimed at producing physically impossible motions in order to carry out an assigned task—for example, imparting a curvilinear motion to the puck to get it to cross both ends of the 90-degree segment of the circular ring without it touching the ring's sides.

It is noteworthy that most of the motions in these experiments are familiar ones that people have observed often enough and that we try, occasionally, to produce. Thus, on the face of things, these ordinary phenomena pose problems of perception, explanation, and prediction for human minds *that usually go unrecognized*.[95] The influence of maturationally natural assumptions is certainly a plausible hypothesis for explaining why naive participants do so poorly with matters with which they have had so much experience.[96]

McCloskey's findings with participants who have had some formal training in physics only enhance that explanation's plausibility. For a large minority of these participants study and reflection were incapable of dislodging at least some of their maturationally natural conceptions. For example, more than one-fourth of McCloskey's *educated* participants thought that in order to hit a target on the floor with a ball that they were holding, they should, as they were walking, drop the ball "straight-down" when it was directly over the target. Subsequent research has indicated that not even practice with hundreds of textbook problems assures that students will overcome the conceptual difficulties with basic mechanics that naive participants manifest.[97] These and other such findings have, understandably, inspired a good deal of research on their implications for the teaching of physics.[98] Of course, such elementary problems do not trick expert physicists, but subsequent research by Dennis Proffitt and David Gilden demonstrates that, without the opportunity to apply their explicit knowledge of the relevant formulae, those experts' intuitions for more complicated motions such as collisions are often incorrect too.[99] Erroneous maturationally natural assumptions can re-infiltrate even the most educated human judgment.

What this research substantiates is that scientific training does not thoroughly stifle the effects of maturationally natural cognitive systems. Other research makes plain that scientists' education and experience does not necessarily liberate them from cognitive foibles and limitations that humans display. Scientists pursue interests and harbor biases like anyone else. Their memory, reasoning, and judgment are fallible. As Walter Gratzer observes, "Scientists, for all their vaunted training in observation and scepticism, are as much a prey to human frailty as anyone else, and their capacity for unbending objectivity is circumscribed."[100] In short, what all of this research shows is that from the cognitive and interpersonal standpoints, scientists are thoroughly normal human beings.[101]

Elaborating on David Hume's insight about induction, Popper argued that science neither proves nor establishes nor confirms anything.[102] Logically, no amount of positive evidence that scientists gather can prove the universally quantified claims (for example, laws) that some empirical hypothesis might advance. Some new contrary finding might always lurk around the next investigative corner. When, however, scientists concur that the responsibility for the explanatory and predictive failure resides with the hypothesis under scrutiny, what they *can* do is employ that contrary finding to *falsify* the hypothesis. According to Popper, the mark of scientific conjectures is their empirical falsifiability.

This is fine as far as it goes, but Popper's analysis contains both limitations and some oversimplifications. As to its limitations, many sciences do not traffic in universally quantified laws but aim, instead, to provide accounts of the mechanisms that are responsible for the patterns to be explained.[103] Accounts of complex mechanisms are not falsifiable all at once, since they can involve dozens of parts and processes that contribute to the mechanism's overall operation. Such considerations also point to possible oversimplifications. Sorting out where the responsibility for explanatory and predictive failure lies is something that active researchers, at least occasionally, never come to agreement about, and scientists have no definitive procedures for settling such disputes. My main goal here, though, is to accentuate how findings about scientific practice diverge from Popper's ideal and, thus, how

cognitively unnatural even its approximation would be. The psychological research points to the penchant of scientific investigators to
exhibit confirmation bias, rather than pursuing the falsification of their
theories.[104]

Ryan Tweney and his colleagues note that confirmation bias can
take a variety of forms.[105] Probably the most obvious is when people
attend to evidence that supports the theories they favor rather than evidence that clashes with those theories.[106] Negative experimental results
rarely lead scientists to drop everything and surrender their theories.
Not only are scientists disinclined to search for evidence that runs contrary to their views, but they also sometimes disregard it or dismiss it
when it turns up. This inclination goes some way toward explaining
why scientists, who favor different hypotheses, often find it difficult to
agree about where the responsibility for a negative experimental outcome lies. Those who prefer the hypothesis under test are inclined to
explain such negative findings away. Rather than blame their hypothesis, they frequently construe the negative findings as artifactual, con-
signing the problem to untidy measurements or to flaws in the apparatus
or in the experimental controls. Gratzer's *The Undergrowth of Science* is
replete with instances of late-nineteenth- and twentieth-century scientists, who, for decades in some cases, steadfastly defended theories of
everything from N-rays to polywater, insisting that widespread failures
to replicate their findings were the consequence of everyone else's
carelessness in the execution of experiments as opposed to any faults
with their proposals.

Tweney and his colleagues supply experimental evidence concerning humans' penchant not only to stick with their own theories but,
much of the time, to ignore alternative theories. People are even less
likely to propose and ponder such alternative theories themselves.[107]
I said before that evidence is always evidence relative-to-a-theory, but
that is no more than half of the story. Tweney and his colleagues' experimental participants also neglected the general admonition that a
proper assessment of theory and evidence depends upon comparing
the probability of the theory that the participants favor, given that
evidence, with the probability of alternative theories, given that same
evidence. When given the choice, instead of seeking information that

would support such comparisons, participants in their studies were far more likely to seek what Tweney and his colleagues dubbed "pseudo-diagnostic" information, which would not support such comparisons. They also showed that participants (incorrectly) thought that such pseudodiagnostic materials would serve to confirm the theory they preferred.

Ironically, Tweney and his colleagues suggest that confirmation bias may not be all bad and that it may be helpful initially. They found that participants who abandoned theories quickly in the face of contrary evidence did not make as much progress in ascertaining the physical principles of a simulated universe as those who were not so quick to bail out. Their most successful participant used confirmatory evidence initially and then explored disconfirmatory evidence to refine his hypothesis, instead of completely overthrowing it.

A scientist's commitment to a theory or model has social consequences.[108] Scientists make considerable investments when they study a theory, explore its implications, and bring evidence to bear, and they often build cooperative relationships with like-minded researchers with whom they share theoretical convictions. On the other hand, scientific investigation also elicits humans' competitive urges. The differential allocation of wealth, power, and prestige on the basis of scientists' achievements occasions competition not just between researchers whose programs are at odds in some way but between the members of cooperative groups too. Science resides in a region of the marketplace of ideas where the opportunities to participate are more costly than most—in time, in education, and in the resources necessary to sustain individuals' endeavors. It is a region where both the norms constraining legitimate participation and the social infrastructure supporting that participation are also considerable. Reward systems sharpen scientists' interests. Research indicates that the resulting interests influence their judgments. For example, when they referee articles that have been submitted to journals, whether the submitted piece concurs with reviewers' positions *does* have an impact on their reviews and recommendations.[109]

Scientists, like all human beings, are also subject to motivated perception. My effort to see what physicians were trying to get me to see in medical images as well as Churchland's exercise designed to help us see the evening sky as Copernicans are mundane examples of what is at stake. In each of these cases consciously pondering the rudiments of a theory to which I subscribe enabled me to see things I had not seen. In the case of the scans, they were often things that I had not seen at all before. In the case of the Copernican exercise, they were things that I now saw differently. So far, this is simply to reiterate that theories affect perception. Questions of motivated perception explore the impact that commitments to theories can have on perception. Once again the social and the cognitive intermingle.

Armed with theories, whether with those that are maturationally natural or with those that we learn from others in the course of study, we find them hard to shake. Fodor argues that what I am calling the maturationally natural assumptions that inform so much of our perception are, in fact, unshakeable from a functional standpoint, if not from an intellectual one. That, recall, is why some illusions persist no matter what. Fodor is making a cognitive point. In *The Structure of Scientific Revolutions* Thomas Kuhn seemed at times to entertain an even stronger claim. Kuhn suggested that the theories that we learn— either from the culture at large or in the course of specialized study— exert nearly as firm a grip on what we perceive and an even firmer grip on what we think. Kuhn's most extreme proposal was that what I am calling the practiced naturalness that experts achieve with comparatively esoteric scientific theories not only largely renders those theories perceptually unshakeable but intellectually unshakeable as well.[110] Consequently, Kuhn sometimes framed major theoretical upheavals in the history of science—scientific revolutions—as much in terms of social dynamics as in terms of rational assessments of evidence. He highlighted scenarios in which a younger generation of scientists, who were advancing a new theory, supplanted their predecessors, who defended the theoretical status quo, and he described transformations of theoretical loyalties within communities of scientists in terms of "conversion."[111] Kuhn's most extreme remarks along these lines provoked a firestorm of criticism, since they seemed to impugn the possibility of scientists' marshaling telling empirical evidence either for or against scientific proposals. Kuhn devoted much of his subsequent work to fine-tuning his claims. Behind the extreme view, though, lurks the more temperate insight that commitment to a scientific theory is, in effect, commitment to seeing the world in a particular way.

Kuhn furnishes wonderful illustrations from the history of astronomy.[112] In the first fifty years after the ascendance of the Copernican view, European astronomers were suddenly able to observe all sorts of changes in the firmament that the previously prevailing Aristotelian conception supposed were impossible. By contrast, Chinese astronomers, without the aid of telescopes but, crucially, also unencumbered by Aristotelian cosmology, had recognized such changes (for example, sunspots) centuries before. Acquiring the Copernican theory introduced possibilities and provided motivations for astronomers in Europe to perceive the night sky anew. On the other hand, the Copernican theory offered no reason for astronomers to expect to find new planets. Consequently, they did not see them, even when one, night after night, was right before their eyes. Kuhn reports that astronomers, in the ninety-one years before 1781, when William Herschel "discovered" the planet Uranus, had spotted it on at least seventeen different occasions. Herschel himself initially announced that he had discovered a new comet until he realized, after months of observing the object's motion, that its orbit about the sun was far more likely that of a planet. Kuhn remarks that once the community of astronomers acknowledged Herschel's discovery, "there were several fewer stars and one more planet" in the skies they studied.[113] But not for long. Herschel's breakthrough opened up new possibilities, and by the middle of the nineteenth century astronomers had identified twenty more objects in planetary orbits, including asteroids and the planet Neptune. According to Kuhn, both the precursors and the influences of Uranus' discovery demonstrate how theoretical understandings motivated perception in contrary directions.

Coda: *Social* Science

We have seen that learning and doing science entails grasping intellectual constructs and procuring cognitive skills that human beings find difficult to acquire, onerous to retain, challenging to exercise, and unnatural all around. Although I will not make the case here, experimental science also involves a host of practical skills, for example, bench skills in the laboratory, that, if not as onerous to retain and as challenging to exercise, are, in their own ways, just as difficult to acquire.

These observations occasion three related questions. First, if the necessary intellectual and practical skills and the radically counterintuitive contents of science issue in something as foreign to the natural proclivities of human minds as I have portrayed, then how have human beings ever managed to do science? Second, if science is so challenging for individual human beings to learn and carry out, then how has it achieved its often celebrated epistemic status? Third, how has it made such progress (especially in the past one hundred fifty years or so)?

With regard to the first question, I suggested earlier that Aristotle's pronouncements about the human desire for knowledge and the pleasure we derive from its acquisition pinpoint the natural wellsprings from which we generate this cognitively unnatural product we call "science." The understandings, the insights about the future, the practical control of features of our environment and the technologies that produce them, and the health, wealth, and power that those controls and technologies support each contribute to science's staying power.

In spite of their cognitive biases and fallibility, humans have managed to do science because of the insistence on the public availability of scientific work and the accordant opportunities to ponder and criticize it. Many scientists have worked in secret for a time—perhaps, in a couple of cases, for their entire lifetimes. Apparently, Flamsteed, that first Astronomer Royal, came very near to that extreme.[114] But even to figure in the history of scientific inquiry, they must leave statements of their work (even if they do so posthumously, as was the case with Copernicus), which have to surface, sooner or later, for public scrutiny by the scientific community. Crucially, that inevitable publicity guarantees that the criticism of scientific work never need turn on the reliability of the cognitive processing of a single individual scientist. Individual scientists may be blind to the weaknesses in their theories, the gaps in their evidence, the mistakes in their reasoning, and the errors in their calculations. They may also manifest a preference for evidence that confirms their hypotheses. Nonetheless, however poor scientists may prove to be as critics of their own views and of views that they favor, the history of science supplies compelling testimony about their abilities as critics of other scientists' views and views that they oppose. Scientists may suffer from an all-too-human penchant to confirm the proposals that they prefer, but they suffer from no such failing when it comes to assessing competing positions.

The expectation that scientific work must ultimately be made publicly available is what links science to literacy. Donald maintains that *"graphic invention, external memory,* and *theory construction"* go hand in hand.[115] Literacy not only permits the storage of ideas, relieving a culture's demands on human memory, but it also introduces the possibility of widespread access to those ideas in a fashion that is beyond their authors' control. It is a prerequisite for the sort of careful, systematic, extended criticism of ideas that is characteristic of science. Science, then, depends upon the invention of external linguistic and mathematical symbols and of an educational system that engenders a facility with such symbols in enough human beings to support a community of scientific inquirers. Science depends upon sustaining a critical mass of literate individuals with the time to study and criticize publicly available proposals about the empirical world and to replicate experiments to see if they produce the same outcomes as those reported.

Like scientists, literate human beings are made, not born. Like science, the ability to read is, most assuredly, *not* a maturationally natural cognitive skill.[116] Is there any intellectual skill, other than science, that requires more practice? Learning to read and write calls not merely for years of hard work and tutelage but for the availability of materials to write on and to read. The extensive availability of both printed materials and systems of schooling continued over many years of a child's life is a uniquely modern phenomenon, which to this day is confined primarily to the wealthiest half of the world's nations. The principal reason that science has been so rare in human history is that the unnatural cognitive accomplishment on which it depends, literacy, has itself been so rare in human history. Most cultures did not develop a system of writing and only a fraction of those that even adopted one have produced a substantial corpus.[117]

The opportunity to criticize written, publicly available theories occasions a need for and fosters the development of a variety of sophisticated but unnatural intellectual skills.[118] It introduces a sense of "literacy" that goes far beyond the mere capacity to decode text or to do basic arithmetic. Over the long haul, engaging in such critical activity in a publicly accessible way yields better theories, arguments, and evidence. Publicly accessible exchanges tend toward standardized forms of presentation in order to make the positions and the reasoning as clear as possible. (This was as true about the exchanges of the medieval schoolmen as it is about those of contemporary scientists.) As I stressed earlier, what the empirical sciences add to these procedures of rational, literate inquiry is a particularly disciplined approach to the collection, generation, analysis, and assessment of empirical evidence. The acquisition and mastery of these additional skills, beyond the literary, logical, and mathematical ones connected with the advanced forms of literacy in question, involve years of training and prolonged apprenticeships.

The public availability of scientific work and the regularization (for clarity's sake) of the presentations of scientific claims are but two of a collection of principles that form the basis for answering the question of how science has achieved its eminent epistemic status. This achievement is not a substantive one about our confidence in settled scientific views in any particular area, but a procedural one about how scientific inquiry works. Science is certainly not the only way for humans to acquire knowledge, but as a knowledge-seeking activity, it is second to none. Scientists have erected all sorts of safeguards to catch and correct the sorts of mistakes that scientific inquirers, indeed, all human inquirers, are wont to make. After recounting the flaws and shortcomings of human reasoners at length, Gilovich, for example, emphasizes the "formal procedures to guard against . . . bias and error" in science, including the use of statistical tools, control groups, random sampling, double-blind designs, independent raters, and so on.[119]

Two of these principles deserve special mention. Of a piece with high standards across all of the academic disciplines, top scientific journals are, in part, defined by their use of peer reviewing. The vast majority of scientific papers submitted to these premier journals are rejected outright on the recommendations of independent referees, who are experts in the fields that the articles address and who provide the journals' editors with written reports laying out their reservations about the papers. Even with those few papers that make it into print, their authors usually must revise their papers, incorporating additional arguments and analyses to meet their referees' objections.

That is how the system works at its best. As cited in the previous section, however, scientific research about this process indicates that referees tend to be gentler in their treatment of papers with which they agree and tougher on papers with which they disagree. One check on the problems these tendencies introduce is for journal editors to engage more than one referee. All of the journals that enjoy the best reputations engage at least two referees for each submission considered for publication, and some enlist as many as a dozen or more. Usually, the refereeing is done anonymously, which means that neither the referees nor the authors are identified to one another, in order to reduce the possibility that decision making turns on extraneous personal considerations. There is some reason to think that only hiding the authors' identities from the referees might be a fairer way to proceed. As a mandatory procedure, though, this practice is rare. Most editors fear that it would make it virtually impossible to obtain referees, who serve voluntarily and are not remunerated. Some editorial policies, however, do permit referees who are inclined to do so to reveal their identities to authors in their reports. These findings about prejudicial refereeing also show how much power journal editors have in their selection of referees. This is why editors at virtually all top journals must provide periodic reports about this process and their decisions to one or more of the journals' readership, the governing boards and the membership of the professional societies sponsoring the journals, the journals' editorial boards, or the representatives of the institutions that publish the journals.

Prejudice and errors, no doubt, tip some decisions unfairly. The process is not perfect, but scientific communities retain an unending interest in finding ways to improve it. On the other hand, like any human activity, science must deal with fraud and deceit. No human pursuit does remotely as good a job of ferreting out such deceptions. That is because, unlike all other human activities, the sciences have developed procedures that are superb at smoking such ruses out, at least eventually. This is due in large part to the second important principle on which all of the sciences stand, namely, the insistence on the replicability of results.[120]

Science does not tolerate secret formulas, special sensitivities, or so-called singularities. Scientists must not only report on intersubjectively available phenomena, but they must also provide accounts of their experiments at a level of detail that permits other scientists to reproduce them. Those other scientists, carrying out the same procedures under the same relevant conditions (as theoretically defined), must be able to get the same results.[121] A failure to replicate findings instantly clouds the findings' credibility. Repeated failures to replicate discredit the report altogether and can raise questions about the ethics of the original researchers, especially if they have continued to defend the findings' soundness.[122] Even claims about often-replicated experimental findings in science remain forever susceptible to questioning, but until some finding is replicated (ideally, by its critics), its position is thoroughly provisional. Of course, since empirical science cannot *prove* anything (recall Hume and Popper), theories and findings never completely cease to be provisional. The frequency with which they become the targets of critical scrutiny may simply decline at some moments compared to others.

The steadfastness with which the scientific community demands the public availability of scientific claims and the replicability of scientific findings are the two most important pillars on which scientific methods' epistemic credibility rests. The sciences' pattern of explanatory, predictive, and technological triumphs and the accelerated pace of those triumphs over the past century and a half only burnish that standing. This leads straightforwardly to the final question I raised at the outset of this section.

Science's epistemic prestige notwithstanding, it provides no guarantees. Science's continuing success, in the face of human beings' flaws and limitations and in the face of so many of human beings' natural cognitive inclinations, depends on its inherently *social* character. The public availability of scientific work ensures that it remains a social endeavor, which is the key to its long-standing pattern of theoretical and practical triumphs. Individuals, including individual scientists, make mistakes. Scientific communities operate with principles designed to catch and correct them. Knowledge, criticism, and decision making are all distributed across the scientific community. They are collective accomplishments.[123]

Since the middle of the nineteenth century, in particular, science has become a fount of explanatory and predictive insights and of technical innovations. During this period, special social arrangements and an institutional infrastructure have led to enhanced scientific productivity. Scientific principles, practices, and projects have become associated with large institutions, which have enabled far greater numbers of people to learn and do science. These include professional societies, university departments, journals, laboratories, research institutes, foundations, systems of government funding, and more. Generally, these forms of support have both facilitated communication between scientists and helped to disseminate scientific work. With a few exceptions (concerned with such things as perceptions of nations' security), these arrangements have mostly served to institutionalize the various compensatory strategies I have discussed for handling the fallibility of individual scientists. Not even the resulting bureaucracies have been able to undo the fact that most of the time these measures have ensured that in science the collective outcome in the long run has proven superior to individuals' efforts in the short run.

4

Natural Religion

The Importance of Being "Ernest"

During the first week of our stay at the University of Oxford in 2007, my wife and I resided in guest rooms at Magdalen College near the northeast corner of the College's Cloister Quadrangle. We had breakfast in the College's hall each day, and high on its north wall looking down on us there was a bust of one of Magdalen's most celebrated graduates, Oscar Wilde.

Wilde came to Magdalen College in 1874, after three years of study at Trinity College, Dublin. At Oxford he was influenced by the teachings of two of its great nineteenth-century aesthetes, John Ruskin and Walter Pater, who championed the intrinsic value of the arts as contributing to a life well lived. In his student years at Magdalen, Wilde was known for his leisurely extravagance and wit, but, apparently, when alone he worked assiduously,[1] so that when he took his examinations, he earned the highest marks, was awarded his degree with honors, and won the Newdigate Prize for his poem "Ravenna." Wilde went on to a distinguished literary career, cut short by his prosecution, conviction, and imprisonment for homosexuality. In addition to his poetry, Wilde produced reviews, essays, stories, and one novel, but he is best remembered today for his plays, especially *The Importance of Being Earnest*.

In that play two young women, Gwendolen Fairfax and Cecily Cardew, who are both prim and preoccupied with romantic ideals, express their mutual preference for marrying a man named "Ernest," a mutual inclination motivated, in part, by their mistaken beliefs that their respective suitors are both named "Ernest." (Jack Worthing and Algernon Moncrieff—their suitors, respectively—have each led his beloved to this mistaken belief.) In order to bring reality into conformity with their deceptions, both Jack and Algy hit upon the idea of being christened "Ernest" by the local vicar, Dr. Chasuable. Once they learn about one another's plans, they debate their comparative suitability to participate in that rite:

Algy: . . . I have just made arrangements with Dr. Chasuable to be christened at a quarter to six under the name of Ernest.

Jack: My dear fellow, the sooner you give up that nonsense the better. I made arrangements this morning with Dr. Chasuable to be christened myself at 5:30, and I naturally will take the name of Ernest. . . . I have a perfect right to be christened if I like. There is no evidence at all that I have ever been christened by anybody. . . . It is entirely different in your case. You have been christened already.

Algy: Yes, but I have not been christened for years.

Jack: Yes, but you have been christened. That is the important thing.

Algy: Quite so. So I know my constitution can stand it. If you are not quite sure about your ever having been christened, I must say that I think it rather dangerous your venturing on it now. It might make you very unwell.[2]

Much of the humor of Algy's rejoinders turns on the fact that some religious rituals, including christening, at least typically, not only do not need to be repeated with the same person, but, in fact, should not be. Once duly christened, a person should not be christened again. Wilde understood that the truth of this assertion, at least in practice, if not theoretically, is obvious to anyone who has even the most elementary knowledge of Christian ritual. (The exchange also discloses Wilde's grasp of some far less obvious points about religious ritual systems, namely, that it is just the kind of rituals in question that can often be physically and psychologically taxing but that repeating some of these nonrepeatable rituals carries some attractions, nonetheless.[3])

Implicitly appealing to the principle that having undergone some rituals renders a participant ineligible to undergo them again, Jack argues that his and Algy's cases differ crucially. Jack, who was a foundling, has never been christened, whereas Algy certainly has been christened already. Jack's unstated conclusion is that, unlike Algy, he is eligible to be christened "Ernest." Algy concedes that he has been christened, but he goes on to note that he has "not been christened for years." As with much comedy, it is Algy's total disregard of the obvious that is a guaranteed laugh line. Every director and every actor in what is now more than a century of productions of this play knows that every audience member with even the vaguest knowledge of religious rituals will find Algy's subterfuge amusing, because what he disregards is so *obvious*.

It is, precisely, its obviousness that I wish to highlight. Wilde's confidence on this point means that Jack does not need to and, in fact, never does cite the principle explicitly. It is not quite accurate to say that *everyone* knows it, but virtually everyone, whether Christian or not, who is aware of not much more than the fact that religious ritual systems exist knows it.

A great deal of knowledge about religion is like this. With only minimal familiarity with some particular religious system or other, people can automatically grasp all sorts of facts and readily infer all kinds of connections among several of that religion's features by virtue of their engaging maturationally natural cognitive systems that make up normal human cognitive equipment.

Some disclaimers. First, while our maturationally natural cognitive systems undergird a great deal of human beings' knowledge about religion—specifically, about its recurrent features—it does not follow from this that they undergird *all* of our knowledge about religion. Second, not everything about religion is cognitively natural. So, third, to repeat a point that I made earlier, the contrast I am drawing between the cognitive naturalness of religion and the cognitive unnaturalness of science is *comparative*: maturationally natural cognitive systems influence religion far more than they influence science. And, fourth, an analysis of the cognitive naturalness of religion, like the one that follows, does not provide a comprehensive theory of religious cognition, let alone a comprehensive theory of religion. In sum, we are cognitive systems, but we are not only cognitive systems. Religions exhibit recurrent cognitive features, but not all of the features they exhibit are cognitive and not all of their cognitive features are recurrent.

Religion and Natural History

Cognitive considerations are not the only ones supporting the view that religion should be understood as a cognitively natural phenomenon. A collection of considerations that cluster around what might be described as issues of natural history also furnish grounds for contending that religion originates from human beings' natural capacities. In the previous chapter I explained various ways in which science and technology differ. But religion and technology have a lot in common that distinguish them from science.

First, unlike science, but like technology, religion dates from the *prehistoric* past. Both archaeological and anthropological evidence indicates that religions require neither writing nor fixed settlements (though both, of course, have contributed greatly to the subsequent development of many religions). Religion predates both of these milestones of civilization. Evidence of ritual sites among prehistoric groups abounds. A massive stone python marks what is reputed to be the oldest known ritual site in the world at Tsodila Hills in the Kalahari Desert of Botswana, which appears to date from about seventy thousand years before the present.[4] In *The Creation of the Sacred*, which looks at what he calls biological "tracks" in early religion, Walter Burkert hypothesizes that the origins of ritual activity may be older yet. Burkert thinks that ritual not only predates literacy, but he also considers the possibility that it may even predate language.[5] Plenty of other species, after all, participate in ritualized behaviors. Religion, like technology, is old. It is prehistoric. Science, by contrast, is new. It is no more than a few thousand years old on the most liberal criteria, and modern science is but four hundred years old.

The second observation about the natural history of religion concerns its *ubiquity*. Religion, like technology, arises in *every* human culture. Religion is a universal phenomenon among human groups, which may well have existed from very nearly the emergence of our species in prehistory.[6] Some religions have long histories, whereas others are short-lived, but religion in some form or other persists in human groups, even when all forms of it are actively suppressed, as was the case in some communist countries throughout much of the twentieth century. This is *not* to assert that every individual is religious, but it *is* to say that religious ideas and practices invariably bubble up and persist in human groups just as the production and use of tools do. Compared to religion and technology, science is not only new, it is also rare. Science has blossomed in very few cultures at any time, and it has thrived in fewer still.[7] Even today, the pursuit of science at its theoretical frontiers occurs in but a few dozen countries at most.

The third criterion is probably the most familiar for deciding if something about human beings should count as natural. That is to look for the trait of interest *in other species*. In chapter one I characterized chewing and walking as maturationally natural skills, in part, by virtue of the fact that these are basic developmental accomplishments in scores of other species. Part of my case for the comparative naturalness of technology hinged on the fact that many other species use and produce tools. The detection over the past few decades of tool use in a variety of species and, in some of them, of tool fabrication as well is a function of the fact that, since Goodall's famous discovery about chimpanzee technology, scientists have spent much more time watching animals in the wild.[8] Since levels of nonhuman enrollment in mechanical engineering programs around the world have held steady at zero, there is good reason to suspect that these various animals have been making or using tools long before any human beings noticed. Scientists have discovered archaeological evidence that chimpanzees, at least, have been making tools for millennia.

Still, no matter what ways religion may resemble technology, scientists have not suddenly begun to return from the field trumpeting startling new discoveries about animal religiosity. That said, though,

Burkert is not alone in touting the affinities between religious forms and patterns of behavior in the animal kingdom. He notes, for example, similarities in the bodily postures of religious participants before their gods (kneeling and bowing in prayer and supplication) and those bodily postures of subordinates before dominant individuals in primate groups. Burkert and Frits Staal, who even earlier spotlighted the affinities between the ritualized behaviors of animals and humans, follow a line of distinguished students of evolution and animal behavior who have advanced similar hypotheses about the human predilection for ritual.[9]

Staal has been especially forthright about what he takes to be the consequences of such a view. According to Staal, rituals are not symbolic. He argues that human ritual does not differ in kind from the compulsive, patterned rituals of animals and that most animals who carry out such rituals are not even remotely plausible candidates for possessing the sort of rich theory of mind that is necessary for the use of symbols. Consequently, Staal infers that all rituals, whether religious or not, are meaningless.[10]

All of this may be true, but in a religious world (and, these days, in an intellectual world) where meaning can turn up *anywhere*, nothing about Staal's analysis prevents religious people from finding meaning in their rituals, bars religious leaders from imposing meanings on rituals, or precludes religious authorities from codifying those meanings officially.[11] If religious ritual does not seem to religious participants to be something fundamentally *different* from ritualized behaviors in animals, at a minimum they surely regard it as something *more* than that. Ritual may not be inherently meaningful in the requisite sense, but nothing Staal argues would demonstrate the inability of people to tack meanings on.

That response may suffice to restore religious meaning to ritual, but it would still concede Staal and others' contentions about its *natural* foundations in humans' evolutionary heritage.[12] I am willing to bet that the vast majority of religious participants hold that religious ritual is something that is fundamentally different from the ritualized behaviors of other animals. The current state of our knowledge is hardly sufficient to settle the question of whether the similarities between religious ritual and animal ritual are homologies or only analogies, but even if religious ritual is inherently meaningful in ways that set it apart from the rituals of other animals, this does not quite settle the question of whether proto-religious sensibilities, thinking, or conduct can be found in other species.

If conventionalized burial of the dead is evidence of the same, then it is *not* obvious that religion is something that has been confined to *Homo sapiens*. Although considerable doubt has been raised about the suggestion that the Neanderthals at the Shanidar Cave in northern Kurdistan buried their dead with flowers, that the Neanderthals buried some of their dead seems to remain the prevailing view among archaeologists.[13] The absence of grave goods (everyday artifacts such as tools and jewelry) at most of these sites and the absence of any uncontroversial evidence for grave goods at any of them implies that Neanderthal conceptions of what they were doing did not coincide with those of *Homo sapiens*. What can be said is that archaeologists have repeatedly discovered specimens of Neanderthals that are virtually complete. Those specimens appear in depressions and other anomalous contexts within the caves where the Neanderthals resided, and this pattern is one found at many sites in southern Europe and western Asia. Whether these considerations jointly rise to the level of conventionalized burial or not, these findings are clearly not random. This placement of corpses is certainly not an optimal way to avoid attracting predators, as some archaeologists have proposed. If that were the aim, burying them far away would have been a better course. By contrast, burying grandpa, in effect, under the living room rug surely guaranteed that the Neanderthals continued to conceive of him as remaining nearby and as a part of their everyday lives. Ancestors, especially recent, prominent ones, matter—even, perhaps, to Neanderthals.

That religious forms have *recurred independently* throughout history across a wide array of physical and cultural settings also points to religion's origins in natural dispositions of human minds. For all of the difficulties associated with defining "religion," the collection of elements by means of which scholars routinely identify religious systems usually invites little controversy. Not every religion includes exactly the same list of elements, but nearly all systems we are tempted to treat as religions share a number of prominent ones (such as myth, ritual, beliefs about agents with counterintuitive properties, sacred spaces, and the like).[14] Furthermore, people have little trouble recognizing less clear cases as such (for instance, certain elite, esoteric forms of Buddhism). All of this is due, in no small part, first, to the fact that those elements have recurred throughout human history in religious systems the world over and, second, to the fact that their recurrence does not depend on the influence of prior systems of the same sort. New religions pop up all the time; however, the ones that last any time at all mostly stir in the same old ingredients.

This observation about independently recurring elements that shape religious stories, beliefs, activities, and artifacts is where maturationally natural cognitive systems step back on stage.[15] I contend that a small number of variations on a limited set of elements lies beneath the assorted myths, rituals, beliefs, doctrines, icons, sacred spaces, and more that humanity's religions present. Our maturationally natural cognitive systems are primarily responsible for those elements and the forms that their variations take.[16]

In the previous chapter, I underscored the *novelty* of scientific tools, of scientific theories, and of the radically counterintuitive representations that the theories of science employ. Religion is different. Their superficial diversity notwithstanding, religions share the same cognitive origins and vary within the same limited framework of natural cognitive constraints. Science overturns those constraints and regularly produces new, original ideas. Religion mainly obeys those constraints and replays minor variations on the same ideas time and time again. The sciences inevitably generate radically counterintuitive representations. Religions inevitably traffic in representations whose counterintuitiveness is quite modest. This is the sense in which Pinker states that "compared to the mind-bending ideas of modern science, religious beliefs are notable for their *lack* of imagination."[17]

The central ideas of *popular* religion are mostly not counterintuitive. The italics in the previous sentence overtly mark a distinction that, for the sake of convenience of expression, I have left and will leave unmarked most of the time. Putting emphasis there on popular forms of religion is a way of calling attention to the fact that I am *not* denying that religion can generate the sort of radically counterintuitive representations that the sciences invent. On the contrary, the elaborated religious representations employed by theological and ecclesiastical elites in *some* religious systems can be every bit as counterintuitive as the most radically counterintuitive scientific representations are.[18] Engaging in religious reflection of this kind connects with what Harvey Whitehouse has dubbed the "doctrinal mode of religiosity."[19] For most everyday purposes people are happy to leave their religious representations and explanations intellectually unmolested, but occasionally, as the result of theoretical competition, extraordinary events, or implacable curiosity, they end up pondering their religious representations' implications at length. When social circumstances are such that entire religious systems are in the grip of Whitehouse's doctrinal mode, they may allocate resources to systematizing religious representations, to formulating doctrines, and to enforcing both.

The most familiar manifestation of the intellectual side of this enterprise is theology. In the course of refining religious formulations to increase their consistency and coherence, theologians avail themselves of many of the same tools that scientists use. Typically, theologians are experts at conceptual analysis and at carrying out the same forms of deductive inference that play such a noteworthy role in science.[20] They often generate convoluted, abstract religious representations that are no easier to understand than esoteric scientific ideas are. Recall Feynman's statement that no one has ever really understood quantum mechanics. The same might well be said about all of the most famous doctrinal conundrums of Christianity (or any other doctrinal religion), such as those proffered for resolving the Christological and Trinitarian controversies of the early Church.

Under some kinds of material, social, and intellectual circumstances, then, some religions are fully capable of provoking (and supporting) extended reflection about the complicated logical, conceptual, explanatory, and empirical issues that religious representations reliably engender. Like science, these conscious, thought-full, theological activities can spawn cognitive representations that depart substantially from the deliverances of our maturationally natural cognitive systems, and, like science, all of the evidence suggests that such activities do not occur in any prolonged, widespread, or systematic fashion without literacy. The key point, though, is that, just as religion does not depend on literacy, religion's existence does not depend on theological institutions, theological reflection, or ecclesiastical hierarchies. The danger here is how easy it is for people in modern, literate societies, which is to say the readers of a book like this one, to forget that plenty of religious systems have existed in human history that never involved any of these institutional arrangements and may not have even involved protracted, explicit reflection about their religious representations on the part of individual participants.[21] Logically, even one case would suffice to establish these negative claims, but by now cultural anthropologists have submitted a bevy of ethnographies about religions in small-scale societies that corroborate them.[22]

What I have referred to as "popular religion," then, stands apart not merely from science but from the activities and representations associated with elaborated doctrines and theology. Religion in its popular, that is, widespread, forms incorporates assumptions that are more common, materials that are more familiar, and judgments that are more intuitive than is the case with either science or theology. Religion in this sense employs ideas and forms of thought that are *naturally appealing* to the human mind, because they are rooted in maturationally natural cognitive dispositions and the kinds of knowledge they support, which are available to most children by the time they reach school age.

Religions as Rube Goldberg Devices

Religious beliefs and behaviors emerge from routine variations in the functioning of components of our normal mental machinery. Crucially, the mind does not contain a specific "department" of religion. Humans' religious predilections are understood as by-products of our natural cognitive capacities.[23]

Religions variously activate cognitive inclinations that enjoy neither a logical nor a functional unity. *Cognitively speaking,* they are like Rube Goldberg devices—the delightful contraptions of the great Pulitzer

Prize–winning cartoonist from the first half of the twentieth century, who became famous for making fun of America's love of everything technological. Goldberg's fanciful devices were marvelously and preposterously complicated mechanisms that achieved some unremarkable goal (such as snapping a photograph) that might easily be accomplished in far simpler ways. (See figure 4-1.) For anything that could be done in one or two steps with the most elementary tools, Goldberg would devise a way to do it in his cartoons that took eight or ten times as many steps and that included a comparable number of disparate, everyday items used in ways for which they were not designed.

Similarly, religions enlist a variety of regular psychological propensities that are otherwise basically unconnected in what are often elaborate arrangements of beliefs and behaviors, many of which are utterly superfluous to handling the practical, intellectual, and social problems on which they are brought to bear.[24] The standard features of religious mentality and conduct are cobbled together from sundry psychological dispositions that develop in human minds on the basis of very different considerations—different both from one another and from anything having to do with the roles they might play in religions. The analogy with Rube Goldberg devices stops there, though, since scientific accounts and procedures can prove far more complex and costly than religious ones.

Those dispositions develop because the largely automatic mental capacities they undergird serve humans well in dealing with a host of

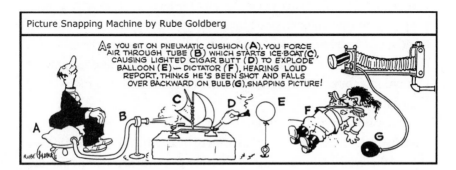

Figure 4-1. A Rube Goldberg device

problems—having nothing to do with religion—that their physical and social environments present.[25] Whether these abilities begin as dedicated, task-specific systems or not, many end up, as the result of ordinary cognitive development, seeming to operate that way much of the time. The abilities to do such things as detect agents, recognize individual humans' faces, understand their utterances, and read their minds from their facial expressions, bodily postures, and behaviors are just the sorts of capacities that not only usually increase organisms' ability to pass on their genes but that also make life a lot more interesting overall. Comparatively early in human development, the mind responds to some stimuli (facial, social, linguistic, and so on) instantly and unreflectively. The resulting knowledge is predominantly intuitive and any underlying principles that might be guiding these behaviors are almost always unconscious.

Specific stimuli evoke these systems' operations. That these mechanisms' exercise often engages a range of human emotions also stands outside the analogy but is, nonetheless, a point worth noting. Often the cuing of such mental systems stimulates powerful feelings in human beings as well as characteristic intuitions and behaviors.[26] Those emotional effects are often transparent not just to observers but sometimes even to the participants themselves. Consider, for example, the feelings and behaviors associated with perceptions of contaminated food or with the inability of an informant who is socially equal to make eye contact or with unfairness in assessments or with the influence of recognized social hierarchies in the distribution of opportunities and resources. All other things being equal, human beings in each of these scenarios typically experience distinctive feelings that can readily propel them into characteristic behaviors—here, acts and attitudes of avoidance, wariness, complaint, and deference, respectively—even though they may be completely unable to articulate those judgments or anything about either their emotional responses or the motives for their actions.

Maturationally natural systems guess straightaway on the basis of what in most environments has proven to be a critically diagnostic fraction of the available information. They are the embodiment of perceptual, cognitive, and action heuristics. Their sensitivities to that fraction of the available information amount to biases in their responses. It is precisely because they are biased that these systems can be hijacked. When conditions mimic the cues to which they are naturally poised to respond and interpret in some specific way, they can leap to erroneous conclusions.

Sperber distinguishes between adaptive cognitive *dispositions* and their various latent *susceptibilities*. If a disposition has been the direct result of a species' evolutionary heritage, that is, it is adaptive in a way that contributed to the fitness of the species' members, then it qualifies as a bona fide adaptation and has what Sperber calls a "proper" domain. A disposition's proper domain is the collection of arrangements that were vital to some ancestral population's successful reproduction, which that disposition came to manage well (enough). The disposition's "actual domain," however, encompasses everything in its proper domain and more. Its actual domain comprises all of the stimuli that will arouse that disposition, whether those responses will contribute to animals' fitness or not.[27] For example, animals, whose evolved cognitive equipment contains a penchant for taking cover at the approach of a stampeding elephant so as to avoid being crushed and to reproduce another day, may also take cover at the approach of United Parcel Service (UPS) trucks, if they fulfill the inexact cues sufficient to trip what had until then functioned as those animals' stampeding elephant detectors. The disposition's proper domain includes stampeding elephants (and, perhaps, rhinoceroses), but its actual domain includes approaching UPS trucks as well. Among a disposition's actual domain, then, are all of the arrangements, in addition to those in its proper domain, that will bring about what Pierre Lienard and Pascal Boyer describe as its "*cognitive capture*," that is, its "activation by signals that are not part of its intrinsic functional repertoire."[28] Some circumstances just push the right buttons. When those circumstances are not the kind that were influential from either an evolutionary or a developmental standpoint, they exploit that system's latent susceptibilities, spawning what are best understood as behavioral and intellectual by-products of that system.[29]

But how do such dispositions outfit human beings for *religion*? A long tradition of theorizing in anthropology stretching back to

Edward Tylor in the nineteenth century, which holds that humans entertain religious beliefs because they explain things, provides one route into this theory.[30] When humans confront phenomena that violate their intuitive expectations they have no plausible intellectual options other than generating *counter*intuitive theories in order to make sense of these states of affairs. Inexplicable, unexpected, counterintuitive experiences inspire counterintuitive representations to make sense of them.

Such experiences are just as capable, from a logical point of view (though, not just as likely, from a psychological point of view), to stimulate scientific speculations as religious ones. As sciences advance, however, they offer up proposals that are substantially more counterintuitive than those of popular religion. One consequence of this general process, as we have seen, is that modern science has increasingly restricted the domains in which appeals to agent causality (of any sort) are deemed legitimate. These two related considerations set science and popular religion far apart. Science and religions both invent counterintuitive representations, and, as I noted in the previous section, theologians, like scientists, sometimes generate religious representations that are radically counterintuitive too. But to explain things popular religions rely overwhelmingly on representations about the states of mind and the actions of *agents*, who exemplify a few (usually very few) counterintuitive properties. (I will, hereafter, refer to these as CI-agents.) Religions deploy modestly counterintuitive representations that appeal mainly to these CI-agents' mental states and actions.

The cognitive considerations I reviewed in chapters one and two carry implications for both the origins and the persistence of such popular religious representations. Burkert, Stewart Guthrie, and Justin Barrett hold that religion's modestly counterintuitive representations about these CI-agents are often the results of cognitive false alarms.[31] The conditions capable of triggering the mental reflexes that I have been discussing do not infallibly correlate with the objective conditions that led to their development. Consequently, when some cognitive disposition's actual domain substantially exceeds its proper domain, it is prone to err, in effect, on the side of caution. Maturationally natural systems are not perfect detectors. Recall hypersensitive agency detection devices (HADD) from chapter two. Even when we have compelling evidence to the contrary, our default hypothesis for explaining unexpected sounds is that they have resulted from some agent's actions. When we do not find those agents, the force of the associated emotions and intuitions leads us to believe that we have failed in our search, that the agents have gone undetected. Barrett and Robert Hinde submit that it is but a short imaginative step from them to empirically *undetectable* agents.[32]

Because every normal human being is susceptible to such emotionally compelling cognitive misfires, every culture has emerged with collections of either ancestors or angels, demons or devils, ghosts or ghouls, or gods or golems possessing counterintuitive properties. Cultures everywhere take forms that manipulate our maturationally natural cognitive predilections. The questions remain, though, why only some of the representations that these false alarms create persist in populations of human minds and why some, but not others, among those that persist, count as religious.

In response to the first of those questions, both Sperber and Boyer hold that, finally, how such counterintuitive representations originate is not the salient issue.[33] They may just reflect random variations in people's mental representations. The more pressing question is why some representations get transmitted to others and, thus, persist. The answer, broadly speaking, is that the persisting representations are the ones that survive the culling wrought by a process of *cultural*, as opposed to natural, selection. What makes representations cognitively and psychologically appealing constitutes the primary selection forces here. This process of cultural selection is based largely on humans' maturationally natural dispositions. Just as humans find some foods particularly good to eat, they find some representations particularly good to think. Religions, like Rube Goldberg devices, tend to capture and enthrall human minds.

Representations get transmitted when they have the following properties. First, they are readily *recognizable* and *attention-grabbing*. For instance, human beings in the wild have interests in attending to middle-sized objects that exhibit vertical symmetry, for such arrangements occur when we are facing some animal, whether that animal is kin or a competitor or a predator or prey. It is not a coincidence that physical structures displaying vertical symmetry are so abundant in culture.[34] Structures of this sort, especially ones with two horizontally aligned spots (resembling eyes), commandeer humans' attentions and influence their behavior, whether they realize it or not.[35]

Second, representations that get transmitted are ones that are *easily remembered*. People, for example, tend to remember verbal representations that exhibit rhythmical patterns and rhyme.

Third, people also have interests in remembering ideas that are *functional* representations that enable them to deal with problems that they face. A representation's promise on this count turns primarily on its *inferential potential*. Inferentially rich representations are ones that have logical and conceptual hooks with plenty of other representations and that are, therefore, deeply embedded in what we know. (I will return to these matters at greater length in the next section.)

Fourth, the ideas that get transmitted are *communicable* (like diseases). Frequently, the features that make a representation memorable will also make it easier to transmit. Usually, tunes are unforgettable precisely because they are so easy to sing, hum, or whistle. By contrast, representations that enjoy none of these features, such as scientific theories, are far less likely to get transmitted spontaneously.

Finally, representations that are well suited for transmission *motivate* people to invest their time and energies in broadcasting them to other people. If we believe God is the secret to happiness and human fulfillment and we want those whom we care about to have happy, fulfilled lives, then we will tend to transmit representations of God to those whom we care about. Or if part of some idea is that rewards will accrue to those who advertise that idea, this will increase the probability that it gets advertised. On this account religions should mostly be understood in terms of distributions in populations of human minds of similar representations, attitudes, and beliefs about CI-agents, where those mental representations figure in a web of causal connections with one another and with a set of public representations (such as statements, rituals, practices, clothing, icons, statues, buildings, and so on).

The eruption of religious representations in populations of human minds relies neither on a uniquely religious set nor even on any integrated set of mental sensitivities or cognitive capacities. Instead, religion—along with such things as folk tales and fantasy, magic and music, and civil ceremonies and superstition—largely results from the responses of fallible perceptual, cognitive, and action heuristics to conditions that are not part of their proper domains but that spark their operations, nonetheless.

Like Rube Goldberg devices, the resulting religious systems have a variety of consequences, and some of those consequences may be useful. In addition to the puffing and popping sounds it would make, Goldberg's picture-snapping machine would also take a photograph. (See figure 4-1.) Religions, like Rube Goldberg devices, may also have some useful consequences either for individual participants, the overall group, or both. However practically and intellectually cumbersome and costly the set of solutions they provide may be, religions can assist individual human beings with their problems by furnishing explanations of puzzling events or offering emotional consolation in the face of tragedies or injustices. They may also aid human groups by engendering social support and solidarity.[36]

What something can do, however, depends on its setting. Had he also outfitted it with a flash, the Rube Goldberg device for snapping pictures of people could just as readily have momentarily illuminated the immediate environment (even if the camera were out of film), so long as something of sufficient weight happened to end up on the seat that initiates the device's operation. Similarly, from one context to the next, religions' consequences may not be the same, even when they enlist about the same list of maturationally natural systems in roughly similar ways. (It is not unreasonable to suspect that quite similar religious forms, from a cognitive perspective, might have some different consequences in traditional, small-scale societies than the ones that they might have in technologically sophisticated, large-scale societies.) A religious device that makes for a peaceful, supportive, but tightly-knit religious community in one setting might make for a violent cell of religious fundamentalists in another.

It does not take much reflection to conceive of means, which are both more efficient and less expensive, for either snapping pictures of people or momentarily illuminating the environment. That, however, does not change the fact that under different circumstances, Goldberg's picture-snapping machine is just as capable of being enlisted for either purpose. Likewise, in a variety of settings, the constellations of maturationally natural systems that religions tap may effect arrangements that have a number of useful consequences—some intended, others, no doubt, not so. There is, by now, a good deal of research on how participating in religious groups can have an assortment of benefits for participants.[37] Rodney Stark surveys advantages that early Christian groups and their members had in their competition with other religions in the ancient Roman world. He traces how piggybacking on structures and patterns familiar to Hellenized Jews of the ancient Diaspora, the organization of its local groups, and its comparatively benign treatment of women and of the sick all contributed to Christianity's rapid growth and eventual dominance in the Roman Empire.[38]

Construing religions as the analogues of Rube Goldberg devices suggests that many features of religion probably did not originate as the direct result of natural selection. Pinker remarks, "For the same reason that it is wrong to write off language, stereo vision, and the emotions as evolutionary accidents—namely, their universal, complex, reliably developing, well-engineered, reproduction-promoting design—it is wrong to invent functions for activities that lack that design merely because we want to ennoble them with the imprimatur of biological adaptiveness."[39] By speaking of "natural religion," I want to stress that much about humans' religious propensities are the unmediated, if latent, consequences of the operations of maturationally natural capacities on items outside their proper domains. To repeat: the mind has no department of religion.

Religion's Cognitively Natural Products

Without a department of religion, that human minds so unhesitatingly adopt religious representations is surprising. That those representations manifest so many *recurring* features is all the more so. The latter point, however, is one that is often overlooked. As with recent cultural anthropology, religious studies has prospered for decades by documenting and looking for common themes in the most minute twists and turns in the beliefs and practices of the world's myriad religious systems. Collectively, this work constitutes an enormous compendium of religious detail, compiled from research on religious groups from every era and every corner of the earth. Without explicitly articulated, testable theories that attempt to identify both the underlying order and the mechanisms responsible for it, though, a compendium risks resembling the haphazard contents of a neighborhood garage sale rather than the ordered displays of a museum.

With respect to the cognitive *products* of religion, in particular, the diversity of religions is, in some pivotal respects, utterly superficial. Cuing maturationally natural systems produces recurrent patterns and forms that underlie multifarious religious phenomena. The patterns and forms recur because these are the religious representations that are readily *transmittable*. Without the aid of critical cultural tools—mainly literacy—representations of any sort, religious or not, are extremely unlikely to get transmitted, unless they mostly square with the biases our maturationally natural predilections exhibit.[40] Those that do recur are the ones that human minds find naturally appealing. Thus, the cognitive products of popular religion involve only modestly counterintuitive representations, at most, that mainly concern special sorts of agents that arise on the basis of normal variations in the operations of garden variety, domain-specific, maturationally natural, cognitive equipment.

Why does popular religion involve only "modestly" counterintuitive representations? It is because those representations involve limited violations of maturationally natural knowledge. Boyer has argued that religious representations are substantially constrained on two major fronts.[41]

The first concerns the domains they address. Boyer maintains that religious ontologies contain violations in three domains that maturationally natural cognitive systems manage—intuitive physics, intuitive biology, and intuitive psychology. The second front concerns the kinds and numbers of violations of the principles governing these domains. It is, of course, precisely these violations of those principles that, by definition, result in representations that qualify as *counter*intuitive.

Boyer maintains that the violations that religious representations incorporate are of two sorts, transfers or breaches. See figure 4-2.

Breaches occur when something transgresses a principle in a domain that ordinarily applies to the item. A "person who walks through walls" violates a principle of our intuitive physics that holds that two objects cannot occupy the same place at the same time, as evidenced by Spelke's young participants, who were disproportionately interested in a ball that appeared to fall through a table. A "person born of a wolf" breaches our folk biological expectations. Similarly, a "person who knows others' thoughts" breaches a basic assumption of our intuitive psychology.

Transfers occur when properties and principles appropriate to one of the domains are transferred to items that are not typically deemed appropriate for that domain. "A mountain that is alive" transfers a collection of biological properties to a nonliving, physical entity.

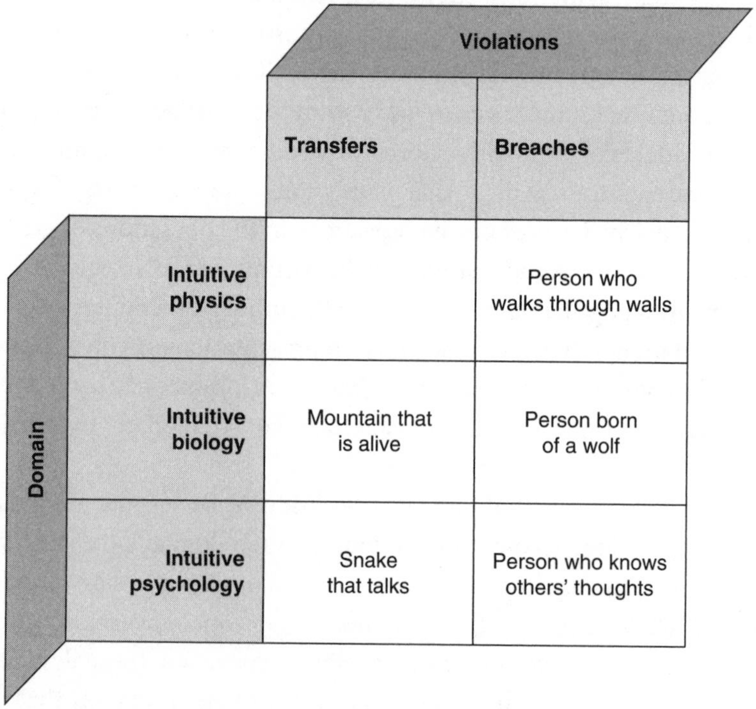

		Violations	
		Transfers	Breaches
Domain	Intuitive physics		Person who walks through walls
	Intuitive biology	Mountain that is alive	Person born of a wolf
	Intuitive psychology	Snake that talks	Person who knows others' thoughts

Figure 4-2. Limited violations in three familiar domains

A "snake that talks" transfers a suite of sophisticated psychological capacities to an organism that does not possess such capacities.

Such transfers exemplify what Mithen aims to capture in his account of the cognitive fluidity of the modern human mind. On Mithen's view, these transfers are not unique to religion.[42] He explains, for example, our species' emergence from the Stone Age on the same basis. Mithen argues that our prehistoric cousins had modularized technological capacities as well as modularized capacities for dealing with problems presented by their natural surroundings. The latter capacities pertained primarily to the tasks of hunting and gathering. Mithen thinks that these now-extinct species of the genus *Homo* had minds with tightly sealed, informationally encapsulated modules. Their cognitive architectures, therefore, permitted little, if any, information transfer between modules. He speculates that the fabrication of tools from a variety of organic materials, instead of from stone and wood only, appeared when the minds of early *Homo sapiens* became capable of exchanging information between these two sets of domains, that is, when early humans became capable of *transferring* the principles and properties governing their technological capacities to plants and animals and their parts. Hence, after a couple of million years of one stone hand ax after another, modern humans began to construct tools from bones and leather as well as from plant fibers and reeds.

Mithen accords chimpanzees some minimal modularized capacities in two domains. He thinks that their knowledge with respect to both their natural surroundings and their social world shows features of modularity. This is to say that chimpanzees have what Mithen calls "natural history modules" and "social intelligence."[43] At least one recent finding about chimpanzees suggests that even they may have limited cognitive fluidity between these two modularized capacities. If so, then that would indicate that they are capable of carrying out at least one cognitive transfer of the same generic sort that the composition of religious representations involves in human minds. Again, Goodall is responsible for writing about the phenomenon in question, but virtually everyone who has spent much time observing groups of chimpanzees has witnessed this behavior at one time or another.[44] I refer to what has come to be known as the chimpanzee "rain dance." That designation is a bit odd, however, since the behavior does not seem to be aimed at bringing rain, and it is not a dance.

Thunderstorms are not much fun for chimpanzees. Basically, they get soaked. Goodall and, apparently, every other experienced student of chimpanzee behavior have observed some male chimpanzees, in the face of thunderstorms, undertaking behaviors that are usually associated with social displays. These individuals vocalize, run around, shake bushes, and generally carry out many of the behaviors that they do when they publicly demonstrate their prowess and social stature. (I have been told by various primatologists that male chimpanzees have been observed undertaking such behaviors in the presence of waterfalls and, in captivity, when large trucks pull up near their compounds.)

My point is not that this conduct is quasi-religious—only that it seems to exhibit exactly the same sort of cognitive fluidity that Mithen implicates in the production of religious representations. In their rain dance, the chimpanzees not only seem to be carrying out a transfer of domain-specific principles and properties (involved in a social display) for managing an item (a thunderstorm) foreign to the domain in question, but they also seem to be carrying out that transfer between the same two domains that many religious representations involve. Like religious participants who converse with and give gifts to invisible deities to deal with droughts, impending volcanic eruptions, and, yes, occasionally even frightening thunderstorms, the chimpanzees utilize a social strategy for managing a problem presented by their natural surroundings.

Boyer argues that the character of human cognition also sets fundamental constraints on the *number* of violations that religious representations involve. Among the features that I outlined in the previous section, Boyer spotlights the need for religious representations to grab people's attention and to be memorable. A moment's reflection on how the transmission of religious representations is accomplished in settings where special tools for their preservation (literacy in particular) are either not widespread or not available at all will clarify why Boyer concentrates on the features that he does. Again, it is easy for contemporary readers to forget that literacy did not exist in the settings in which religion had its beginnings and that it has, otherwise, been a comparatively infrequent attainment in the course of human history and that even where it has existed, it was usually restricted to an elite group.

What complicates all of this is that being attention-grabbing and being memorable can be at cross-purposes with one another. The more breaches and transfers a religious representation incorporates, the more attention-grabbing it is likely to be. On the face of it, a snake that can carry on conversations *and* that can slither through solid walls (a transfer *and* a breach) will be more attention-grabbing than a snake that is simply garrulous (a transfer only). Experimental evidence hints, however, that even this small boost in attention-grabbing potential comes at a price. Counterintuitive representations that implicate as few as just two violations, instead of only one, prove more difficult to remember. In cross-cultural experiments Boyer and Charles Ramble asked participants either to imagine themselves as future diplomats preparing for tours of duty by visiting an intergalactic museum with various exotic items from distant planets or (depending on their culture) to imagine themselves as orphans who went off to seek their fortunes in distant villages and who returned to tell about what they had seen.[45] Among the items in the museum or in the distant villages are (1) regular (intuitive) items, (2) *minimally* counterintuitive items such as statues that hear what people say (a transfer), and (3) *less* modestly counterintuitive items that include both a breach and a transfer, such as a piece of furniture that only remembers things that did not happen. Boyer and Ramble found that across cultures participants remembered the minimally counterintuitive items significantly better than they remembered the others.

Using another experimental procedure, in which participants recalled a narrative, Barrett and Melanie Nyhof provided evidence that minimally counterintuitive items are recalled significantly better than common (intuitive) items both in the short term and at a three-month retention interval.[46] In a related experiment, they also obtained evidence that participants recalled minimally counterintuitive items in a narrative significantly better than they recalled items that were merely exotic but not counterintuitive, such as leaves that are as big as tables. One of Barrett and Nyhof's most intriguing findings was that not only were the minimally counterintuitive items recalled much better than the exotic ones, but that participants tended to transform the exotic items that they did remember into ones that were minimally counterintuitive. More than half of their participants who, three months later, recalled the bright pink newspaper, which, in the narrative, had been blown by the wind (somewhat exotic but not counterintuitive), remembered it, instead, as walking or running. Not only, then, do minimally counterintuitive representations seem to possess mnemonic benefits; they also seem to attract human attention more than items that are simply unusual.

Highlighting such modestly counterintuitive representations' memorability and their ability to attract attention goes some way toward explicating the point that not only do the cognitive products of popular religion involve only modestly counterintuitive representations but also that they involve such representations "at most." Representations that reveal decidedly greater counterintuitiveness may, in some cases, do an even better job of grabbing our attention, but the experimental evidence indicates that they sacrifice much of their memorability in doing so. The balance that such modestly counterintuitive representations achieve between their ability to seize human attention and their memorability, however, does not exhaust their cognitive advantages.

Religious representations are properly described as "modestly counterintuitive at most," because they are mostly *not* counterintuitive. The third advantage of the modestly counterintuitive representations that surface in popular religion is that they are *easy to use*.[47] By nearly always presuming, in any particular context, one or, very occasionally, two violations of intuitive knowledge (Moses, after all, held a conversation with a burning bush that was not consumed by the fire), these religious representations permit participants to utilize a huge range of *default inferences* that accompany our maturationally natural ontological knowledge. On this score transfers and breaches work differently.

Barrett has pointed out that, although any single instance of a transfer, for example, in a religious narrative, will mention only one transferred property explicitly, these violations typically presume the large-scale importation of the associated default expectations.[48] Thus, a living mountain will presumptively exhibit all the generic properties of living things. It will likely breathe and sleep and require water and nourishment. Similarly, a snake that talks is also a snake that has beliefs, that schemes, and that tempts, which is to say that it is a snake that also thinks and acts and is accorded the status of an intentional agent. Transfers overtly relocate one property and covertly relocate (at least some large subset of) the collection of default expectations connected with things that normally possess that property.

Unlike transfers, breaches are specific. They violate one principle only. Everything else we know will still hold. Instead of transferring all of the default inferences to some anomalous item, religious representations that depend on a breach preserve all of those inferential principles, save the one that they violate. So, even though some person may be able to read others' minds, this would *not* automatically entail that he or she is also capable of remembering every input perfectly or of predicting everything that people will utter or of monitoring, let alone holding, ninety-four thousand conversations simultaneously. A breach of one principle leaves everything else the same.

Human beings' maturationally natural cognitive systems endow these modestly counterintuitive representations with an abundant inferential potential. For example, knowing that something is an *artifact* allows us to infer that it has a determinate size, shape, and weight, that human beings have had some influence on its current state, but also that it does not indulge in respiration, contemplation, or copulation. On the other hand, knowing that some thing is an *agent* allows us to infer that it has goals, desires, and preferences, that it finds some attitudes and behaviors offensive, and that it is disinclined to help anyone who manifests such. That some agent has biologically counterintuitive origins (a breach of folk biology) does not block our ability to draw all of the standard inferences about that agent's mental states, aims, interests, values, and likely behaviors, which we can draw about any other agent.[49]

Most prominently, religions proliferate agents. Most popular religion depends upon activating human beings' theory of mind capacities and introducing anywhere from one to hundreds of surplus agents who are ordinarily invisible at least, if not downright impossible to detect by any means. Whitehouse contends that violations of intuitive knowledge about animate beings enjoy a selective advantage, and Barrett stresses that representations of intentional agents demonstrate the greatest inferential potential.[50] That is not just because, in addition to their psychological properties, agents have physical and biological properties too. It is also because agents *do* things. They activate our most readily accessible mental machinery for explaining what goes on around us, namely, our conception that agents cause things to happen. They can bear responsibility for what would otherwise be inexplicable events.[51] A plethora of invisible agents or only one omnipotent one is an inexhaustible font of explanatory resources. The gods do what they do or fail to do what they fail to do, because they have beliefs, values, interests, preferences, and so on. Bad things happen unexpectedly, because offended gods purposely let them happen or because more easily perturbed gods make them happen. Aloof gods could not care less (so we do not have to worry as much about them). The requisite explanations focus on particular incidents, not general classes of events, because agents act in specific circumstances.[52]

Notably, all of these default inferences that our maturationally natural systems supply is knowledge that we get *for free*. It comes built into our maturationally natural proclivities. It does not rely on reflection, instruction, or artifacts. This is knowledge that nearly all human beings have command of by seven years of age, and it is knowledge that they can easily use in reasoning about the mental states and behaviors of *any* agent, including all of those that religions supply.

It is the instant availability of this immense body of default knowledge, then, that constitutes an additional cognitive gain for these modestly counterintuitive representations that religions offer. Their minimal counterintuitiveness notwithstanding, these are representations that human beings find *natural* to contemplate and reason about. Boyer argues that popular religion's minimally (or nearly minimally) counterintuitive representations approach a cognitive optimum that approximates the highest levels of attention-grabbing and inferential potential that can be achieved concurrently.[53] Arguably, Boyer and his colleagues' findings suggest that the optimum they approach balances not only attention-grabbing and inferential potential but considerations of memorability as well. This makes religious representations simultaneously ideas that are good to think and, hence, ideas that are likely to spread among a population of human minds.[54] Religious representations' resonances with our maturationally natural cognitive systems' pronouncements about the world are what make them so *believable*.

Why have I characterized the violations in the operations of this garden variety cognitive equipment that religious representations involve as *"normal?"* The answer, in short, is because such violations arise in many other contexts. Modern human minds' maturationally natural dispositions have rendered them susceptible to generating and retaining a variety of representations, beliefs, and practices that presume modestly counterintuitive arrangements. These include *representations* of fairy godmothers, talking wolves that can plausibly be mistaken for elderly women, and Superman; *beliefs* in everything from Lassie, Santa Claus, elves, and leprechauns to ancestors, angels, and gods; and *practices* such as parades, theater, and ritual. These variations appear in everything from folktales, fantasy, and fiction to comic books, commercials, and cartoons.

What precise forms these representations, beliefs, and practices take are mostly a function of what is in the air locally and, needless to say, not all of them are religious. So, what I have been describing is only part of the story about religion, but it is an important part. In the non-religious cases as well as in religion, human beings effortlessly comprehend these modestly counterintuitive representations (about agents mostly) and carry out inferences about them unhesitatingly, in order to explain and predict events and, in the case of religions, to reason about their transactions with CI-agents.[55] In contrast to science, then, which operates with radically counterintuitive theories that thwart our maturationally natural knowledge and have largely abandoned explanatory appeals to agent causality, religion, at least in its popular manifestations, employs only modestly counterintuitive representations that overwhelmingly rely on the default inferences that are automatically available to us when we engage our maturationally natural cognitive systems—especially our theory of mind.

Religion's Cognitively Natural Processes

I have suggested that although maturationally natural systems may not begin as domain-specific capacities, that is certainly what they look like once they have developed. If that is true, then the cognitive processes that religions recruit will prove every bit as diverse as the various maturationally natural systems they engage. Let me lay out some examples.

Undoubtedly, the principal maturationally natural system that religions utilize, but by no means the only one, is theory of mind. But let's first examine two others: language and the management of contaminants.

Scholars have debated whether natural language is a mental module more thoroughly and at greater length than any other cognitive process. Its status as a maturationally natural perceptual, cognitive, and action system, however, is uncontroversial. As Noam Chomsky and his followers have argued, children's creative use of language shows that they acquire formidable competence with their natural languages even though those languages exhibit patterns, forms, and structures that depend on theoretical constructs that are every bit as complex as those employed in the most esoteric areas of science. Even those theorists who disagree with Chomsky about this do not substantially disagree about the levels of children's linguistic accomplishments. They simply explain them differently. Although disputes about natural language swirl with unabated vigor, that it should count as a maturationally natural cognitive system is surely one of the least contentious issues. It is not mere coincidence that we speak of "*natural* language."

That religious systems largely depend on linguistic communication comes as no surprise. So does science. Religion is a human undertaking and human beings are indefatigable language users. There is nothing exceptional about that. In what instances, then, does religion peculiarly draw on language as a maturationally natural system? Perhaps the most striking example is speaking in tongues.

When religious people speak in tongues they produce utterances that appear to be linguistic, at least to an uncritical ear.[56] From its beginnings Christianity has included speaking in tongues, but it is by no means the only religion to do so.[57] Accounts in the Christian Bible of humans producing what appear to be miraculous linguistic utterances come in at least two varieties. The second chapter of the book of Acts reports that the apostles displayed *heteroglossia* (or *xenoglossia*), that is, they spoke known languages that they had never learned. According to this passage, they produced utterances that recognizably sounded like utterances in at least thirteen different languages. The other famous reference to exotic religious utterances is in St. Paul's first letter to the church in Corinth. In that letter's twelfth chapter, among the various gifts of the Spirit that he lists are "divers kinds of tongues" and "the interpretation of tongues." This has generally been construed as referring to *glossolalia*, in which people appear to speak in unknown languages that are putatively extinct or divine in origin and, therefore, demand comparably inspired interpretation in order to be understood.[58] Under regular circumstances, no one understands them. Pentecostal Christian groups regard the production of glossolalia as evidence of the speaker's baptism in the Spirit. Across religious systems, spirit possession or trance, of more and less orthodox forms, often accompanies xenoglossia and glossolalia.[59] On the most prominent conception of possession, in which the possessing spirit displaces the host, this entails that it is someone other than the host who is doing the talking. Of course, it is someone who might very well speak a different language too.[60] If not theologically, then, at least, functionally, the interpretation of such utterances is usually a more sober undertaking. Translations are often considerably longer and more complex than the utterances that inspire them.[61]

Examining these phenomena in divergent cultures, Felicitas Goodman and William Samarin, separately, explain why these phenomena only *appear* to be linguistic. What make such utterances fascinating is their ability to cue maturationally natural dispositions of the human mind that kick a variety of inference engines into gear. The operations of those inference engines condition both the utterances that are produced and the way they are perceived and understood. This approach to speaking in tongues not only explains many of these utterances' features but makes corresponding, testable predictions about them as well.

The first of these predictions is that these extraordinary utterances will largely resemble the affected individuals' native languages.

Each natural language utilizes only a subset of the wide range of speech sounds that humans are capable of making. In the first months of life normal infants can distinguish all of these speech sounds, but they progressively lose their sensitivities to many of these distinctions as they rapidly hone in on the sounds that their caretakers use and become insensible to many phonemic distinctions that only figure in other languages.[62] Features of what we hear as non-native speakers' accents in their pronunciation of *our* native tongues are a function of these acquired limitations. The inability, by the time they reach adulthood, of native speakers of Japanese to distinguish the sounds typically associated with the letter "r" and the letter "l" in English is a familiar illustration for native speakers of English. The morphophonemic properties of a natural language concern the combinations of sounds that its grammar allows. Sounds only come in some orders and not others. In English, for example, the phonemes typically associated with the consonants "t" and "b" never immediately follow the sound of a hard "g." The same will be true when someone whose native language is English speaks in tongues.

Instead of producing unused or novel sounds in curious combinations, the people speaking in tongues that Samarin studied neither produced different sounds from other languages with which they may have had some familiarity nor even all of the sounds of their native languages. Their glossolalia and xenoglossia manifested only a subset of the phonemes of their native languages. In their production of these utterances, Samarin comments that his participants seem to do "what comes naturally." Putatively miraculous utterances notwithstanding, the Spirit only incited routine sounds in routine combinations from a speaker's native language.[63]

The account on offer also helps explain why apparently fluent xenoglossia and glossolalia have the rhythmic features and inflections that they do. The concomitant prediction here is that these utterances will usually involve patterns of articulation with the pitch contours and intervals, timing, stress, and intonations that are characteristic of utterances in the speakers' native languages. This seems to be the case, at least once a speaker performs beyond an initial level of what Samarin calls "abortive glossolalia," which is characterized by "stammering, babbling, or uttering [a very small number of] syllables repetitiously."[64] As noted, Samarin found that both the xenoglossia and the glossolalia that he studied displayed the same dominance patterns among consonants that prevailed in the participants' natural languages.[65] As to their overall rhythmic and sonic character, Goodman's findings indicate that, again, these utterances incorporate only a limited set of the available options in the speakers' natural languages, which results in greater regularity among these utterances.[66] Although fluent glossolalia is not necessarily transparently formulaic on these fronts, it is a good deal more repetitious than most ordinary language. But, of course, that is also true of other characteristically religious uses of language as well, such as chanting, singing, and praying.

These considerations disclose a salient respect, then, in which these utterances (and many other religious uses of language) differ from much everyday use of language. But what Samarin at one point describes as their "disguised" repetition does not, alone, show that they do not merit inclusion within the *proper domain* of the relevant maturationally natural systems.[67] In fact, most of Samarin's participants believe that these special, religiously inspired utterances are instances of language use. Still, according to Goodman and Samarin, xenoglossia and, certainly, glossolalia differ from natural languages in two closely related and glaringly obvious respects. First, unlike natural languages, their sounds are not subservient to their meanings, since, second, there are no standard meanings for these utterances![68] (The languages that xenoglossia allegedly involves are, conveniently, ones that no one knows or, at least, ones that no one present knows very well. English speakers may have impressions of what French *sounds like*, but, unless they know French, they do not know when French or what French is being spoken.) Both St. Paul and contemporary Pentecostals handle the parallel problem with glossolalia by appealing to the gift of interpretation, but, crucially, those interpretations establish no systematic relationships between sound and meaning and, regardless of how similar or how diverse the utterances may be, Samarin, at least, reports that the proffered interpretations that he witnessed were virtually always highly standardized fare.[69]

Fodor underscores how little access our conscious minds have to the workings of mental modules. When conditions in the environment trigger these systems, they deliver their products to our conscious mental life as unanalyzed wholes. Consequently, Fodor notes, "not only must you hear an utterance of a sentence as such, but, to a first approximation, you can hear it *only* that way."[70] What I am arguing is that the recurrence of these special religious utterances across different religions and different eras points to a related fact, namely, that humans not only *must* hear utterances that mimic enough properties of speech as speech, but, to a first approximation, they can *only* hear them that way. (Describing an informal test he ran with colleagues, Samarin states that, upon first hearing him read a transcript of glossolalia, even professional linguists initially presumed that it was language. Some Malayo-Polynesian language, they suspected.[71]) These special kinds of religious utterances exploit humans' thorough-going inability to hear other human beings' articulation of not-obviously-repetitive sounds within the framework of plausible rhythmic structures and sonic inflections as something other than the use of natural language. As Goodman comments, when people hear glossolalia and xenoglossia, "they fit the audiosignal into a previously prepared category, namely language."[72]

Fit into that category, these utterances bring an added bonus for grabbing human attention. They unleash some prominent default inferences associated with anything that this maturationally natural system deems "exposure to spoken language." Specifically, they occasion the inference from the assumption that this is language to the conclusion that it must, therefore, be meaningful. Carrying out that inference jump-starts further inferential machinery, setting listeners on a quest to ascertain the meanings of these enigmatic utterances. These are activities that will greatly occupy human minds, at least for a while, particularly in circumstances like those where people typically confront glossolalia and xenoglossia, where it is assumed that these utterances not only possess meaning but carry great religious significance. Listeners automatically begin searching for plausible connections between sound and sense (for example, listen for cognates!) and will entertain hypotheses about these utterances' contents based on any evidence they have at their disposal, including conventional interpretive paths that have become well worn through generations of use.

A second group of domain-specific competences that religions engage concerns coping with contaminants. Wariness about what substances an organism comes into contact with and, especially, about what ones it ingests wears its prudence on its sleeve. Knowing what things in the environment are toxic or virulent is a tremendous advantage when the decisive criterion is whether an animal survives long enough to reproduce. The problem is that, other than overt symptoms in the diseased and occasional bitter tastes, noxious smells, or bright colors (for example, in frogs) in the poisonous, these harmful traits are not conspicuous. On balance animals adopt a winning strategy when they treat unknown substances and items carefully and keep their distance from known contaminants and sources of contagion. Animals with minds that normally develop such cautious dispositions, and in which the perception of contaminants or sources of contagion will induce strong negative emotional signals, would be more likely to produce offspring than their more reckless brethren.

Paul Rozin, Carol Nemeroff, and their colleagues have studied what people feel and think about such dangers and how they react to them.[73] Although what counts as a contaminant for any given person can depend, in part, on *cultural* inputs (in the same way that what languages babies learn to speak does too), researchers have marshaled experimental evidence that, independent of culture, humans have similar *feelings* and *intuitions* and exhibit similar *behaviors* in the face of what they perceive as contaminants. Those feelings (primarily disgust), intuitions, and behaviors conform to specifiable principles that seem to be universal among adults.

First, *any* contact with a contaminant or a source of contagion is capable of transmitting *any* characteristic of that source. It follows, then, that any contact with such a source is capable of transmitting the peril it harbors. Those contacts are potent in a second respect. The size of the dose does not matter. Even the most limited contact can suffice to contaminate. One touch is enough. A third measure of their potency is not only that one contact is enough to contaminate but that it is enough to contaminate *fully*. As a result of these maturationally natural intuitions, powerful feelings of disgust animate humans, when they are in the presence of perceived contaminants or infectious items and especially when they are contemplating the possibility of their ingestion.

In Nemeroff and Rozin's view these principled intuitions long predate the rise of modern scientific insight about these matters, but, as with other maturationally natural systems, they get some important things right, at least for most practical purposes.[74] So, for example, a fourth principle is that the source of the hazard need not be perceptible. Long before the discovery of the germ theory of infectious illnesses in the nineteenth century, people feared invisible airs and vapors that transmitted contaminants and diseases. People knew to be guarded about what they inhaled long before they knew about invisible, airborne microbes. Just as McCloskey's research demonstrated that maturationally natural presumptions about objects' motions can persist even after people have had training in physical science, Rozin and his colleagues have shown a similar persistence of these maturationally natural dispositions about contaminants. A fifth principle underlying humans' intuitions about these matters, to the effect that the consequences of contamination tend to be permanent, illustrates this.[75] Participants across a variety of cultures will continue to reject previously contaminated items, even when they know that they have subsequently been purified. They will not drink, for example, from a glass that has come in contact with a cockroach, even though it has subsequently been cleaned and disinfected. Boyer argues that this shows that, their cultural infiltration notwithstanding, these systems are adapted to ancestral circumstances in which "there was no such thing as thorough disinfecting."[76] These systems' imperviousness to modern scientific developments is evidence that, although they are tuned *by* contemporary cultural conditions, they are not tuned *to* contemporary cultural contents. In short, they enjoy a measure of informational encapsulation.

These principles of contamination and contagion provoke some fairly obvious inferences. Most assuredly, infectious substances should not be swallowed or inhaled or touched. It is even better to maintain a "safe" distance from a contaminant, as this will substantially reduce the probabilities of becoming contaminated. People should either give these items and substances a wide berth or shield themselves from their effects. And people certainly should handle them, when they absolutely must, with profound care and, if at all possible, cleanse themselves in special, appropriate ways afterward. Principle five often rules this out, so in some cultures persons who are charged with such tasks are members of an untouchable caste.

Rozin and his colleagues' empirical findings nicely conform to one further feature of maturationally natural systems. In cross-cultural research with children, they found a consistent pattern. Children younger than three years appear to be utterly oblivious to these concerns about contaminants. Children between the ages of three and ten show increasingly greater sensitivity to questions of contagion, contamination, and the possibilities for purification, and by ten years of age, the principles previously described seem to be firmly in place. This too is an ordered body of knowledge over which children have gained command well before the onset of adolescence.[77]

Armed with this knowledge, children are perfectly prepared to perceive, understand, and interact with religions' sacred spaces and objects. Religions the world over exploit these proclivities of the human mind. Like all maturationally natural systems, once they are in place these mental systems work automatically and fast. The cues sufficient to trigger their operations, however, are not perfectly reliable. All maturationally natural systems sacrifice a little reliability in order to gain speed. Just like HADD, these contamination management systems are susceptible to false positives. Religions have repeatedly evolved in ways that cue these systems' operations. The activation of contamination management systems instantly bestows on religious participants a virtual instruction manual about how to conduct themselves around sacred spaces and objects. (Religions are not the only systems that take advantage of these cognitive resources. The state frequently exploits such dispositions as well. People had just as good an idea about how to conduct themselves in Lenin's mausoleum as they have about how to conduct themselves in their religions' holy places.)

Religions mark such special places and things off from the mundane world. Typically, these spaces and objects merit uncommon treatment on the grounds that they enjoy a comparatively direct connection with CI-agents. Religious myths often testify to those connections, but they can be ritually established as well. These can be spaces the gods inhabit (Mount Olympus) or things with which they are alleged to have had (contagious) contact (relics such as the Shroud of Turin). They can be locations in which exchanges with the gods are appropriate (the altar constructed in the Agnicayana ritual) or materials which they have endowed with extraordinary powers (holy water). They can be places that the divine periodically visit (such as Fatima or Conyers, Georgia) or items (either artifacts or natural objects) that *are* the gods themselves (statues or mountains). Whether those CI-agents are benevolent or malevolent, religions cue human beings' contamination management systems to activate information about how they must conduct themselves around the places and objects in question. They should exercise care about where they go, what they touch, and how they handle things.

How does such cuing occur in religious contexts? No differently from the ways it occurs in everyday settings. Humans will immediately pick up on the fact that someone has diverted his or her path of motion around some place, whether it is an oil spill, roadkill, or an altar. Attention will only be keener when no visible obstacle necessitates that diversion. Humans will notice whether gardeners walk around a patch of ground that they have just treated with an herbicide or religious participants walk around an empty chancel just to get to the other side. Obviously, coordinating abruptly altered behaviors, such as the cessation of conversation, brief bows, and so on, with distinguishable points in those diverted paths may enhance these psychological effects, but they are almost certainly unnecessary. Unexpectedly and systematically diverted paths suffice to alert the mind to the possibility of contamination or danger. Other kinds of behavior, in addition to diverted paths of motion, can also be straightforwardly tied to the management of contaminants or contagious items, and observing those behaviors will also alert the relevant systems. These range from restricting access to something or someone, to monitoring them (and especially monitoring them frequently), to undertaking special motor routines suitable to handling contaminated or contagious items.

None of this is to suggest that these religious items or places are construed as contaminating in the normal sense. If anything, religious arrangements usually *invert* the orientation of the contamination management systems. The danger is not that these special places or objects will contaminate participants, but, instead, that the participants or the mundane world will contaminate these sacred spaces and objects! (If a priest drops or spills one of the Eucharistic elements, it will not simply be left for the janitor to vacuum or towel up after the Mass. The problem is not that Jesus's "blood" has soiled the carpet but rather that the carpet has, in effect, contaminated Jesus's blood.) These inversions serve to clarify just what is being cued and manipulated, namely, a system of inference, and to highlight its key role in these religious dealings. Cuing humans' maturationally natural contamination management systems provides participants, straightaway, with default inferences about how to conduct themselves with these objects and in these settings, regardless of the source or the direction of the hazard.

That inversion of orientation is manifested in other ways. Since, according to the fifth principle, the effects of contamination tend to be permanent, the possibilities for purification are limited. Consequently, as noted earlier, the task of dealing with contaminants in some societies is often left to a negatively marked caste. If purification is an option, it depends on special cleansing after contact with the contaminant. In the religious cases, however, these features are turned on their heads. There, since it is the religious participants who are the potential contaminants, they must cleanse themselves before they deal with sacred spaces and objects. It is no coincidence that so many rituals across so many religious systems involve cleansing and purification, which dependably come *before* more direct dealings with the gods and with their possessions and abodes.[78] Although the persons who are entitled to deal directly with items in these special spaces frequently fall into an "untouchable" caste in these religious cases too, we are now using that term in a very different sense—this time with a positive valence. Priests and other religious officials are set apart from everyone else on the basis of their peculiar ritual histories. Since they have a closer relationship with the divine, they are untouchable in this different sense. They often reside in special quarters removed from the everyday world. Often members of such groups are supposed to be celibate. Only priests and other religiously stipulated persons can traverse these duly demarcated areas and handle these special objects without danger. Those privileges are just the kinds of signals that serve to cue other mental systems concerned with the detection of social prestige. These signals mark those persons off as a uniquely qualified and influential group that merits cultural learners' attentions.[79]

Rozin and his colleagues identify a sixth principle, which is that people construe negative contagious effects as more potent than positive ones.[80] The most deleterious effects of contaminants carry a finality whose import for survival and reproduction no naturally occurring beneficial substances can match. Under most conceivable conditions, death and contagious causes of widespread death are costs that are radically disproportionate to any benefits that any naturally occurring substances can confer. For humans to be warier of contaminants than they are attracted by putative sources of positive contagion makes sense in the world that our predecessors inhabited. Just the same, some religions, including some of the most popular ones over the centuries, have lassoed this inference system and managed to upend one of its features too. The counterintuitive variation these religions introduce is the possibility of a *positive* contagious effect, arising on the basis of securing proper contacts with the divine, which is every bit as potent as the most negative contagious effects that threaten us in the natural world. Eternal life, acquired by means of the positive contagious effects of contact with the gods (or the gods' duly authorized representatives), is a proper antidote to the finality of death and the dangers inherent in any contaminant or negatively contagious item in the environment.

Theory of Mind and Myth

The most transparent way in which religion enlists the aid of maturationally natural systems is in its pervasive appeal to inferences grounded in theory of mind. Religions engage domain-specific knowledge about agents, their states of mind, and relations between them that virtually all humans have command of by the time they reach seven or eight years of age.[81] Those appeals are pervasive, because religions are filled with agents, from gods, goddesses, and ghosts to demons, angels, and ancestors, who exhibit counterintuitive properties and whose beliefs, attitudes, and actions are vitally important to participants' lives.

In chapter two, we saw how the acquisition of theory of mind entails a series of cognitive accomplishments. It begins with infants' recognition of animacy and goal-directed behaviors and proceeds over the next few years of a child's life to attributing intentionality to agents and according them particular perspectives and rich mental lives. No other maturationally natural mental system provides humans with a more versatile set of tools for making sense of the world. It is no coincidence that humans regularly conceive of the people who make up groups (whether gangs, clubs, ethnic groups, political parties, or nation-states) collectively as individual intentional agents. Journalists and pundits regularly speak of what France "thinks" or what Iran "wants" or how the White House sees matters. The agent causality that theory of mind encompasses is the root notion of causality that humans share. Agents are the pivotal causal variables in our social world. Consequently, agents are the mind's *natural* candidates for making things happen in the natural world as well. Religions' CI-agents not only constitute a source of additional explanatory capital. By virtue of their counterintuitive properties (they are agents who are physically undetectable, or who are not limited by physical barriers, or who are immortal, or who have full access to everyone's thoughts and so on), they constitute what is, in effect, a vast source of explanatory capital.

With the right kind of stimulation, the various components of theory of mind, like all of our other maturationally natural systems, can misfire. Its actual domain exceeds its proper domain. Each of the relevant systems errs on the side of liberality—from infants' susceptibilities to detect animacy and goal-directedness in disks moving on a computer screen to humans' susceptibilities to anthropomorphize just about anything in sight.[82] In order to make the world readily comprehensible, we are inclined to find in it a human face. But even when there is no face to be found, human beings are still inclined to spot in it the workings of an agent's mind and the consequences of an agent's actions. That is especially true in cultural settings, where the characteristic effects of intentionality—whether tools, symbols, or institutions—are omnipresent, but it is also true in natural settings where the evidence is more equivocal. Outfitted with HADD, human minds are poised to detect agents and draw inferences about their mental states and actions, no matter how circumstantial the evidence.[83] Mithen remarks that when children play with dolls, they not only wield this intuitive knowledge, but they also seem "utterly compelled to do so."[84] And recall Dennett's observations, cited earlier, about the *comfort* that humans derive from such attributions.

With experience and reflection, humans learn to discount many of HADD's promptings quickly, especially in familiar situations. They must. Spending a lifetime systematically checking out each one of its false alarms would waste a great deal of energy and leave much less time for other valuable activities. With experience, however, some events that were once unexpected are no longer so, and with deliberation some events that were once unexplained are no longer so either. Kelemen's research indicates that children subscribe to promiscuous teleology, but experience and education eventually rein in that inclination, at least somewhat, in adults.[85] Still, when stimuli activate adults' theory of mind systems, they, no less than children, will heed default inferences and display promiscuous teleology.

Religions regularly assemble stimuli that carry out such cognitive capture. I discussed previously how religious representations of agents with modestly counterintuitive properties enjoy mnemonic advantages. Their ability to transfix various theory of mind systems is a major part of what it means to describe such representations as "attention-grabbing." Cuing these systems about agents is also what gives these religious representations' their abundant inferential potential. Kick-starting them makes a body of default inferences available when pondering the ways of the gods, and it ensures an ease of cognitive processing with religious representations that only enhances their explanatory allure. These susceptibilities incline human beings to acquire religion, to depend on religion, and to fill both the world and events in their lives with religious meaning. The limitations that modern science has imposed on the legitimacy of agent-explanation have been gradual, hard won, and, as subsequent discussion will hint, often ineffective at superseding the online, rapid-fire deliverances of our maturationally natural theory of mind.

What is noteworthy, from the standpoint of cognitive *processing*, is that those special religious agents' counterintuitive properties notwithstanding, they are, otherwise, perfectly normal agents. They exemplify all of the standard sorts of interests, motivations, and states of mind that we recognize and acknowledge in our fellow human beings. Their conformity to virtually all of our default assumptions about psychologies and social relations enable even the most naive religious participants to reason about them easily—which is to say children who have reached school age and who, by that point, have their basic theory of mind systems in place. We can deploy the same folk psychology that we utilize in human commerce to understand, explain, and predict the behaviors and states of mind of religions' CI-agents.[86] The maturationally natural system of assumptions about the workings of agents' minds that enables us to negotiate safely (most of the time) on the streets as drivers, cyclists, and pedestrians is every bit as suitable for our negotiations with the rulers of the universe.

Religions traffic in myths. Religions employ stories whose comprehension turns overwhelmingly on possessing theory of mind and on understanding the agent causality that it entails. Agents' intentional states and actions are the threads that stitch episodes together both in narrative lines and in human memory. From those intentional states and actions that our theory of mind serves up, we weave the patterns in the fabric that constitutes our social and personal worlds and many peoples' understandings of their physical surroundings as well.[87]

It is through appeals to these covert intentional states that we can most readily organize temporal series. We arrange a series of events in a narrative, and we understand those stories in terms of agents, their states of mind, and the sequences of their actions. This is the sense in which myths and stories serve as tools for cognitively integrating the diverse materials of experience. By organizing events in time, story lines order the past and offer grounds for coherent recollections, as opposed to random ones. Donald emphasizes that with such cognitive tools at hand, an animal's experience of the world is no longer merely one episode after another, and memory is no longer just the chance recollection of such episodes nor just the recollection of frequently repeated, similar episodes organized in terms of a schema.[88] We gain a mastery of the concepts and skills required to manage such materials, quite literally, while sitting at our parents' knees, and we organize our own lives accordingly. These are the same tools with which we construct our life stories and forge our sense of self. Myth, history, and a sturdy sense of self depend upon the formulation of representations in conformity with the principles of theory of mind, in terms of which episodes may be categorized, comprehended, organized, and remembered.

Our knowledge about agents, intentionality, and actions strings events together into causally related strands. What we know about agent causality enables us to make predictions about the world and supplies an overarching strategy for bringing it under control. That is because the things that we are most disposed to treat as agents, whether mortal, divine, or mechanical, tend to act *rationally* under a wide range of circumstances. They generally conduct themselves, in short, as intentional systems. Within this framework, reasons serve as causes, and rationality serves as the salient principle underlying this causal order.[89] In these respects, myths constitute proto-theories for making sense of experience—past, present, and future—and for seeing how to acquire some influence over the course of events.[90] This narrative form of "theorizing" that myths and stories epitomize predates the scientific theorizing that is shorn of appeals to agent causality.

The appeal of myths and the ease with which we reason about them continue to trump all comers. Tversky and Kahneman's findings concerning participants' reasoning about Linda, the feminist bank teller, illustrated how in our cognitive processing the representativeness heuristic routinely overshadows a norm pertaining to the probabilities of conjunctions. Arguably, the cognitive biases associated with theory of mind cast an even bigger shadow, for they seem to be what stand behind the representativeness heuristic. (Participants' responses, after all, turn on their speculations about the most plausible *story* to be told about Linda's future, given the information that is available about her preferences and activities when she was in college.)

Narrative activation of theory of mind systems can imbue an *utterly improbable* chain of events with a plausibility and fascination that human minds not only find engaging but convincing. The probability of a long sequence of events is no more probable than its least probable component (and it is usually even less probable than that). In some contexts humans have no trouble recognizing that truth. For example, people have little problem understanding that a chain is only as strong as its weakest link. When, however, people are confronted with a *story*, its general consonance with theory of mind instantly purchases it coherence, memorability, and a measure of plausibility. Stories also invite humans' emotional involvement. Since we use the same principles to make sense of both others and ourselves, we do not find it difficult to project ourselves imaginatively into various characters' positions, to ponder their judgments, and to react emotionally to them and their situations. Humans' responses to science fiction and to fantasy literature, no less than to myths, demonstrate the power of stories, no matter how far-fetched their details, to inhabit our minds. People regularly say that they "lose" themselves when they are consuming stories.

This susceptibility to the influence of stories, including fantastic ones, is the source of many of our chief entertainments, and, as I commented earlier, the same underlying cognitive tools enable us to make sense of the social world, ourselves, and much about the natural world as well.[91] Those cognitive tools permit people to comprehend and recall highly improbable series of events that, without those principles and inference engines fitting them into an intentional framework, would otherwise appear as nothing more than an unmanageable collection of unconnected episodes. That characterizing sequences of agents' actions as a "highly improbable series of events" should seem so odd at first glance is itself testimony to the centrality of theory of mind in apprehending our social worlds. Like our other maturationally natural perceptual and cognitive systems, it provides the unreflective assumptions in terms of which we ordinarily perceive and understand the world. (Science reliably comes to question those intuitive assumptions by exploring alternative, counterintuitive proposals in atypical environments where the predictions of these two different sets of assumptions diverge or where our maturationally natural systems are mute.)

Massimo Piattelli-Palmarini has dubbed this general susceptibility to the ordering that is imposed on the world in stories by our theory of mind capacities the "Othello effect."[92] In Shakespeare's tragedy *Othello*, Iago exploits this penchant of the human mind, as he lures Othello along to the play's grim and pitiful ending. At times Iago manipulates events, but what he does even more skillfully is to use his command of intuitive psychology to shape how events *appear* to Othello, Desdemona, and other characters in the play. With subtle indirection Iago accomplishes that by framing these events within an emerging narrative structure, the automatic plausibility of which in cites Othello to develop suspicions based on flimsy evidence, to accept interpretations hastily, and to undertake actions that are precipitous and rash. Piattelli-Palmarini comments on the power of stories to make highly improbable sequences of events plausible:

> We fail to notice this progressive attenuation of probability. The story takes over from reality. The last link seems ever truer to our mind, and our increased facility in representing or imagining makes that last link seem ever more probable. The trick— which is one of the oldest in the book—is to find the narrative path by which the last, *and most implausible*, link can be made imaginatively compelling. . . .
>
> . . . The implausible becomes plausible, indeed certain. Give us a little story, a script, something born of our own imagination, and our own natural tendencies, cognitive or emotional, do the rest.[93]

Narratives not only make the improbable feel plausible. Notwithstanding the improbability of each event that makes up a story, let alone the even greater improbability of the succession of all of those events, stories often manage to convey a feeling of *inevitability*. This is, perhaps, the most compelling testimony about the firmness with which theory of mind grips our organization of experience.

Narratives, in effect, are intuition pumps. They trip the switches on our theory of mind machinery, readying myriad assumptions and default inferences about mindful agents and their actions that drive our interpretations of these histories, stories, and myths. They entice us to presume and accept information without reflection. Religious myths orient people in these ways unconsciously. Because the assumptions that myths and religious stories elicit are so elemental to our everyday understandings of events, we are usually unaware of how pervasive and how influential that collection of assumptions is and of how they automatically *entitle* the representations of CI-agents that populate these narratives. In the course of relating CI-agents' actions, religious myths, like any other stories, give us information about those agents' personalities, interests, and motives. The same variables that influence how we assess such matters in human affairs serve perfectly well here. So, for example, knowing about the gods' kinship relations will enable us to predict some of their paramount preferences and interests. Or knowing that, like us, the ancestors need provisioning dictates that we supply them with food in rituals of sacrifice.

Theory of Mind and Ritual

Such transactions with CI-agents introduce a second way in which religions implicate theory of mind. They will invariably elicit human beings' intuitive understandings about their social relations. Sooner or later, religious rituals always involve presumptions about some very special agents—but the fundamental point is that simply construing them as *agents* with whom humans can interact is every bit as important to grasping the structure and character of religious ritual systems as anything about their special counterintuitive properties. Religious ritual systems highlight *transactions* with such agents that have import for participants' *quasi-social* relationships with them. Participants' understandings of their religious rituals rely on standard cognitive equipment for the representation of agents and their actions. These components of theory of mind furnish the basic framework for explicating the logic behind participants' ritual interactions with the gods, and they are ones that even children understand.[94]

In a world amply populated with both predators and nefarious characters, it is not difficult to see how vital to humans' survival it is that they quickly learn to distinguish agents from other things in the world and actions from other events. Of course, many animals can detect predators and prey, but the detection of the bad guys among your own kind requires more.[95] That depends on an ability to discern others' intentional states. Developing a more sophisticated version of theory of mind that comprises, among other things, the capacity to read disreputable characters' intentional states establishes someone as qualified to participate in human society—but not in human society alone. They are qualified to interact with any intentional agents who will have them. Armed with the ability to ascertain others' intentional states, we recognize a subset of agents with whom we can interact in complicated ways and whose aid we might be able to recruit. Religions introduce CI-agents to the membership of that subset, and religious rituals are the principal means by which humans interact with those additional intentional agents.

In religious rituals humans move their heads, limbs, and bodies in coordinated ways or they move around in the kinds of paths that suggest that their movements are both goal directed and intentional. They bow their heads, kneel, and lift their hands; they pile stones, circle designated spaces, lift objects, lay out food, pour liquids, and, especially, wash and clean people and things, even when they obviously do not need it. In addition, people often emit formulaic utterances in the course of these movements.

Lienard and Boyer have laid out far-reaching and insightful proposals about ritualized behaviors in our species that apply the same general explanatory strategy that I have advanced in this chapter.[96] They argue that various cultural arrangements' cognitive capture of evolved dispositions of the human mind is responsible for numerous features of religious rituals. These range from the fact that they must be carried out just right each and every time, to the fact that they require concentration at each point on the particular components of the action at hand, to their focus on a comparatively small set of recurrent themes, having to do with such things as managing problems of contamination (hence, all of that cleaning and washing) and creating and maintaining order and boundaries, both physical and social.

One example of such cognitive capture in religious rituals— arguably, the most basic example of all—is the ability of religious rituals to mimic enough features of everyday intentional action to engage humans' mental equipment for representing it as action carried out by intentional agents. The motions and the utterances that people execute in religious rituals give the appearance that intentional agents are doing things. Tom Lawson and I have argued that this activation of the human cognitive system for the representation of action imposes fundamental, though commonplace, constraints on religious ritual form.[97] Attention to these constraints enables us to look beyond the variability of religious rituals' culturally specific details to some of their most general underlying features. Religious rituals, despite what often seem to be their bizarre, inexplicable qualities, are conceived as intentional actions too, and human beings bring the same representational apparatus to bear on them as they do on all other actions.

That is quite a feat, since, construed as actions, religious rituals do have some counterintuitive properties. The fact that in many religious rituals participants interact with perpetually undetectable CI-agents is only the beginning. Unlike their everyday actions, the ritual actions religious participants undertake also have no transparent instrumental aim. Why, for example, must some person be cleaned, when it is clear that they have already gone to great lengths to cleanse themselves and are adorned in their finest clothing? Why must people be kneeling when they drink from a cup? Why must initiates be put through all sorts of excruciating tortures? The repetitions with which religious rituals are replete only magnify their lack of instrumentality. Why must pilgrims climb a mountain seven times? Why must a priest walk around an altar three times instead of only once, especially since no matter how many times he does so he ends up where he started? Whitehouse observes that in this respect rituals resemble art—the performing arts, in particular. Rituals, like theater, dance, and music, have no "technical motivation."[98] This is one of the reasons that both ritual and artistic performances can often be repeated time and time again, where the idea is precisely that the same act is carried out each time.

Rituals are like works in the performing arts in a second respect. The connections between peoples' intentional states and their actions in rituals and plays are indirect at best. Caroline Humphrey and James Laidlaw have stressed that many features of people's actions in these marked cultural settings take the forms that they do not as a direct result of the ritual participants' (or the actors') occurrent states of mind but because they follow a culturally prescribed script.[99]

Whitehouse's observation[100] that this intentional indirection in rituals poses unending interpretive problems for our mind-reading machinery is, no doubt, true. The disconnect in religious rituals between agents' actions and their intentional states, however, occurs at another point as well. Not only can ritual participants be thinking about something else entirely (for example, when they know their script cold), at one important level it does not matter. That, at least, is what Lawson and I have argued for a set of rituals that stand at the core of each religious ritual system.[101] These religious rituals are effective not because of human participants' states of mind but, putatively, because of these ritual acts' forms, which have been specified by the CI-agents whom those rituals engage. The prescribed scripts for these rituals disclose the gods' wishes about how they and humans are to interact. Thus, properly qualified participants cannot fake those core religious rituals. If a properly qualified ritual practitioner carries out one of these rituals on an appropriate ritual patient, the ritual has been performed, regardless of what thoughts the practitioner or the patient might have been entertaining. Many religions certainly exhort ritual practitioners and participants to adopt a proper state of mind when carrying out these rituals, but, for practical purposes, it cannot matter, since participants' states of mind are not definitively discernible—except, of course, to the gods. Where people distinguish between what Barrett has dubbed "smart gods," who can, among other things, read participants' minds, and "dumb gods," who cannot, they often dispense with the niceties and acknowledge that, in effect, going through the ritual motions will suffice with the latter.[102]

Even minimal assumptions about humans' cognitively distinctive representation of actions, as opposed to their representations of other events, disclose avenues for understanding recurrent properties of religious rituals and religious ritual systems across cultures.[103] For more than a century, anthropologists and scholars of religion have underscored particular patterns among rituals and ritual systems, but it has only been an appeal to cognitive considerations that has yielded a unified theory capable of organizing and explaining that collection of properties and patterns.[104] Assuming no more than that the representation of actions will comprise slots

- for agents,
- for the acts that they carry out (and the instruments they employ in doing so),
- for the patients of those actions, and
- for the properties and conditions sufficient to distinguish these various items

will provide a framework for organizing, explaining, and predicting these features and patterns pertaining to religious rituals and religious ritual systems. However extraordinary religious rituals may appear as actions, they call for no unique representational apparatus. They enlist the same maturationally natural cognitive capacities that children use in the representation of actions, whether real or pretend. They do incorporate representations of agents with some modestly counterintuitive properties, but in that respect, they countenance nothing more than what is at stake in the comprehension of folktales and fantasy.

Agents do things to other things, including other agents. Since all of the religious actions that constitute what I have referred to as a religious system's "core" rituals involve agents acting upon patients, the cognitive representation of a religious ritual will contain three ordered slots. These slots represent the three fundamental roles that must be filled in that core religious ritual—the ritual's agent, the act that is carried out (with instruments optional), and its patient. All of a religious ritual's critical details fall within the purviews of one or the other of these three roles. Accommodating the rest of the details about the ritual's form, then, amounts to nothing more than elaborations on the entries for these three slots. My and Lawson's claim that all *core* religious rituals are represented as actions in which an agent does something to a patient departs from widespread, less restrictive assumptions about what should count as religious rituals. Priests baptize babies, ritual participants burn offerings, and pilgrims circle shrines. But people also carry out religious actions that have no patients. For example, they pray, sing, chant, and kneel. Even though such activities may accompany core religious rituals, such activities, in and of themselves, do not qualify as core religious rituals in our sense. Religious rituals—in this narrower, technical sense—involve CI-agents doing things to ritual patients or participants doing things to or for those CI-agents. These rituals are inevitably connected sooner or later with actions in which CI-agents play a role and which bring about some change in the religious world, the recognition of which is available to some public or other.

We certainly recognize that lots of other actions in religious contexts constitute ritualized behaviors in Boyer and Lienard's sense, but the distinction Lawson and I draw is not arbitrary.[105] A variety of theoretically independent considerations triangulate on the same set of religious actions as a religious system's core rituals. I have already mentioned that these core religious rituals *cannot be faked*. People can pretend to pray, but a priest in good standing cannot "just go through the motions" when baptizing an eligible patient. If those motions (and pronouncements) are gone through by a duly ordained priest, then the patient is baptized, regardless of what anyone intended. This feature is closely related to what I have just described in terms of these rituals' public availability. The consequences of carrying out these core rituals are available to at least some participants, though usually to the public at large as well. Under the appropriate publicly observable conditions, any participants who are privy to performances of these rituals can know what has been accomplished. Therefore, these core religious rituals, unlike other religious acts and ritualized behaviors, bring about recognized changes in the religious world (temporary changes in some cases, permanent ones in others). This is by virtue of the fact that these rituals involve transactions with CI-agents. How people act subsequently and the categories they employ change as a result of the alterations in someone or something's religious status that performances of these core rituals achieve. In particular, they bring about changes in participants' eligibility to participate in additional (core) rituals. While participating in anything other than entry-level core religious rituals (in the sense that we intend) turns unwaveringly on having performed earlier core religious rituals, carrying out other sorts of ritualized behaviors and religious actions does not. So, for example, a Jew must have gone through his bar mitzvah in order to qualify to become a rabbi but that ritual accomplishment is not a necessary condition for him to pray.

What sets religious rituals apart from other actions is the introduction of CI-agents into at least one of the slots of their action representations. (See figure 4-3.) It is the insertion of these agents possessing modestly counterintuitive properties into the slots of religious rituals' action structures that is, in fact, both distinctive and determinative. It distinguishes the subset of those events that qualify as core religious rituals, and it determines what type of core religious ritual is at stake and, thus, what properties it will exhibit. What Lawson and I call the Principle of Superhuman Agency (PSA in figure 4-3) holds, in effect, that which role a CI-agent is accorded in a religious ritual's action structure is the key consideration for predicting a number of that ritual's features.[106] The role that a CI-agent assumes in the action representation of a religious ritual may arise on the basis of that CI-agent's direct participation in the ritual or through the direct participation of the

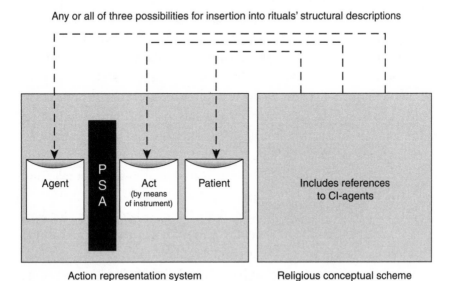

Any or all of three possibilities for insertion into rituals' structural descriptions

| Agent | P S A | Act (by means of instrument) | Patient | Includes references to CI-agents |

Action representation system   Religious conceptual scheme

Figure 4-3. Possibilities for inserting representations of CI-agents into representations of religious rituals

CI-agent's ritually established intermediary (typically some religious specialist such as a priest).[107]

In rituals in which representations of these CI-agents arise first in connection with the agent-slot (for example, in Christian baptism, where the priest as intermediary baptizes the ritual patient), the ritual in question will normally be performed on each individual patient only once. These are what Lawson and I have dubbed "special agent rituals."[108] After all, when the gods do something—even through their intermediaries—it is done once and for all. The gods do not have to do things to the same patient over and over. Since the CI-agents act, whether directly or by intermediaries in special agent rituals (baptisms, confirmations, and bar mitzvahs as well as weddings, ordinations, investitures, consecrations, and so on), the consequences of these rituals are what Lawson and I describe as "super-permanent."[109] Their effects can extend beyond or can even occur completely outside of the time of the ritual patient's earthly existence.

Anyone with even a passing familiarity with a religious ritual system understands most of this implicitly. Human beings readily comprehend that except under extraordinary circumstances, special agent rituals should only be performed once per ritual patient and to perform them with the same patient more than once violates the assumptions underlying *any* religious ritual system. Not unlike how speakers' knowledge of the grammars of their native languages enables them to spot ill-formed utterances instantly, participants in religious ritual systems know without reflection when such anomalies occur. In both cases such knowledge is supported by the interplay in human cognitive development of a maturationally natural system (the human capacities for language, on the one hand, and for theory of mind, on the other) and its cultural infiltration (by a particular natural language or religious system, respectively).

This is why in *The Importance of Being Earnest* Algy's pretext for why Dr. Chasuable should christen him "Ernest"—namely, that he has not been christened in years—is, as I noted earlier, a guaranteed laugh line. Even those with only the most basic knowledge of Christianity recognize that Algy owes an explanation for a second christening. Audience members understand (tacitly, at least) that God has done something to the ritual patient of a christening, and since CI-agents do not need to do things twice, it follows that the baptismal ritual is not a candidate for repetition with the same ritual patient. As evidenced by both his forceful assertion of his own suitability for this rite and his observation that Algy has already been christened, Jack clearly signals that he has made this inference and, thus, comprehends that Algy has an obligation to supply a rationale for a second christening. Wilde also makes it clear by the fact that Algy immediately offers an explanation, when Jack, in effect, challenges his suitability for another christening, that he too understands that he faces this obligation. What Algy must show is that his situation constitutes one of the unusual circumstances in which a special agent ritual can justifiably be repeated.[110]

Where the humor lurks in Algy's rationalization for his hastily scheduled christening is in his utterly ignoring the conspicuous feature of special agent rituals that provokes his need to provide an excuse for his second christening in the first place, namely, that repeating these rituals with the same patient is unnecessary and inappropriate. (It is unwise to toy with the gods.) Algy's comment that he has not been christened in years is funny because of its thorough disregard for the ritual's most transparent consequence, namely, its super-permanent effect on the status of the patient. In more than a century of productions of *The Importance of Being Earnest*, directors and actors know intuitively how and why this scene works. They know how to play it. They know how audiences who possess even the most rudimentary knowledge of Christian ritual will respond to it. They can count on all of this, because of the near ubiquity and the ready availability of this knowledge, which results, ultimately, from how religious ritual systems exploit theory of mind.

Under most circumstances, people intuitively comprehend the sufficiency of these special agent rituals to effect lasting changes in ritual patients. The danger, however, is that those ritual patients may notice that often little, if anything, really, has been done in the course of the ritual's performance. Consequently, these special agent rituals are more likely to incorporate features that will convince their patients that something remarkable has transpired. This is why successful religious ritual systems invariably evolve in a direction that ensures that these rituals contain comparatively high levels of sensory pageantry aimed at seizing the patient's attention and arousing his or her emotions. What counts as "high levels of sensory pageantry" in any particular religious community is relative to local standards, but special agent rituals are more likely to engage both more means and more extreme means for stimulating the senses than other types of religious rituals. In many religious systems these rituals will routinely include (or, at least, be accompanied by) special foods and drinks, music, dance, flowers, oils, incense, and more. The term "sensory pageantry" is intended to be inclusive. The means for eliciting appropriately receptive states of mind are not always confined to arousal through stimulating the senses.[111] For example, some religions administer psychotropic substances to ritual participants. Nor do special agent rituals always employ appealing forms of sensory stimulation. Deprivations and torture are every bit as effective at arousing emotion and, thereby, seizing attention as the more pleasant examples—and, generally, they are cheaper.[112]

Ritual patients in heightened states of emotional or other forms of psychic arousal are more likely to concur that something important is happening to them in those rituals. They are, after all, directly experiencing those rituals' effects. And in such fraught circumstances, if someone is convinced that something profound has happened, human minds, infiltrated with mythological narratives that say so, often leap to the conclusion that someone with some remarkable properties must be responsible.

These special agent rituals evolve to manipulate precisely the variables that research in experimental psychology has suggested are pivotal in generating particularly salient memory for specific events.[113] Any of a variety of means, but especially emotional arousal, can intimate that some event may be noteworthy in the life of an individual. By itself, though, that is not enough. We regularly forget events of high emotion, if, for example, they turn out to be false alarms or if we have no reason or occasion to rehearse or recall them subsequently. If, however, the event produces emotional or cognitive arousal,[114] *and* the individual is a *direct participant* in the event, *and* the individual has occasions to rehearse the event in memory or to describe the event to others, *and* community members acknowledge the event's import for the individual and for the community as a whole by categorizing and treating the individual differently, then the event is likely to stand as a prominent benchmark in that individual's life story.

These are just the sorts of conditions that special agent rituals produce. These are also just the sorts of circumstances in which experimental studies indicate that people actually do have some justification for their extreme confidence in the accuracy of their memories.

The distant memories about which people typically have such confidence have come to be known in the literature of experimental psychology as "flashbulb memories." Flashbulb memories have conventionally been understood as those that people possess about where they were, what they were doing, and who they were with when they learned of some surprising news of considerable social import. The best known are memories of when people learned about such events as the bombing of Pearl Harbor, the assassination of John Kennedy, the destruction of the World Trade Center, and the bombings of the Madrid and London transportation systems.[115] Generally, people report having especially vivid and reliable memories associated with hearing the news about such events in comparison, say, with their memories of the day before each one of these events occurred.

Ulric Neisser has, for decades, been famously skeptical of the confidence people express about such memories.[116] In a study of American participants' recollections of how they heard about the explosion of the space shuttle *Challenger*, Neisser and Nicole Harsch submitted compelling evidence that many participants' recollections of how they heard about the *Challenger* disaster were as thoroughly wrong as they could be, even though the participants expressed high levels of confidence in the accuracy of their memories.[117] Strikingly, though, in a subsequent landmark study, Neisser and his colleagues obtained considerable evidence of genuinely reliable flashbulb memories.[118] They collected statements shortly after the Loma Prieta earthquake in California (the earthquake that disrupted the 1989 World Series), both from participants who directly experienced the earthquake in the San Francisco and Santa Cruz areas and from participants in Georgia who had only heard about it or seen pictures of its effects on television. They brought most of these participants to their laboratories a year and a half later to test how well their recollections squared with the statements that they had given to the experimenters shortly after the earthquake. What the experimenters found was that on all of the dimensions that they had measured the Californians had virtually total recall for the associated events that they experienced directly. They accurately recalled where they were, who they were with, and what they were doing at the time, and they were justifiably confident about the accuracy of their recollections. As Lawson and I subsequently argued, learning the news about some arousing event is not the same thing as participating in an arousing event.[119] Jennifer Talarico and David Rubin subsequently supplied experimental evidence that suggests that memories for learning the news about some surprising event do not differ substantially from memories for many normal activities.[120]

Neisser and his colleagues' findings, in effect, demonstrated that emotional arousal was not necessary for such flashbulb memories, since some of their participants in California were outdoors when the principal shock occurred, were not in any danger, and reported that they felt no particular emotional arousal. Such circumstances are not especially rare in California, where earthquakes are not uncommon. What they and all of the other participants in California did experience, though, was a sense of the earthquake's significance for their communities, as news about its impact emerged over the next day. This news was attention-grabbing, even if many participants did not find it especially arousing emotionally. (Special agent rituals stir ritual patients' emotions, setting off cognitive alarms, since they cannot count on events like earthquakes to grab their attention.) In addition to viewing dozens of damaged areas over the subsequent days and weeks, area residents had also learned about the collapse of the Nimitz Freeway and of a section of the Oakland Bay Bridge, which would take a long time to repair. Thus, they had persisting reminders that they had, themselves, participated in an event of considerable consequence.

It appears that experiencing surprising events, especially ones that might threaten safety like earthquakes or terrorist attacks, firsthand and, thereby, having a sense of having *participated* in what proved to be a socially meaningful event were fundamental variables shaping these participants' extraordinary recollections.[121] But, of course, that litany of conditions faithfully describes the situations in which the human patients of special agent rituals often find themselves. This general pattern also offers some insight about why initiations, especially in many nonliterate, small-scale societies, frequently involve deprivations or torture![122] Moreover, the heightened levels of sensory pageantry associated with those rituals and the emotional and cognitive arousal that sensory pageantry produces will only enhance those rituals' abilities to seize patients' attention, to increase their sense of direct participation in these events, and, thus, to increase those rituals' mnemonic impact.

Core religious rituals of other sorts secure their memorability differently. When a representation of a CI-agent first arises in a ritual's action structure in connection either with that ritual's instrument or with its patient, it occasions a contrasting constellation of properties. These "special instrument" and "special patient" rituals, unlike their special agent counterparts, are capable of repetition (with the same instrument or patient) and can sometimes even involve what can seem like incessant repetition. So, for example, Christians may bless themselves repeatedly in the course of a day or partake of the Eucharist regularly, even though they are typically baptized only once. Special instrument and special patient rituals are the ones that participants perform so frequently that performance of these rituals feels habitual. Ritual performance often becomes the exercise of a well-rehearsed skill like any other, such as riding a bicycle, using a telephone, typing on a keyboard, or reading a book. The levels of sensory pageantry associated with special instrument and special patient rituals are usually notably less than those associated with special agent rituals within the same religious communities.

Why do people normally repeat these rituals? These are rituals, such as sacrifices, where humans do things to or for the gods (or ancestors, saints, or so on), customarily for the purpose of influencing their states of mind and, consequently, of increasing the probabilities that they will conduct themselves benignly. But, in the case of special instrument rituals, since humans' failures are unending, they are always in need of further help. Another blessing never hurts. Or, in the case of special patient rituals, humans' abilities and resources are limited, while the appetites of the gods are insatiable. The gods *never* cease to want their share of available material wealth.[123] Therefore, religious participants typically perform these rituals over and over. Obligations to repeat these rituals often can consume considerable time and resources. Consequently, religious ritual systems are more likely to permit a wider range of substitutions for ritual elements in rituals of these forms. When times are tough, it will be acceptable for a Nuer to sacrifice a wild cucumber as a substitute for an ox.[124]

Lawson and I have argued that performance frequency, levels of sensory pageantry, and participants' cognitive representations of religious rituals' *forms* along the lines I have just described are the psychologically influential variables that largely determine the shape of religious ritual systems. Religious rituals can be situated in an abstract three-dimensional space of possible ritual arrangements that these three variables define. (See figure 4-4.) Two regions in this space act like magnets. Such regions are known in dynamical systems theory as "attractors." Most religious rituals occur at one or the other of these two attractors,

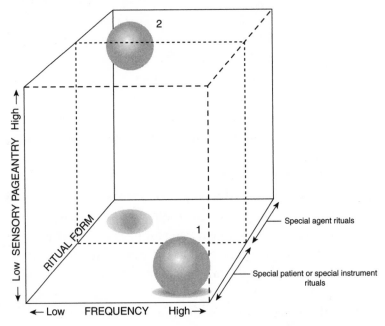

Figure 4-4. Two attractors in an abstract 3-D space of possible ritual arrangements

because the conditions those two positions represent are virtually guaranteed to enhance memory for these rituals and because they cohere with participants' cognitive representations of the actions in question.

These two attractors make sense of the paradoxical associations most of us have about religious rituals. The first region captures our notion that rituals are routine actions that are performed so frequently that participants are often said to carry them out "mindlessly." Special instrument and special patient rituals typically rely on the sheer frequency with which they are performed to ensure that participants recall them.[125] For reasons both psychological and economic, they usually do not enlist high levels of sensory pageantry. On the other hand, we also think of religious rituals as highly stimulating events that mark some of the most important and most memorable moments of our lives. Those rituals cluster at or near the second attractor. So, although special agent rituals are infrequently performed (under most circumstances, participants serve as the patients in these rituals only once), they characteristically recruit high levels of sensory pageantry, which help to grab attention and, thereby, help to establish both prominent episodic memories for the events in question and a conviction that the patient has been touched by the gods.

In what Whitehouse calls "doctrinal" settings, these memories associated with special agent rituals are regularly infused with an elaborate conceptual overlay. Doctrinal religious systems furnish participants with well-codified interpretations of what has been achieved. By contrast, the religious systems of traditional, small-scale societies, especially prior to the introduction of literacy, offer participants little explicit direction about what they should make of such rites. Whitehouse terms the latter "imagistic" arrangements and proposes that such rituals remain objects of ongoing wonder and speculation for participants, occasioning what he calls "spontaneous exegetical reflection."[126] In either case, serving as the patient of such special agent rituals dependably manufactures salient, memorable events that contribute to participants' understandings of themselves and of their lives' stories.[127] These rituals and the culturally available narratives that surround their performance become integral to participants' identities.

The inherent mnemonic advantages of rituals at these two attractors increase the probability that participants will transmit them and the religious systems in which they are embedded. Memory for rituals that is sufficient to secure a collective sense of continuity is vital for transmission. People cannot transmit what they cannot remember. People will not transmit what they regard as spurious.

The consequence of this point, in modern societies containing doctrinal religions, is that printed books (including ritual manuals) and widespread literacy may be overemphasized. The archaeological evidence suggests that religious beliefs and activities predate the invention of literacy by tens of thousands of years. Across the course of human history, the transmission of religious representations has overwhelmingly relied:

(1) on nonliterate (or illiterate) peoples' appreciation of public representations—both material items and practices[128]—and,

(2) on those publicly available items' abilities both to lodge related representations in human memories and to motivate human agents to transmit them to others.

Such nonliterate public representations were the *exclusive* vehicles of religious transmission throughout human prehistory, and they remain the most influential vehicles of religious transmission in historic times as well, as literacy is only about six thousand years old and large literate populations, beyond small privileged elites, are a much more recent phenomenon of the past two centuries.

The availability of literacy notwithstanding, nearly all[129] religious rituals gravitate to one or the other of these two attractors. This is as true in the so-called major world religions as it is in the religions of traditional, small-scale societies. That is because these patterns are rooted in pan-human psychological propensities. Thus, it is no surprise that these patterns recur even in the ritual systems of theologically sophisticated, doctrinal religions in the modern era. The underlying psychological variables that inform those attractors' positions also constrain ritual innovation.

Occasionally, ethnographers have been able to document processes of ritual innovation and evolution from start to finish. A recent case exhibits key trends described earlier. Whitehouse recounts in his ethnography, *Inside the Cult*,[130] the story of the rise and fall of a group that has splintered from the Pomio Kivung, a cargo cult on East New Britain Island. Especially in the decades after World War II, numerous cargo cults arose independently across Melanesia. By that time Melanesian peoples had firsthand experience both with Christian missionaries and with the vast material wealth that the militaries of the warring powers possessed. Cargo cults are new millennial religious movements. They hold that once a proper relationship is achieved—usually, by various ritual means, between cult members and the group's ancestors—those ancestors will return with enormous quantities of cargo for the cult members, inaugurating a new heaven on earth.

In apparent violation of the patterns that I described, the customary ritual system of the Pomio Kivung, from which this group splintered, is atypical in that its ritual system only employs rituals of special patient and special instrument forms. It seems to have no special agent rituals. As Whitehouse's ethnography testifies, however, this group has experienced periodic splinterings that involve the creation of new high arousal rituals that, as my and Lawson's theory predicts, take the form of special agent rituals. These splinter groups have reliably crashed, since their new high arousal, special agent rituals are never sufficient to precipitate the ancestors' return. Splinter group members, however, are welcomed back into the mainstream Pomio Kivung movement. The various splinter groups' failures notwithstanding, participants return to the Pomio Kivung revitalized and enthusiastic. It appears that unless religious ritual systems possess rituals at both attractors, their survival is less likely. As the case of the Pomio Kivung demonstrates, however, there is more than one way to achieve such balance in a religious ritual system. Most religious ritual systems consist of rituals at both attractors that are typically performed alternately during the same intervals of time. Whitehouse's ethnography, though, demonstrates that in rare instances, such as with the Pomio Kivung, rituals of each sort may instead be performed nearly exclusively in serially alternating cycles. The Pomio

Kivung group that Whitehouse studied alternates between periods of stability in which special patient and special instrument rituals prevail and splinterings in which the group primarily performs new special agent rituals.[131]

Whitehouse's report indicates that *all* of the splinter group's novel rituals are high arousal rituals that take the form of special agent rituals. That certainly fits. In one case the story is more complicated, but it is a story that fits too. Whitehouse witnessed the evolution of a ritual during the splinter group's reign that corroborates the connection between religious ritual form and comparative levels of sensory pageantry. The splinter group's ring ceremony shifts over time from a special patient ritual in which members ceremoniously give offerings to the apotheosized splinter group leader to a special agent ritual in which, after a magnificent feast, that same leader takes all of the splinter group members into a newly constructed and consecrated roundhouse for hours of singing and preaching, awaiting the ancestors' return that very night. The ritual fails to bring back the ancestors, but that outcome only provides one of those rare occasions for repeating the performance of a nonrepeated, special agent ritual. (Recall Algy's dilemma.) If the first performance failed, then it must be performed again, and the reason for the failure of the first (and the second and the third and the fourth and so on) performance must be ascertained. The splinter group's leaders show remarkable ingenuity in devising reasons that this ritual continues to fail night after night, while steadily increasing the sensory pageantry associated with these ritualized vigils. The crucial theoretical point, though, is that with the change in the ritual's form from a special patient to a special agent ritual comes a huge increase in its associated level of sensory pageantry and resulting emotional arousal.[132]

The elementary considerations grounded in theory of mind that I have reviewed in this section suffice to account for the forms that religious rituals assume when they occur at one or the other of these two attractors. That religious ritual systems encompass rituals at both attractors—rituals in which participants do things to or for CI-agents as well as rituals in which CI-agents do things to or for humans—comports with human beings' conceptions of social relations, which presume some reciprocity in agents' transactions. In the next section I will explore evidence that the influences of such maturationally natural dispositions of mind frequently swamp the reflectively acquired conceptual schemes that doctrinal religious systems supply. This results in what Jason Slone has dubbed "theological incorrectness."[133]

Theory of Mind and Theological Incorrectness

The third and most obvious respect in which religion engages theory of mind arises from the fact that the gods mostly think and act like us. This claim gets at one of the less obvious implications of anthropomorphic theories of religion, of which Guthrie's *Faces in the Clouds* is a prominent recent articulation.[134] That book explores humans' proclivities to anthropomorphize—in perception, primarily, but also in thought, and action—and it is filled with examples, both visual and verbal, of how we are inclined to construe the nonhuman world in human terms. Guthrie provides dozens of illustrations from nature, from art, from cartooning, from advertising, and from technical design[135] of people either discovering or imposing human-like forms on natural phenomena (those faces in the clouds) and on artifacts (for example, construing a door of the Palazetto Zuccari in Rome as a wide-open mouth of a large face).

The maturationally natural capacities underlying people's dispositions to construe the nonhuman in human terms are no less conditioned and shaped by culturally and socially peculiar circumstances than are those underlying the tuning of visual perception, face recognition, or the acquisition of natural language.[136] Still, anthropomorphism recurs across every culture, and it is no less outstanding in religious representations of CI-agents, from household icons that religious people have produced for thousands of years the world over to the high art of the Renaissance (consider Michelangelo's portrayal of God on the wall of the Sistine Chapel). Typically, CI-agents' resemblances to us in their physical appearance is uncanny. Except for their wings, depictions of angels look like the people that populated college campuses throughout the 1960s and 1970s in different attire. (Even in the respects in which they are not like us—for example, they are often portrayed with wings—they resemble familiar birds, never pterodactyls or Boeing 747s. The *modesty* of religious representations' anomalies extends not just to their sheer counterintuitiveness but also to these other respects in which they might stand apart.)

Guthrie identifies ample evidence of humans' interest in the shape of the human body. In his discussion of protective mimicry in nature, he notes that various species (caterpillars, moths, butterflies, fish, and so on) have evolved to take advantage of most animals' (not just humans) concerns with what look like pairs of eyes in their environments.[137] Since those eyes may belong to either predators or prey, many animals attend to such stimuli. The bodies of these comparatively defenseless creatures that Guthrie discusses include patterns that resemble the eyes (and, sometimes, the faces) of other animals that are considerably more capable. Their protective mimicry persists because it gives their potential predators pause.

Humans have additional grounds for an interest in eyes, at least the eyes of other humans. Infants' ability to monitor where other humans' eyes are directed greatly expedites their capacity for joint attention. Tomasello argues that establishing joint attention is critical to understanding others' communicative intentions and, thus, to the acquisition of language. The near-preoccupation most parents have with making eye contact with their babies tunes a maturationally natural proclivity of those babies' perceptual systems, rendering them particularly sensitive to patterns that resemble pairs of eyes embedded in shapes that resemble human faces.

Material representations of CI-agents sometimes involve no more than faces and eyes. In plenty of small-scale, traditional societies, skulls not infrequently stand in for spirits and ancestors.[138] During one of the periods in Ely Cathedral's tumultuous history when particularly abstemious Protestants were in ascendancy, they set about to disfigure all of its icons. The point is that it sufficed, quite literally, to deface them. These Protestant enthusiasts did not demolish the icons from head to toe. They simply smashed their heads. Obliterating their faces and eyes was quite enough. The same underlying cognitive focus on eyes and faces reveals itself in other parts of the world. Hinde remarks on how Mesopotamian votive statues with eyes of exaggerated size that are all directed at an image of a deity serve both to focus attention on it and to intimate its awesome import.[139] The Taoist "opening of the eyes" ritual speaks even more directly to the psychological salience of faces and eyes than do the icons themselves. When priests install the image of a deity in a Taoist temple, they not only invoke the spirit of the deity to inhabit the icon, but they also perform a ritual in which the image is painted. Specifically, it is the painting in of its *eyes* that transforms this artifact into a CI-agent capable of participating in rituals and responding to worshipers' requests.[140]

As Rochat's research on three-month-old infants' responses to moving dots on a computer screen demonstrates, however, infants' minds are also alert to appearances of goal-directed behaviors in their environments, regardless of whether the agents who display those behaviors take human forms.[141] Rochat's findings show that at this early age infants distinguish the irregular, self-propelled, goal-directed motions of the items in their environment that appear to qualify as animate agents, regardless of those items' shapes. Within another year they have become fairly clear about the subset of those items that will count as fully intentional agents. On the most conservative interpretations of the experimental findings, children, around their fourth birthdays, readily comprehend stories about intentional agents of all kinds of shapes and sizes in fairy tales, folklore, religious myths, and Disney films. Children deploy theory of mind effortlessly, and they can do so independently of stimuli that physically resemble human beings. Thus, the influence of these underlying maturationally natural systems on religious representations extends well beyond the fact that icons frequently have faces and human forms. Some religions, after all, including many forms of Islam and some Protestant Christian groups, permit no truck with icons or pictorial representations of CI-agents. Nonetheless, such restrictions do not preclude participants from knowing a great deal about the *mind* of God.

Experimental investigations of religious cognition demonstrate just how consistently people count on the gods to think and act like us. These studies display how in online, implicit cognitive processing human beings reliably assume that the gods *do* think and act like us. The "us" here is not just generic. Nicholas Epley and his colleagues argue that individuals implicitly presume that God believes what they believe.[142] Of course, if these individuals take themselves to be devoted followers of God, as many of Epley's participants probably do, then such an outcome is not startling. What Epley also found, however, is that when, unbeknownst to the participant, an experiment manipulates his or her beliefs about something, that participant's view of God's beliefs on that matter changes proportionately in the same direction. Epley and his colleagues had done research showing how humans' use themselves to anchor their estimates of others' beliefs.[143] His new studies, however, show that participants judge their beliefs closer to the beliefs of God than to those of other people generally and to those of various celebrities.

In the light of Guthrie's and his various predecessors' proposals, however, even *that* may come as little surprise. The significant contribution of other recent cognitive research is that religious participants assume that the gods are like us regardless of what those participants say explicitly about the character of their religious beliefs and representations, when they are asked to reflect on them.

The best known of these studies is Barrett and Frank Keil's exploration of religious participants' representations of the familiar CI-agents of their religious systems.[144] Barrett and Keil designed an experiment that taps how people carry out reasoning about CI-agents. In the experiment's first stage, Barrett and Keil interviewed participants about their religious representations. Consciously pondering their questions in a reflective, offline mode, participants furnished the experimenters with conventional, non-anthropomorphic conceptions of CI-agents as characterized in the religious traditions they knew. Their responses manifest what Barrett and Keil call "theological correctness." Their participants advanced the complex propositions that constitute orthodox belief in their doctrinal religious systems. Many participants in this first part of Barrett and Keil's study quite willingly proffered claims to the effect that God, for example, is omniscient, omnipotent, and omnipresent. In effect, they consulted, if not quite recited, their catechisms.

Such catechisms, doctrines, and statements of faith are, quite commonly, formulae that theological and ecclesiastical elites have carefully devised to work through various conceptual, theoretical, and political thickets. They are designed to clarify what will count as acceptable belief, to corral wayward-thinking participants, and to direct theologically minded disputants. In doctrinal religious systems, participants are assiduously drilled in these tenets of faith just as routinely as they are expected to perform various rituals. Such formulations, as Boyer proposes, constitute something like trademarks for religious brands.[145] The more open a religious market is, the more emphasis on their functions as *trademarks* such doctrines are likely to receive and, often, the more rigorously they are likely to be policed.[146]

Before pressing ahead with the subsequent stages and findings of Barrett and Keil's experiment, it will be helpful to take a short detour to make a few comments about the cognitive status of such theological endeavors. Up to this point the target of my analysis has been the cognitive status of *popular* understandings about religious belief and action, as the corresponding representations are entertained and as religions' rituals are carried out by ordinary participants. It has been a discussion of religion at the retail level. And it is retail religious thought and practice that I have been and will be comparing with science. I have had much less to say about the leadership, either political or intellectual, of religious groups. These are, metaphorically speaking, the founders, the executives, the boards of directors, and the think-tank members who, in so many cases, attempt to steer these religious enterprises. Practitioners of the cognitive science of religion generally give these figures less attention than they are customarily accorded in conventional religious studies. That is because if, in fact, most cultural transmission is constrained by maturationally natural dispositions of mind, then we probably overestimate the influence such leaders have on the forms that popular religion takes.[147] As will become apparent shortly, Barrett and Keil's findings offer support for the cognitive scientists' caution about such matters.

Doctrinal formulations of the sorts that Barrett and Keil's participants presented deal in what are, not infrequently, the radically counterintuitive representations resulting from esoteric theological exchanges. In some important respects, such theological projects are on a par cognitively with science. Carefully crafted theological formulations—for example, the classical Christological doctrine that Jesus is both fully

God and fully human simultaneously—that make up the doctrines of so many religions of literate peoples have arisen from processes of argument and debate that are similar in many respects to those carried out in other scholarly inquiries, including scientific ones. Theology, like science, is done most readily, most thoroughly, and most memorably when it is a literate endeavor. We, quite literally, have few, if any, traces of any theology in nonliterate cultures.[148] The literature theologians produce, like the literature of science, is theoretical, polemical, analytical, and synthetic. Just like science, theology does not rely on narrative. Theologians normally marshal evidence for their views, which they propound with as much order and clarity as they can. Theologians are most likely to resort to stories precisely on those occasions when they enter the world of popular religion—for example, when they assume the role of preachers.

Theologians ordinarily employ the same tools of conceptual analysis that philosophers do and carry out the same kinds of inference (deductive, probabilistic, inductive, and sometimes even abductive inferences) that scientists do. Since the appearance of direct government support for science in the seventeenth century in England and France and the growing cultural prestige of modern science, many theologians even look to some of the same theories and bodies of evidence that scientists do in formulating their positions. This is akin to the late medieval theologians' fascination with the recovered works of philosophy and science of the ancient Greeks.[149] Like scientists, theologians occupy themselves with forms of reflection that are difficult to learn and difficult to master and that occasionally even issue in representations that are just as cognitively unnatural.[150] Theology is one of the few academic undertakings that can result in formulations that are very nearly as distant from and as obscure to humans' common understandings of the world as the most esoteric theoretical proposals of science are.

As a characteristically literate undertaking, theology too requires the mastery of a host of intellectual skills. Fully qualified participants in theological disputes depend on formal credentialing, just as scientists do. In its most august versions, theology, like science, requires extensive education in programs and institutions specially dedicated to such forms of study. Just like science, it is quite typical for trained specialists to pursue these rarefied matters in settings far removed from the general public. Theology is usually no more of a spectator sport than science is.

I am not, of course, claiming that theology and science are alike in all respects, either cognitively or intellectually. At least three differences stand out. First, theologians may occasionally demonstrate a concern for the consistency of their proposals with the available empirical evidence, but their proposals are rarely empirically testable.[151] Generally, theological formulations do not stand or fall on the basis of any experimental findings, let alone any experimental findings that they inspire. That is because they rarely inspire empirical interrogations of the world. As noted previously, although some contemporary theologians attend to bodies of empirical evidence that the sciences have generated, theologians do not *produce* such evidence themselves. To date, anything described as "experimental theology" has exhibited far more vitality in the fictional world that Philip Pullman describes in his novel *The Golden Compass* than in the world in which flesh and blood theologians carry out their projects.[152]

The second difference is substantive. In the previous chapter I remarked on the increasing restriction of domains, over the history of modern science, in which appeals to agent causality are taken seriously. Progress across the past four centuries in the physical, biological, and psychological sciences has gradually circumscribed the areas of empirical research in which claims about agents' conscious intentional states undergird scientifically viable explanatory schemes.

This is not to say that theoretical progress in science has eliminated agency from every corner of scientific research. In many areas of psychology and the social sciences theoreticians continue to call upon human agents' conscious preferences and intentions to illuminate and explain behavior patterns—both individual and collective. The point is simply that over time the sciences have shown a clear trend toward explanations in terms of physical mechanisms[153] and, in the face of that trend, a comparably clear retreat from explanations that rely on the conscious decision making of intentional agents. As the discussion of the Boxing Day tsunami illustrated, geology, but other sciences too, such as oceanography and meteorology, have eliminated appeals to agents in favor of theories about tectonic plates, deep ocean currents that serve as thermal conveyors, low pressure systems, and the like. Scientists use these representations to explain why such things as the cooling or warming of the South Pacific can cause droughts in such far away places as the southeastern United States. Science painstakingly devises such counterintuitive mechanisms to explain both unexpected, catastrophic events, which religious specialists exhibit a compulsion to frame and moralize about, as well as common, everyday events in these domains, in which religious persons of all stripes usually find much less to pronounce upon. This tendency to dispense with intentional agency, whether of the counterintuitive or the human varieties, for deep explanations of the world, is no less true for the biological sciences (including evolutionary biology and neuroscience) and for much work in the psychological and cognitive sciences. It is the proximity to and logical conflicts with maturationally natural dispositions of mind concerning topics in folk biology and folk psychology, however, that have rendered these mechanistic accounts far more problematic in the public eye than the advances in the other sciences.

This second difference between science and theology is far-reaching but not absolute. At some of its esoteric edges theology has also surrendered appeals to CI-agents once in a while, even in the Christian tradition. Paul Tillich, for example, held that religion was, finally, best understood in terms of "ultimate concern,"[154] which may or may not require otherworldly agents. Of course, these edgy formulations are just the points where arcane theology decisively parts ways with the more popular manifestations of religion with which I am primarily concerned.

Historically, a third crucial difference between theology and science is that theologians, as part of an educated elite in societies (whether or not those societies possessed science as well), were typically supported and aligned with powerful ecclesiastical and political leaders. Sometimes the same individual has filled more than one of the relevant roles. Some ecclesiastical leaders such as Saint Augustine were also famous theologians. Others, such as Cardinal Richelieu, secured considerable earthly power. Theologians and ecclesiastical leaders were often political leaders' close kin. Popes Leo X and Clement VII were, for example, members of the most prominent family of sixteenth-century Italy, the Medicis, as was Leo XI.

In *Guns, Germs, and Steel,* Jared Diamond argues that throughout human history chiefs, kings, and the political leaders of states have repeatedly enlisted religion to render rationales for their kleptocracies.[155] The most straightforward route was simply to apotheosize monarchs the way the ancient Egyptians and the Incas did and the way that many Japanese still do. For millennia, if they were not elevated to the level of the gods, monarchs were, at least, alleged to rule by *divine* right. Religious thinkers and theologians have been the people who have supplied ruling elites with such rationales. From William of Ockham and Martin Luther to Billy Graham and Pat Robertson, religious specialists and theologians in the Western world have obtained wealth, power, prestige, and protection as rewards for either creating, sustaining, or, at least, tolerating ideologies that certify the machinations and the schemes of potentates and politicians. Theologians' connections with ecclesiastical and political elites have often endowed them with greater power than scientists, but that has not infrequently come at the price of some of their intellectual independence. Prior to the Enlightenment, particularly, their influence and, often, their lives depended on the health and political fortunes of their sponsors, as George Gilbert Scott's Martyrs' Memorial at the base of St. Giles Street in Oxford commemorates in the cases of Thomas Cranmer, Nicholas Ridley, and Hugh Latimer. Those three lost their lives with the ascension of the aptly named Catholic queen, Bloody Mary Tudor, to the English throne.

In our own time major scientists have occasionally accepted appointments in government. Barack Obama, for example, appointed the Nobel Prize–winning physicist Steven Chu as Secretary of Energy. Few if any such appointments, though, have turned on kinship or patronage, and, of course, the public does not have the sort of widespread engagement with and support of the sciences that, say, the medieval church often enjoyed.

The theologically correct religious beliefs that their participants furnished in the first stage of Barrett and Keil's experiment almost certainly sprang either from their indoctrination in their various religious traditions or from the parts of those traditions that have seeped into the broader culture. Their participants provided Barrett and Keil with accounts of their beliefs that contained either bits of those historic, avidly negotiated, finely stated catechisms and creeds or the obvious logical consequences thereof.

After these opportunities to reflect on and articulate their beliefs about standard religious topics and about the nature of God, in particular, participants were presented with the experiment's second task. In this second stage Barrett and Keil simply asked participants to read carefully through a group of passages that described interactions between human beings and God. Since the experiment would be testing participants' recall for the passages they had just read, Barrett and Keil introduced, as nearly all experiments testing participants' recall do, a third stage before the memory test in which participants carried out a distracter task. In this case they answered a series of easy questions on unrelated topics. The fourth stage of the experiment was the test phase. Barrett and Keil asked participants to recall as best they could the passages that they had read in the second stage of the experiment.

Following is an example of one of those passages.

> A boy was swimming alone in a swift and rocky river. The boy got his leg caught between two large, gray rocks and couldn't get out. Branches of trees kept bumping into him as they hurried past. He thought he was going to drown and so he began to struggle and pray. Though God was answering another prayer in another part of the world when the boy started praying, *before long God responded by pushing one of the rocks* so the boy could get his leg out. The boy struggled to the river bank and fell over exhausted.

The critical point about all of these passages was that they were *fully consistent* with the theologically correct conceptions that participants had affirmed only a few minutes before in the first stage of the experiment. Each passage, however, incorporated one or more critical details that readily lent themselves to more than one interpretation. I have italicized the pivotal material in this passage, but, of course, it was not italicized in the copies of the passages that the participants read.

What Barrett and Keil found was that in the online memory task participants recalled the passages in a manner that was inconsistent with their theologically correct, consciously available, religious representations. Instead, their memories of the passages squared with their maturationally natural conceptions of agents. So, for example, in this case, participants recalled the passage in a way that indicated that the short delay between the boy's prayer and God's response was either because God (rather more like Superman) required some time to relocate, however fast he might be able to do it, in order to deal with the boy's plight or because God, even if omnipresent, had to finish answering another prayer before attending to the boy. This trend to remember passages that were consistent with participants' avowed theologically correct beliefs in a theologically *incorrect* fashion was pervasive. Virtually all of their participants manifested such biases in their recollections of the passages. The passages were neutral between theologically correct and anthropomorphic, theologically incorrect readings. Barrett and Keil's participants, who reliably reported that they subscribed to theologically correct beliefs, nonetheless completely abandoned those beliefs when they carried out everyday problems in cognitive processing, such as reading and recalling the passages. In their *online* cognitive processing they opted instead for interpretations of these passages implicating quite modestly counterintuitive representations that conformed to the deliverances of their maturationally natural cognitive systems concerning embodied agents rather than the radically counterintuitive representations that their theologically correct, reflective beliefs entail. (This squares well with Barrett's independent findings about religious participants' petitionary prayers. There he discovered that what participants thought it made sense to pray for was thoroughly constrained by "completely nontheological activities of mental tools."[156] Petitioners' prayers, for example, reflected reasoning to the effect that it was much easier for God to change individuals' minds than it was to rearrange biological or physical circumstances.)

Two additional considerations support this view of Barrett and Keil's results. First, the distracter task proved irrelevant to the experimental outcome.[157] When, after completing the initial experiment, Barrett and Keil tried skipping the distracter task, they still got the same findings. Participants would interpret the passages in accord with the dictates of their maturationally natural cognitive dispositions instantly. The effects that Barrett and Keil found were not a function either of the distracter task itself or of any memory decay it might have caused. Participants automatically opted for the modestly counterintuitive representations that are overwhelmingly consistent with their maturationally natural cognition, even though, shortly before, in stage one of the experiment, they had faithfully rehearsed and, thereby, primed their theologically correct beliefs cognitively. This is just what the account of religious representations as rooted in maturationally natural capacities of mind that I have advanced in this chapter would predict.

The second consideration bolstering this analysis concerns the religious diversity of the participants that Barrett and Keil have tested. Initial indications, at least, signal that religious and cultural differences do not alter these findings. Barrett and Keil got the same results with Jews that they got with Christians in Ithaca, New York. The agnostics and atheists among their participants there manifested the same patterns in their responses, even though they did not share the religious participants' *convictions* about the representations in question. Barrett also replicated these findings with Hindus and Muslims in India. This is hardly a comprehensive inventory of the world's religions, but it is a creditable initial sample, which includes religions with different histories from different parts of the world and from different cultures.[158]

The substantially counterintuitive, abstract, theologically correct representations that doctrinal religions market turn out to be as delicate, cognitively, as the radically counterintuitive representations in which science traffics. Even students who are rigorously schooled in such representations drop them in a flash at the first sign of circumstances that cue the operation of a maturationally natural system. Participants may assent to theologically correct claims, they may listen to extensive explications of those theologically correct formulations, they may even memorize all sorts of propositions about them, but it does not follow that the mysteries and paradoxes those claims involve are anything that connect with those participants' day-to-day thought or reasoning about the matters in question.[159] Religious participants are prone, in short, to theological incorrectness.

The lesson of McCloskey's research about the withering of science students' laboriously acquired, radically counterintuitive scientific representations applies, apparently, with equal force to many theological materials. The extensive intellectual exercises that constitute formal training in science or doctrinal religion usually prove insufficient to trump the impact on their unguarded thinking of participants' maturationally natural dispositions of mind. In naked cognition both scientific and theological representations are vulnerable to being swamped by the same sort of automatic, intuitively compelling recognition and reasoning that overtook Mr. Quiverful.

Except, perhaps, for experts some of the time, neither science nor theology are likely to displace humans' most entrenched maturationally natural cognitive systems.[160] The lesson of Tversky and Kahneman and their followers' discoveries about the susceptibilities to maturationally natural heuristics—even, at times, in the thinking of highly trained experts— suggests that reasoning in conformity with orthodox theology will often prove difficult. Human minds' deepest maturationally natural dispositions are profoundly difficult either to shake or to correct. So far, anyway, correcting their deliverances has been the job of science; however, *both* science and theology have investments in shaking them. The testimony of history, of findings like those of McCloskey and of Tversky and Kahneman concerning the difficulties surrounding the cognitive processes and products that science engages, and of findings like those of Barrett and Keil concerning the ease surrounding the cognitive processes and products that religions enlist do not engender optimism about their prospects on this front.

Of course, all of this poses far less of a threat to popular religion than it does to science. First, whether they favor some particular religious or scientific account of things, all partisans are liable to confirmation biases. Without a community like the kind that animates scientific inquiry, which is dedicated to unearthing previously unknown evidence and to evaluating it systematically, popular religion successfully avoids most serious confrontations with negative evidence.[161]

Second, the entire burden of this chapter has been that popular religion sails on unencumbered with these maturationally natural winds at its back. (By contrast, science must tack vigorously to make any progress with a mostly uncomprehending public.) My case has not been that humans are naturally religious,[162] but rather that their maturationally natural cognitive systems develop in ways that make people thoroughly receptive to religions, to their myths, to their rituals, and to their representations. Humans do not have natural mental dispositions to acquire religion. But they do have susceptibilities, based on maturationally natural dispositions of mind, which exist for utterly unrelated reasons, that make them cognitively ready to leap at, swallow, and digest religious stories, actions, symbols, and settings like a hungry frog will leap at, swallow, and (attempt to) digest a ball bearing that flies within reach through its visual field. Like the ball bearing, religious materials trip enough of the switches in these organisms' naturally developing cognitive systems to attract their attention, engage their cognitive apparatus in characteristic ways, and often, literally, to set them into action.

Barrett, Kelemen, and Jesse Bering have all argued that young children are particularly well prepared mentally for the acquisition of religious representations.[163] Barrett's arguments focus on such things as the fact that until they are in their fifth year of life, children cannot pass a verbal version of the false-belief task. Possessing something less than a fully tuned theory of mind, they seem to find infallible minds unproblematic.[164] Kelemen argues for the same broad conclusion on related, but different, grounds. She emphasizes the penchant of young children for advancing promiscuously teleological accounts of the world. She argues that children, only slightly more readily than their elders in their own incautious ruminations, presume design intentionally imposed on things throughout their natural surroundings.[165] Bering and his colleagues have done a variety of studies that suggest that school-age and, on some counts, even younger children are thoroughly receptive to notions of invisible agents and the psychological persistence of dead agents' minds.[166] School-age children have little difficulty figuring out invisible agents' psychological states and carrying out inferences about them.

On this account of human cognitive development, which I have been pressing too, it is atheism, not religion, that humans must work to acquire. Compared with atheism or science, popular religion's modestly counterintuitive representations of agents that involve only limited, familiar variations and that preserve most of our maturationally natural default knowledge make comparatively light cognitive demands on human minds. The crucial point is that possessing these everyday, maturationally natural capacities and concepts equips people, including children, to acquire religion in a way that is not at all true of science.

Surprising Consequences

Traditional Comparisons: Turf Wars or Peace at a Price Too High

I promised a surprise ending, and we are almost there. But, first, I want to say a few words about traditional comparisons of science and religion.

Most such comparisons have not danced to cognitive tunes. Traditionally, most scholars (whether philosophers, scientists, or theologians) have focused on science and religion's comparative epistemological and metaphysical merits. This is to say that they have focused either on how each activity does or does not contribute to our knowledge or on what each discloses about reality. Two trends have emerged. Generally, the champions of science have tended to headline its epistemological strengths. They tout the fact that science stands unmatched in its ability to increase and improve our knowledge.[1] By contrast, defenders of the faiths, in the face of what they see as the metaphysical severity of science, usually commend religions' metaphysical abundance. Those guardians concur that assumptions about invisible sources of agency, both in us and in other kinds of beings, help to make sense of human experience, to undergird what they see as proper moral and social arrangements, and to frame the most daunting questions human face, concerning their own mortality, in particular.

An examination of these enterprises' cognitive foundations not only provides new views of science and religion, it also explains these trends. From the standpoint of popular, commonsense conceptions of the world, science can appear metaphysically hobbled. Science bears substantial burdens in the marketplace of ideas (let alone everyday marketplaces) selling radically counterintuitive representations whose appreciation requires painstaking cognitive processing that takes years, if not decades, to master. Cognitively awkward representations that are inconsistent with the representations that human minds most readily deploy are never a quick or easy sell. In particular, scientific abandonment of agent causality in a progressively wider set of domains inevitably leaves human minds, in at least some of those domains, floundering and incredulous. Over the past fifty years the sciences of the mind/brain have even begun to constrain appeals to invisible sources of agency *within us*.[2] Undoing agency in the biological realm, however, has been a political flashpoint. The battles that rage over Darwinian evolution are concerned, first and foremost, with the place of the deity's agency in shaping the biological world.

Science's major selling points come into play when its effectiveness at explanation, prediction, or control is timely or when related technologies either thrill or fascinate. When scientists develop effective vaccines for deadly diseases, predict celestial events, explain the genetic mechanisms of inheritance, or inspire the latest advance in computing, the public is less inclined to challenge science's epistemic authority, even if science's shifting verdicts and its underlying metaphysical commitments utterly perplex the general public.

By contrast, the recurrent metaphysical commitments of religions are far easier to swallow. They overwhelmingly square with the deliverances of our maturationally natural cognition, and they capitalize, especially, on the penchant of human minds to presume that noteworthy events result from the actions of intentional agents. Proliferating agents present no special cognitive problems for human minds in standard operating mode. I have examined how religious representations incorporate modest violations of humans' maturationally natural presumptions. Their minor conflicts with human intuitions permit us to draw on all (but one or two) of the default inferences we associate with the categories in question. As I outlined in the previous chapter, Boyer holds that the representations of popular religion approximate cognitively optimal arrangements, at least from the perspective of making sales in the marketplace of culture. Such representations go a long way toward solving the problem of simultaneously attracting human attention, enhancing human memory, and increasing inferential potential. That is another way of saying that standard religious wares sell comparatively easily, which is why in relatively open religious markets, like that in the United States, so many vendors of religious goods and services thrive.[3] It is also a way of saying that religious representations probably never completely lose their natural attractiveness, regardless of humans' intellectual training. The most valuable evidence here is not the steadfast denials of the nonreligious about their conscious mental lives but, rather, indirect tests that tap cognitive influences and activities that operate below the level of consciousness. Unshakeable, subterranean forces are the more interesting marks of some representation's natural cognitive allure.

The downside, though, is that ease of swallowing from a cognitive standpoint does not guarantee ease of digestion from an intellectual standpoint. Enduring texts permit systematic assessments of whether the claims those texts make are true. Since it presents the opportunity for prolonged, methodical reflection about ideas, literacy renders the logical and empirical problems that religious representations and their violations of ontological intuitions entail all the more conspicuous. Such conditions spawn theological reflection and proposals, which can end up appearing nearly as convoluted as the most puzzling claims of science. Because theological and scientific claims part so substantially from our maturationally natural knowledge, people often find them perplexing at best. Once the claims of popular religion undergo inspection in a literate culture, though, the conundrums they generate can become uncomfortably clear to thoughtful participants and, often, laughable to outsiders. The claims of popular religion, especially those in behalf of religious experience, cannot easily bear the unencumbered scrutiny of a highly literate public and the rigorous application of methods employed to study other areas of human conduct.[4] In these precincts the religious and, all too often, even scholars of religion break into special pleading, which is not a recipe for creating durable or persuasive arguments.[5]

These two trends among conventional comparisons of science and religion often lead people to parcel out the pertinent intellectual territory between them. Probably the best known advocate of that strategy in our time has been Stephen Jay Gould. In his book *Rocks of Ages*, Gould assigns science and religion to two different "magisteria." He asserts that "the ... magisterium of science covers the empirical realm" while "the magisterium of religion extends over questions of ultimate meaning and moral value." This strategy for dividing up the turf is popular, because it promises intellectual peace. Gould stresses that "these two magisteria do not overlap," which eliminates possibilities for conflict.[6] In this two-state strategy, each, according to Gould, rules in its own realm.

This strategy for achieving peace faces problems, though, on at least two counts. First, it is not obvious that science and religion are the sole authorities in the respective magisteria to which Gould assigns them. For example, what specific religions have to say about meaning and morality always ends up turning, sooner or later, on their particular contents, commitments, and practices. The problem, if these religious systems' recommendations are to be persuasive to anyone other than their followers, is that these distinctive features of religious traditions carry little, if any, authority precisely where they need to—namely, *beyond* the confines of that particular religious system's subscribers. These contents, commitments, and practices must retain their credibility in a complex and diverse world, if they are to supply any basis for either general, morally obligatory prescriptions or what people, across cultures, take to be meaningful arrangements. Arguably, a particular religion is exactly what any grounds for binding moral authority cannot depend upon, if rational and psychological purchase *across* religious systems and cultures is the aim.[7]

On the other hand, although science is second to none in the empirical realm, that is not the same thing as claiming that it is the exclusive or the exhaustive authority with regard to empirical matters. Science is young, it operates with limited resources, it is difficult to learn, our lives are short, and the world is vast and complicated. We have hardly even begun to question the world scientifically. Furthermore, science is a neverending process. As we do better science, we learn that much more about what we do not know and, as noted earlier, some of the conclusions invariably change as science progresses. Over the last few decades larger numbers of people around the world have had sufficient time and material support to learn some science, and, occasionally, the particularly diligent get the opportunity of consulting informed, up-to-the-moment scientific judgment, but we should not be embarrassed about the fact that so much of the time we are stuck with relying on little more than our maturationally natural intuition in our dealings with the world. It is the inevitable consequence, in the face of the practical necessity of getting about from day to day, of the immense variety of problems that we face, of our limited resources, of the fallibility of our inquiries, and of the substantial intellectual challenges required to comprehend the sciences.

The second reason that purchasing peace at this price may prove too dear is that it involves some normative sleight of hand. The particular norms that I have in mind here are about the application of the concepts "religion" and "science." Following are two related examples. First, one of the easiest ways of minimizing the tensions between science and religion is simply to deny that religious people, who remain especially exercised about apparent conflicts with science, deserve to be designated as "religious" in the first place. This dismissive attitude lurks behind all gentle and seemingly conciliatory talk of "true" religion among the faithful, among theologians, and among academics. This includes, for example, claims that the terrorists who attacked New York, Madrid, and London in the first years of the twenty-first century were not *true* representatives of religion or, more specifically, true representatives of Islam.[8] My point is *not* that I think that they are true representatives of Islam or of religion, more generally, but rather that with respect to religious disagreements, *no one* is entitled to use such idioms. The pressing questions are: (1) Who gets to say whose religiosity is or is not true or whose version of Islam (or any other religion) is the right one? and (2) On what rationally convincing basis do they get to say it? In light of these questions, consider Gould's declaration that "creationists do not represent the magisterium of religion."[9] Gould proceeds as if the religious, let alone the logical, sensibilities of literally hundreds of millions of people should not count when sorting these matters out. Gould and his allies here invent prejudicial norms where norms of the sort they desire are not to be had.

The fact that defenders of religion focus on its usefulness for morality amounts to a tacit recognition of that fact. This asymmetry between the status of norms pertaining to the applications of the concepts "religion" and "science" is not coincidental. As I shall argue in the next section, science and theology have different relations to the maturationally natural moorings from which they are born. Theology, like Lot's wife, cannot avoid the persistent temptation to look back—to look back to popular religious forms. By contrast, the radically counterintuitive commitments at which the sciences inevitably seem to arrive commonly produce unbridgeable gaps with the intuitive assumptions underlying our commonsense explanations. The sciences fairly quickly get to a point where they can no longer look back to our maturationally natural predilections for inspiration. Theology is largely devoted to making sense of and bringing some logical order *to* the claims of popular religion. Science, by contrast, follows wherever its inquiries lead and that has reliably been *away* from the automatic deliverances of the maturationally natural mental systems that inform our commonsense understandings of the world.[10]

Peoples have routinely construed their own conflicts as conflicts between the gods. The invention of literacy not only made proselytizing religions possible, it also created the possibility for reflection on conflicts about different religions' comparative intellectual and moral merits. It is not for lack of trying that no religion has yet made a case for its truth that comparatively disinterested observers from around the world find persuasive.

This contrasts with the way that huge majorities of the world's professional scientists do find the resolutions of so many of the controversies in their fields of study convincing, at least provisionally, given the current state of the evidence. Scientists regularly arrive at such views on the basis of relevant evidence and without epistemologically troublesome coercion (from governments, corporations, religions, and so on). That, of course, is not to say that they *always* do so or to say that they *ever* do so completely independently of extrascientific social influences. The difference here between science and theology is not trivial, but it is not absolute either. That is because the sciences' verdicts, even their most fundamental ones, are constantly eligible for reconsideration and because, as noted, once in a while evidence emerges that the influence of scientifically arbitrary forces has *not* been negligible or unimportant.

These considerations lead to a second, related illustration of how designating nonoverlapping magisteria for religion and science carries problematic normative consequences. Gould urges both science and religion "to stay on their own turf."[11] On his account science is concerned with explanations of empirical phenomena while religion covers morals and meaning. Religions certainly do try to make sense of our lives and of the world in which we find ourselves. The problem, though, is that that process of making sense of things inevitably involves appeals to explanations about the origins, the makeup, and the behavior of things generally and about our origins, makeup, and behavior in particular. Religious meaning-making, indeed *all* meaning-making, always makes explanatory assumptions, for example, about what makes human beings do the things they do. Some of those assumptions, such as those creationists proffer, are explicit. Many more, connected with such maturationally natural cognitive systems as theory of mind, are implicit.[12] But in either case meaning-making depends on, among other things, explanatory accounts of how things hang together, of how events are connected, of how the world works, and of how human beings operate. Whether advocates of exclusive magisteria like it or not, all religions explicitly traffic in explanations some of the time, and religious meaning-making makes explanatory presumptions all of the time. Much of the time those explanations are superfluous from the standpoint of scientific accounts, if they are not downright inconsistent with the claims of science. The attempt to buy peace by designating exclusive magisteria requires either (a) ignoring the place of explanations, whether religious or scientific, in the processes of finding or assembling meaning or (b) ignoring the logical tensions between the explanations that science and religions favor or (c) ignoring both.[13] Gould's conception of the relation between science and religion is not exactly peace at any price, but it does seem, in light of these normative problems, to be peace at a price too high.

Although the discussion that follows will touch on some of these traditional issues, I promised a surprise ending, and I hope not to disappoint. Not every item will astonish every reader, but most interested parties should find at least one or two of these claims surprising. Here are the seven consequences:

- Traditional comparisons of science and religion are cognitively misbegotten.
- Theological incorrectness is inevitable.
- Science poses no threat to the persistence of religion.
- Relevant disabilities will render religion baffling.
- Science is inherently social.
- Science depends more fundamentally on institutional support than religion does.
- Science's continued existence is fragile.

Discussion of the first of these consequences will frame all that follows.

Traditional Comparisons of Science and Religion Are Cognitively Misbegotten

Comparing science and religion has become an intellectual cottage industry over the last hundred years. The tensions between science and religion have been clear even to the casual observer. Contributors to the debate have been anxious either to dissolve those tensions or to emphasize them as grounds for extolling one of these activities or (like Gould) for extolling both. Such epistemological and metaphysical preoccupations are perfectly legitimate concerns and perfectly understandable philosophically. No matter how legitimate and understandable, though, these preoccupations only clarify some things. They blur others. Traditional comparisons of science and religion are, from a cognitive standpoint, misbegotten in two respects.[14]

Anything can be compared with anything. Still, science and popular religion diverge on two kindred cognitive criteria that suggest that conventional comparisons are less revealing than is typically presumed. Those criteria permit science and religion, along with theology and commonsense explanations of the world, to be distinctively situated in a two-by-two table. (See figure 5-1.) The first criterion, represented vertically at the left of figure 5-1, contrasts the relative prominence of two types of cognitive processing in any of these enterprises. Cognitive undertakings that tilt toward reflective, offline, cognitive processing and away from maturationally natural cognition are across the top (that is, cells 1 and 2), whereas those that rely more prominently on maturationally natural, online, cognitive processing that tends to preempt conscious, offline reflection are in the bottom row (cells 3 and 4).

Reflective, offline cognition is the most plausible candidate available for thought that is under conscious control. Literacy has played a

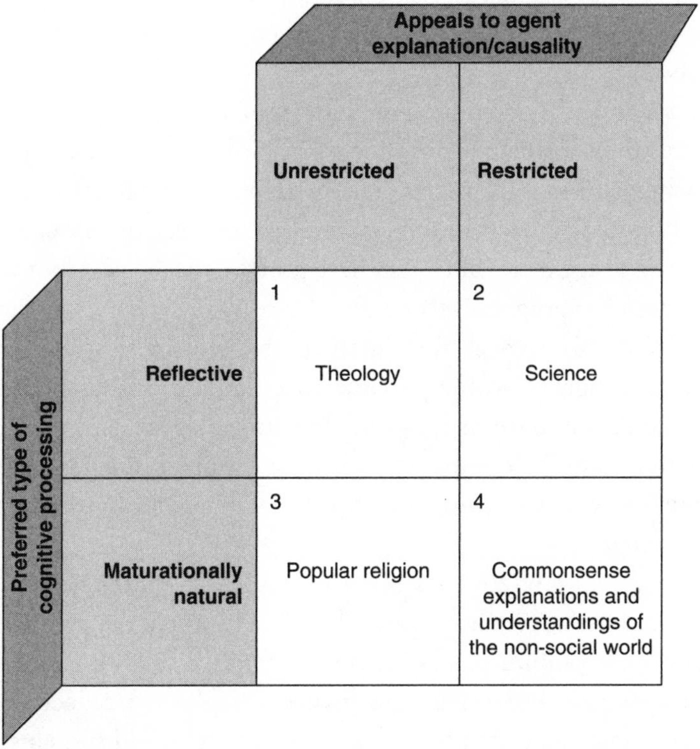

	Appeals to agent explanation/causality	
	Unrestricted	**Restricted**
Reflective	1 Theology	2 Science
Maturationally natural	3 Popular religion	4 Commonsense explanations and understandings of the non-social world

(Preferred type of cognitive processing)

Figure 5-1. Cognitive asymmetries

pivotal role in its enrichment, since the external representation of such thought in publicly available texts permits conscious minds to produce and contemplate the elaborate ideas and extended arguments that arise in the most sophisticated forms of reflection. The only naturalness that can ever accrue to these forms of cognition is a practiced naturalness. One of the most familiar kinds of practiced naturalness in an intellectual domain is associated with reading. For experienced readers, reading is automatic. But for inexperienced readers, it is a struggle—one that requires lots of practice to overcome. Prolonged exercise at reflective activity in some field can yield a practiced naturalness on some intellectual fronts. With considerable experience, experts obtain comparatively detailed intuitions about their areas of expertise. The research on lapses in deductive and probabilistic reasoning and in the application of scientific theories and concepts that I discussed in chapter three indicates that such practiced naturalness in intellectual matters is both hard-won and, often, surprisingly inflexible. Recall that small shifts in an otherwise familiar scenario can even drive the performance of experts off a cliff.

The second criterion represented horizontally at the top of figure 5-1 concerns the explanatory prominence accorded agent causation. This distinction arises from my earlier observation about the increasing restrictions that, over its history, science has imposed on the legitimacy of appeals to agent causality. As I have noted, over the past four centuries science has progressively confined the use of such explanations— in the physical sciences first, then in the biological sciences, and now increasingly so in the psychological and sociocultural sciences. Scientific abstemiousness regarding intentional agents and their putative actions is to be compared with what I argued in chapter four is religions' pervasive recruitment of theory of mind and appeals to agent explanations.

Although its discrete cells seem to imply differences in kind, the differences are merely in degree. The table captures the comparative priority each venture places on these cognitive variables. Its layout situates religion and science relative to theological reflection and commonsense understandings of the (nonsocial) world and illustrates two telling asymmetries.

Concerning cell 2—I have argued that science is a reflective activity involving forms of thought and types of representation that depart radically from the pronouncements of our maturationally natural cognitive systems. The progress of science has gradually but steadily whittled down the areas in which the most accurate and comprehensive explanations for phenomena involve taking the intentional stance. The prohibition of agent causality from physical and biological science has, in effect, become a tacit methodological maxim.[15] Still, this contrast should not be exaggerated. The success of mechanistic modeling in the cognitive sciences notwithstanding, the psychological and sociocultural sciences continue to call upon agents, their mental states, and their resulting actions.[16] In fields such as social psychology, classical microeconomics, and cultural anthropology, theories and models about intentional agents, their preferences, and their actions remain the standard mode of analysis and explanation. Thus, even in science the use of agent causality is unlikely to wither away completely, at least for the foreseeable future.

Concerning cell 4—remember that not all of the verdicts of maturationally natural cognitive systems involve summoning agent causation or theory of mind. In fact, most do not.[17] By school age, human beings seem to possess all sorts of detailed dispositions about matters as various as the basic physics of solid objects, grammatical form, fair distributions of resources, kin, and the avoidance of contaminants. What makes many of our commonsense understandings and explanations common is precisely that they arise from maturationally natural dispositions that human beings share. Certainly, humans are not incapable of reflection about such matters, though it rarely occurs to them to undertake such musings. But in many situations, especially those that call for quick judgment or fast action, these intuitive systems and the accompanying emotions they often involve kick into gear before opportunities for conscious deliberation even arise. For example, when people feel cheated, it dominates their awareness and emotions and it drives their bodily states and actions immediately. Sometimes such dramatic circumstances cue these cognitive systems' automatic operations, but far more mundane matters can trigger dispositions that also have nothing to do with theory of mind either. Recall McCloskey's research in which large numbers of naive participants attempted actions that were aimed at producing physically impossible motions in order to carry out the requested task. So, for example, when asked to roll a puck in such a way that its path crossed both the "entrance" and the "exit" of a curved "passage" drawn on a flat surface, many of McCloskey's participants attempted to make the puck curve to follow the arc of the curved passage. See figure 5-2.

Concerning cell 1—*nothing* that I have said anywhere in this book rules out offline, reflective activity in domains that have no inherent restrictions on appeals to the intentional, of the sort that constrain the physical and biological sciences. Theology is not the only kind of intellectual project that falls within this cell. It also contains traditional

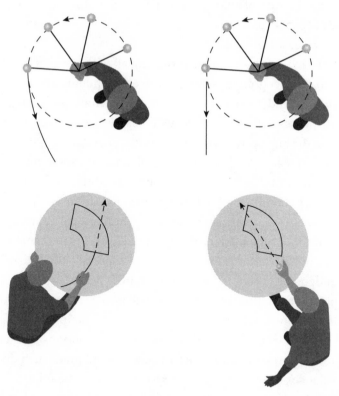

Figure 5-2. Participants attempt physically impossible motions (after McCloskey 1983)

moral philosophy and somewhat more rarefied areas of contemporary philosophy such as action theory. With respect to matters religious, though, such reflection occupies theologians primarily. In the literate cultures where they arise, theologians regularly carry out the same forms of inference that philosophers and scientists do (deductive reasoning, chiefly, but probabilistic and abductive reasoning too). They also brandish representations that can sometimes be as counterintuitive as those that scientists use. The suppositions of popular religion tend to be only modestly counterintuitive. By contrast, theologians have been generating radically counterintuitive representations for millennia. Attributing esoteric, abstract properties such as omniscience, omnipotence, and omnipresence to some gods leaps to mind. As do the conceptual recalibrations required, for example, of Christians to accommodate what are far more fundamental notions. Understanding God as a triune entity (each person of which is alleged to have had temporary, divergent physical manifestations) presents all of the conceptual challenges that the modern psychological account of multiple personality disorder demands and more.

Concerning cell 3—I argued in chapter four that popular religion enlists humans' maturationally natural cognition and that it engages theory of mind especially. Thus, it falls in cell 3. Folklore, fairy tales, and fantasy literature fall into this cell as well, but religion is the more interesting case. Popular religious forms, including icons, sacred spaces, rituals, priestly status, CI-agents with full access to people's thoughts, and more, variously activate mental systems that develop early in human minds. Those mental capacities do not operate as they do in order to manage religious inputs, but, instead, arise in human cognitive development to handle problems of perception, cognition, and action that are far more basic to human survival. Particularly central to making our way in religious worlds are the default inferences and intuitive calculations about agents, their intentional states, and their actions. These happen to be particularly central to making our way in our everyday social worlds as well. These mental tools are what make religious materials captivating for human minds. They are also what, by school age, equip human beings to grasp religious forms and enable them to acquire religion.

My aim here is to underscore how traditional comparisons of science and popular religion on epistemological and metaphysical grounds can be downright misleading about the underlying cognitive factors that give them their shapes. From the standpoint of cognition, science and religion are asymmetric on two crucial counts. First, they mostly operate at different cognitive levels. One is primarily dependent on the natural proclivities of human minds and, hence, recurs in every human culture, whereas the other is a function of comparatively rare social arrangements that require (a) mastery of both norms of reasoning and radically counterintuitive conceptions and (b) the public availability of the pivotal processes, products, and evidence. The second cognitive asymmetry hinges on their critically different default assumptions about the way the world works. Religions presume that the most penetrating accounts of the world will always, ultimately, look to agent causality. Science does not.

Nor, in all domains, do our commonsense understandings of the world. That observation hints at how the lack of interest in these cognitive and cultural considerations can obscure some revealing connections. For example, from a cognitive standpoint each of science and popular religion are more similar to each of theology and commonsense explanations (of the nonsocial world) *than they are to one another*. Consider science first. As I just noted, neither scientific nor commonsense approaches to accounting for the nonsocial world assume that agent causality, finally, provides the most telling explanations. On the other hand, both science and theology are reflective activities that are mostly (and most credibly) pursued by highly trained specialists. Popular religion, by contrast, shares neither of these properties with science. On both of the cognitive considerations just reviewed, though, it too is more like both commonsense explanations and theology than it is like science, though in exactly opposite ways. It is their mutual emphasis on maturationally natural cognitive capacities that link religion and commonsense understandings of the world, while it is the priority they set on agent causality in their explanations of things that popular religion shares with theology. There is a respect, then, in which the long-standing interest in the comparison of science and religion is, from the perspective cognition, somewhat misbegotten. Without systematic attention to these cognitive questions and explicit discussion of the place of theological reflection and commonsense views of the world as well, conventional comparisons of science and religion seem a bit contrived.

In his book *Inevitable Illusions*, Piattelli-Palmarini discusses findings from experimental psychology indicating humans' penchant for relying on their maturationally natural cognitive systems even when their deliverances are thoroughly contrary to the norms of deductive and probabilistic inference. He asserts that "we have come to see that our minds spontaneously follow a sort of quick and easy shortcut, and that this shortcut does not lead us to the same place to which the highway of rationality would bring us." A few pages later he adds that "our spontaneous psyche is not a kind of 'little' or lesser reason, nor is it an approximate form of rationality."[18] Piattelli-Palmarini's observations counsel that the cognitive affinities between science and maturationally natural commonsense explanations should not be overestimated. As I have argued throughout this book, behind these two approaches to the world lurk differences that make a difference cognitively. The symmetries that figure 5-1 displays suggest that if that is true, then neither should the cognitive affinities between theology and popular religion be overstated. Systematic reflection generates intellectual working space beyond that which our maturationally natural tendencies supply. The maturationally natural cognitive processes and inferences that prevail in popular religion are no more a "'little' or lesser" version of systematic theological reasoning than are the intuitive shortcuts of our commonsense explanations a "'little' or lesser" form of scientific reasoning. The framework figure 5-1 represents and this observation about its contents point to the second unexpected consequence I wish to consider.

Theological Incorrectness Is Inevitable

What is surprising is not that the eruption of theologically incorrect religious representations occur but rather that such eruptions will be both recurring and *inevitable*. In religious systems with carefully formulated doctrines, chock-full of radically counterintuitive propositions over which theologians have wrangled, in some cases for centuries, the predilection to revert to cognitively natural religious representations results in what Boyer calls the "tragedy of theology."[19] His position, in short, is that no matter how meticulously theologians articulate doctrines or how strenuously ecclesiastical authorities police orthodoxy, human minds will regularly follow paths and introduce variations that more closely harmonize with their natural cognitive prejudices. This is just what Barrett and Keil's participants did. In addition, what is striking about their findings is that this is what their participants did immediately after recounting and thereby activating their consciously held, theologically correct beliefs.

Doctrinal religious systems undertake the explicit codification, logical organization, and systematic formulation of religious ideas. Literacy may not be strictly necessary for such developments, but no doctrinal religious systems exist in nonliterate cultures that have not had contact with doctrinal systems from literate cultures (most often, missionary Christianity).[20] Intellectually, doctrinal religions rely on offline, theological reflection. Socially and politically, they rely on ecclesiastical leaders and institutions to inculcate and enforce doctrine. Leaders teach the creeds and exploit a variety of cultural tools—texts most prominently—to transmit them. Priests' first duties are to protect the integrity of the brand and to inculcate brand loyalty. Two clarifications may be helpful here.

First, none of this talk of doctrinal religious systems requires very much ecclesiastical organization or regulation. Consider, for example, Emma Cohen's research on spirit possession in a small, urban, Afro-Brazilian religious group. Part of a loose confederation—in fact, a lineage—of spirit possession groups, the *terreiro* Cohen studied in Belém, a city of 1.8 million in northern Brazil, is modest in size and scope. Although some hundreds of clients and followers had passed through it over the years and many clients continued to consult with the leader (invariably either about their health or about their romantic or financial prospects), this religious community involved only twenty or so core followers during the eighteen months that Cohen spent with them.[21]

With increased literacy and the publication and dissemination of works discussing the religious, historical, and theological dimensions of various Afro-Brazilian religious groups, much of what had once been prized, esoteric knowledge delivered from the specialist's mouth to the novice's ear, was now openly available. Possessing such secret knowledge had imbued cult leaders with prestige, enabling them to check the ambitions of aspiring young protégés. It also provided them cover for gaps in their own knowledge. Now with the widespread availability of much of that knowledge in print, they were under pressure to demonstrate their theological and philosophical acumen by delivering sermons and lectures that were both insightful and inspiring.[22] In the newly emerging religious economy, leaders not only need to offer convincing evidence of their intimacy with the *orixá* (traditional African spirits) and *entidades* (all other spirits), but they also find themselves under increasing pressure to exhibit their theological perspicacity. The leader of the group Cohen studied submitted such homilies and stated his desire to devote most of his time to studying theology. His closest followers rated learning the cult doctrines (*fundamentos*) as one of their two most important religious activities of ten that Cohen surveyed, but, as is so often the case in doctrinal settings, most followers usually found the leader's theological disquisitions uninspiring.[23]

Such conditions, however, are all it takes. Cohen's account establishes how no more hierarchy than this furnishes a perfectly satisfactory medium for the widespread generation of theologically incorrect representations. The issue on which she focuses is how participants ascertain who is responsible for a host's various behaviors during episodes of possession. For both participants and for scholars, the most conspicuous problem associated with this issue is simply deciding whether someone is possessed or not. For participants that is a metaphysical question. For scholars it may or may not be. But the ethnographer confronts an additional independent question, namely, whether the leader and the participants *believe* that the host is possessed or not. It does not take extensive experience with the group to foresee problematic scenarios, such as when the same spirit manifests glaringly different traits from one host to the next. Such a state of affairs invites theological complications.

The group leader's solution has been to advance a conception of spirit possession as the fusion of the possessing spirit with the mind of the host. The spirit slowly acquires some of the host's characteristics while the host simultaneously acquires characteristics of the possessing spirit. A bit of reflection on the ability of this proposal to address the conundrum at hand speaks to the leader's theological creativity. Possession as fusion also proffers a neat solution for members' inclinations, simultaneously, to accept that some host is possessed yet to attribute many features and behaviors, especially unwelcome ones, to the characteristics of the host.

Cohen argues, however, that this notion of spirit fusion does not square with folk psychology and supplies little inferential potential to guide judgment on the ground, that is, with putative possessions here and now. The notion of fusing spirits does not sit very well with our theory of mind. Think, for example, about Hollywood movies about minds that move between bodies. Typically, these films involve either the exchange of minds (in the comedies, such as *Freaky Friday*) or the suppression or displacement of one by another (in movies like *The Exorcist*). What follows from the view that two fully active minds simultaneously share a single body is unobvious, even after conscious reflection. What it means for them to fuse is even less clear.

Cohen is maintaining, in effect, that the leader's doctrine of spirit fusion is a theologically correct formulation that is substantially counterintuitive. If so, then we should expect that his followers will have difficulties adhering to such a strongly counterintuitive view in their online cognitive operations, at least. In fact, what Cohen has found in the course of interviews and conversations with participants in the group is that even in offline reflection they regularly describe possession as the *displacement* of the host spirit by the possessing spirit, instead of in terms of the spirits' fusion.[24] In addition to Cohen's ethnographic evidence about the popularity of this cognitively natural, but theologically incorrect, innovation among participants, she has also obtained experimental evidence that humans in other cultures opt for a displacement view when faced with questions about possession.[25]

This is not to say that this conception of spirit possession as mind displacement presents no interpretive problems. Where, for example, does the displaced host spirit go when its body is possessed by the possessing spirit? But participants apparently find that a much easier question to answer than explaining what claims about spirit fusion might entail. So, some, for example, say that the hosts go to sleep when they are possessed and, thus, have no memories of their possession experiences and must, therefore, be told what has happened after the fact. Theologically incorrect representations will proliferate in the face of orthodox religious representations that are substantially counterintuitive, no matter how small the religious system.

Second, the notion of theological incorrectness in play here is not about heresies or schismatic ideas. Those disputes address alternative, explicitly formulated religious representations about which specialists may submit intricate arguments. Rather what I mean by the inevitability of theological incorrectness concerns the constant, unconscious intrusion in participants' online cognition, no matter how well they have learned their catechisms, of *modestly* counterintuitive religious representations that generally agree with our theory of mind.[26] It is these representations from popular religion, rather than the intellectually subtle representations of theologians, that normally figure in the thinking of ordinary religious participants and carry personal significance for them.[27]

Variability in cultural representations is inescapable. As Sperber argues,[28] the accurate reproduction of mental representations is the rare exception in the transmission of ideas, even with the cultural scaffolding that texts can supply. Consequently, circumstances that appear to attain faithful cultural transmission pose a key explanatory problem. How is such fidelity of representation achieved? Recall Boyer's contention that such modestly counterintuitive religious representations approach a cognitive optimum. By incorporating only one or two violations of our natural ontological assumptions, these representations attract attention, are comparatively memorable, and secure considerable inferential potential. People find such representations both appealing and easy to use, which makes them more likely to last. This is why the eruption of such representations in populations of human minds is both recurring and inevitable.

Religions' modestly counterintuitive representations cluster at an attractor within the space of possible cultural representations.

The notion that modestly counterintuitive representations huddle there is a metaphor. It is not, itself, an explanation. The psychological considerations (memorability, inferential potential, the ability to seize attention, the capacity to motivate further transmission, and so on) that characterize the location of that attractor in that abstract space are what furnish the explanatory insight. Religions do not own that particular corner though. Folklore and comic book superheroes congregate there too. Their appeal rests on the same psychological foundations.

None of this is to claim that popular religious representations always fulfill these criteria. But the probability of some variant's successful transmission is mostly a function of how well it does. To persist over time variants will either migrate in the direction of that attractor or require extensive, targeted, cultural support to endure.[29]

Systems of explicit theological propositions share these cognitively optimal representations' implicit commitments to agent explanation. Like scientific ideas, however, theological proposals are formulated on the basis of offline reflection and conscious deliberation and, hence, are substantially more counterintuitive than popular religious ideas. Ordinary participants in religious systems may dutifully learn and even memorize theologians' radically counterintuitive formulations that their leaders codify and insist upon. My claim, however, is that those formulations will prove unstable in participants' online religious thinking, including their understandings of their day-to-day religious activities. No matter how much effort religious authorities put into standardizing, inculcating, and regulating religious representations, participants will re-construe them, mostly unconsciously, in their online cognition in ways that are theologically incorrect. Abstruse theologically correct formulations will require extensive cultural support, from the intellectual and educational activities of theologians and ecclesiastical authorities to the printing of theological texts and the maintenance of theological schools and libraries. Theologically incorrect but cognitively natural representations, by contrast, arise among populations of adherents, even when religious authorities inveigh against such "simple-minded" misunderstandings of sacred doctrines.

Findings about the persistence of theologically incorrect representations in religious cognition have inspired Tremlin's arguments for a dual-processing model of religious cognition.[30] Such models contrast a rapid, intuitive form of information processing that relies on easy-to-use heuristics with a more ponderous form of conscious thought that includes systematically reasoning in conformity with explicit principles.[31] I have, of course, in this book further subdivided the intuitive form into two sorts of cognitive naturalness, maturational and practiced. (See figure 1-1.) People's tendencies to re-construe reflective theological notions in maturationally natural idioms leave them with two sorts of religious representations. Their spontaneous, theologically incorrect representations unconsciously inform their online cognitive processing and, as Cohen's findings indicate, sometimes their conscious offline ruminations as well (depending, for example, on how much or how little effective policing a doctrinal religious system can marshal). For anyone other than experts, though, their hard-won, often radically counterintuitive, theologically correct representations are, by contrast, difficult to deploy in much more than the social and intellectual contexts in which they are well practiced. Those reflective theological notions demand a great deal more work to acquire and sustain; as with any cognitive product, though, they can acquire a *practiced naturalness* in the minds of experts, who work with them on a regular basis, that is, professional theologians.

Barrett and Keil's findings about theological incorrectness are basically parallel to McCloskey's findings about what we might call "scientific incorrectness." Religious participants revert to theologically incorrect but intuitively appealing representations when facing everyday cognitive tasks (like the processing and recollection of narratives). Similarly, some students of high school– and college-level physics classes, who served as participants in McCloskey's experiments, also revert to their scientifically incorrect but intuitively appealing conceptions of motion when managing common cognitive tasks (like anticipating the paths of moving objects). If they do not acquire a solid command of physical theories, most academically successful students of physics, presumably, gain at least a measure of familiarity with them in the course of their studies. But McCloskey's research discloses a resurgence of maturationally natural conceptions of objects' motions in the minds of many participants, who have successfully completed at least one high school– or college-level course in physics. For example, many of McCloskey's participants resorted to their pre-Galilean, maturationally natural intuitions about falling objects in their online physical thinking. The point is that, from a cognitive perspective, they do so in a fashion that basically mimics the penchant of religious participants to rely on their more cognitively congenial, theologically incorrect representations.

In short, theological and science educators face many of the same problems.

Science Poses No Threat to the Persistence of Religion

The cognitive comparison of science and religion also furnishes grounds for maintaining that, whatever their intellectual frictions, science poses no threat to the persistence of religion. The contemporary campaigns against religion based on an admiration of science and of scientific rationality, by the likes of Sam Harris, Richard Dawkins, Christopher Hitchens, and Daniel Dennett, will not meet with much success.[32] Correspondingly, religious defensiveness either about those campaigns or about science in general is needless trouble, at least with respect to either the fate of any particular religious system or the fate of religion overall. Depending upon material and cultural conditions, religion may wax or wane, but religion will never go away. Campaigns to make it go away will not work. Resisting those campaigns is unnecessary.

By claiming that science poses no threat to the persistence of religion, I do *not* mean to say that there are not logical conflicts between the claims of science and plenty of religious claims. There certainly are, as I stressed in the discussion of Gould's "non-overlapping magisteria." Gould's position is but a further instance of a long-standing, but unsustainable, program that insists on a rigid separation of values and facts, on the basis of an unyielding barrier between meanings and explanations.[33] Note, my objection is *not* to the claim that, in any specific setting at any specific moment, most values and facts and most meanings and explanations are, for most purposes, distinguishable from one another. Instead, what I object to is Gould's stronger claim that the conceptual walls between values and facts and between meanings and explanations are forever impermeable.

Gould's position, however, would not even be plausible if it did not at least capture some truth. Science, after all, *is* primarily concerned with describing, explaining, predicting, and manipulating the empirical world. Religions *do* display recurrent interests in standards for human conduct and in accounts of the meaning of human life based on presumptions about empirically inaccessible agents. But those truisms do not rule out frictions between the two. Although no airtight case for peace between science and religion is to be had, these propositions can endow an argument for a somewhat less ambitious conclusion:

(1) The findings of science concern the (intersubjectively available) empirical world.
(2) Almost all gods are (alleged to be) empirically inaccessible almost all of the time.
Therefore: (3) Scientific findings, indeed empirical findings of any sort, will not ordinarily have any direct bearing on claims about those gods' existence.[34]

This argument suggests that we should expect limits on the impact that any scientific findings are likely to have on religious claims for the existence of the gods and for their conduct.

The continual complication, however, is that religious people, including theologians, regularly backslide about the truth of that argument's second premise. They do so in order to certify participants' putative experiences of their gods and to render their gods as bona fide agents in the world and, thus, as capable of bearing explanatory responsibilities. That means construing the gods or at least the consequences of their actions as empirically detectable after all.

Barrett's research on petitionary prayer shows that religious participants often follow paths that forestall any precipitous backsliding on this count.[35] He found that when multiple solutions to a problem were conceivable, participants in his study usually reported praying for their gods to employ extremely-difficult-to-measure and not-normally-intersubjectively-available psychological means over far-more-easily-recognizable biological or physical interventions. They were significantly more likely to pray, for example, that their gods ensure a surgical team's mental alertness than that their gods heal the patient in some biologically inexplicable way that would render the surgery unnecessary. These trends in petitionary prayers, however, are only that—trends. Even in Barrett's study, participants often reported employing religious representations that would seem to imperil the truth of premise two.

Even when the religious boldly violate the truth of premise two, they can still wield theological defenses to insulate their claims from empirical refutation. Available shields include such moves as insisting that their preferred CI-agents, in fact, just happen to act by means of natural processes as scientifically understood or that as genuinely free agents, the CI-agents they endorse do not act in ways that scientific means detect. Such dodges drain their claims of all empirical refutability and, thus, of all empirical interest, but that has no impact on their continuing cognitive (and religious) appeal.[36]

Gould and his allies protest that all such conduct on the part of religious people is only appearance or that, when it is not mere appearance, it somehow should not count as genuine religiosity. As I argued earlier, though, those assessments issue from norms that Gould and company can only pretend to possess legitimately. Furthermore, indulging in such pretense is, in effect, to traffic in theology. (There is nothing wrong with trafficking in theology. We just need to be clear about when we are doing so.)

Appealing to such norms about genuine religiosity in the academic world echoes ecclesiastical leaders' insistence on orthodoxy in the religious world. Viewing these matters from a cognitive standpoint discloses why: both moves resist the natural predilections of human minds to explain current events, whether community disasters, timely rains, or some individual's misfortune, on the basis of what are often theologically incorrect representations of CI-agents' intentional states and actions. The floorboard of his porch collapsed and he broke his ankle, because his patron saint wished to warn him about his recent moral failures. St. Joseph will facilitate real estate sales, if sellers bury an image of him somewhere on the premises. It was Jesus himself who directed the man's progress through the flames of the burning building to the exit through which he escaped. These explanatory forays frequently implicate theologically incorrect representations of CI-agents that overwhelmingly conform to humans' natural expectations—save one or two in any given case. The normative import of proclamations—whether by academics or by religious leaders—about the religious illegitimacy of such explanations and of the theologically incorrect representations to which those explanations appeal is essentially the same. On this front Gould's comments about inauthentic religion differ little from the pronouncements against theological incorrectness by doctrinal religions' theological constables.

The psychological literature on judgment and decision making over the past few decades supplies no encouragement to Gould and other champions of bloodless, abstract religious thought and scrupulous theological reflection. Its enduring message is that reasoning about substantially counterintuitive abstractions is not easy, even when people have had extensive training and experience with such matters. It is immaterial whether that reasoning concerns scientific or theological matters. Both require the exploration of remote conceptual provinces that are quite distant from the domains that human beings' maturationally natural cognitive systems are built to manage. So, my grounds for contending that science does not endanger the persistence of popular religion are very different from those Gould cites. Of course, from here on that claim's import is empirical rather than philosophical, and the basis for its support to which I am pointing is cognitive rather than conceptual.

The same considerations that informed my criticisms of Gould's proposal figure here as well. Paradoxically, perhaps, the inevitability of theological incorrectness is just as likely to frustrate the campaigns of the critics of religion as it is those of ecclesiastical and theological authorities or those of conciliatory academics. The religious leaders and the conciliatory academics are bothered by the inevitability of theological incorrectness. By contrast, the projects of the critics of religion are largely undone by the inevitability of the religiosity of theologically incorrect conceptions. The latter implication is transparent in Burkert's characterization of just the sort of explanatory uses that people routinely make of religious representations: "Danger is overcome by constructing or reconstructing a world of meaning. . . . irrational associations and expectations, especially in matters of health and disease, persist to the present time. Modern science . . . will not easily prevail. People prefer to cling to the surplus of causality and sense, and there is no lack of mediators to explore the hidden connections."[37] Or to put it another way, corresponding to Boyer's tragedy of theology is its mirror image—the futility of antireligious polemics. The upshot of my case for religion's natural cognitive appeal is that although such polemics may unravel some individual believers' religious convictions, they will not dismantle entire religious groups, nor extinguish the eruption of new religious ideas in human populations, nor eradicate spontaneous representations about modestly counterintuitive agents in people's minds. Ghosts, for example, seem to be a form that recurs in every culture.

The long march of human history aside, pollsters, sociologists, and news reports about popular culture furnish an unending stream of evidence for the popularity of such ideas in our own, putatively secular, time. Religious self-description is, by no means, a perfect measure of the popularity of religious ideas, but it provides a plausible first approximation. Large majorities of the populations of nearly every country in the world, and of every country in the world where we have reason to think that such statistics are reliable, identify themselves as adherents of some religion or other.[38] But the point is not one merely about the popularity of conventional religious ideas attached to recognized religions. Polls show, for example, that tens of millions of Americans believe in ghosts (41 percent) and witches (31 percent) as well as more conventional notions such as miracles (79 percent) and angels (75 percent).[39] Not only do some measures indicate that interest in such ideas is, if anything, on the increase in popular culture,[40] but one study even advances evidence that obtaining a college degree *increases* the probability of belief in such ideas.[41]

No doubt the openness of the American religious market abets the proliferation of such ideas. Plentiful competition has honed superior salesmanship among distributors of religious ideas. Consequently, over the past two centuries America has served as one of the world's most prolific religious incubators. That the social and political arrangements in the United States have fostered some particularly successful new religions is uncontroversial.[42] If the cognitive analyses I have offered in this book are on the right track, though, the persisting suspicion, among northern European colleagues especially, that Americans are somehow outliers on this count does not wash. They allege that Americans' pervasive religiosity is peculiar. A cursory glance at national statistics will show, however, that it is the lower percentages of religious affiliation among the citizens of various northern European countries that stand apart from most of the other nations of the world, including most other first-world countries.[43] Still, that assumes that the surveys have got the facts right. They may not. That many northern Europeans have abandoned state-supported religions seems plain enough, but that alone does not rule out the possibility that susceptibility to religious representations may still be widespread but no longer conventionally expressed among the populations in question. Xinshong Yao and Paul Badham report that although less than 10 percent of Chinese report being Buddhist, more than half have prayed to a Buddha or bodhisattva within the last year.[44] Obviously, these topics deserve further research, and these standard sociological measures that I have cited certainly do not settle these matters. The patterns that these ordinary quantitative measures reveal in virtually every nation on earth, however, suggest that conventional religious ideas, let alone the nonconventional ones, retain considerable charm.

Though they lack quantitative precision, two further considerations also point to an inevitable futility of antireligious polemics. The first of these returns to more purely intellectual matters and pertains to the logical relations between science and theology, that is, to the relations between two sets of substantially counterintuitive representations. The historical evidence seems to testify to the fact that, given enough time and enough theological ingenuity, there is no particular scientific claim that theologians and, therefore, doctrinal religions cannot accommodate. And those are the only religions that have much interest in accommodating them. Those accommodations mostly turn on the frequency with which religious believers, including theologians, vacillate about the empirical detectability of the gods' works and of the gods themselves.[45] After a time, theologians have devised intellectual means for tolerating even the most revolutionary scientific claims.[46]

The second consideration is psychological and concerns the overall stability of these patterns. When construed as means for cuing and enlisting maturationally natural cognitive systems, what is so striking about the modestly counterintuitive ideas and practices of popular religions around the world and throughout history is how little variability they exhibit (at least, by comparison with the radically counterintuitive novelty of the ideas that have arisen in the history of science). Modestly counterintuitive, theologically incorrect representations are ideas that human minds find good to think. This is why these ideas and forms recur across vastly different cultural and material circumstances.

What is so striking is how often people, not the least among them religious people, ignore all of this!

Ideas, principally about the thoughts and actions of CI-agents, flourish in human groups, even in the face of antireligious polemics and even when religions are actively suppressed. (This is a point that most of world's communist regimes never adequately appreciated and, hence, some, to this day, continue such repression.) Because they ignore the sorts of phenomena and patterns of human behavior that I am pointing to, many evangelical Christians in America think that they must steadfastly resist both science education and the findings of science more generally, because of what they see as science's potential to undermine religion and religious belief. Oddly, some of religion's most outspoken contemporary critics seem to share this conviction with those evangelicals. Their aims, of course, are diametrically opposed, which is to say that these critics think that deeper, but especially wider, science education *will* help to undermine religion and religious belief.

However sympathetic I am to the aim of eliminating the automatic public deference that is accorded religions and religious beliefs, I hold out no great hope for getting "the culture of credulity to evaporate" as Dennett puts it.[47] People are rarely argued out of beliefs that they were not argued into in the first place. As Tversky and Kahneman's research shows, even when we recognize the force of sound reasoning, we find it difficult to shake the intuitive hold that naturally appealing ideas exert on our minds.

The contemporary critics of religion underestimate the vital importance of three cognitive dynamics that influence the relations between science and religion. First, they underestimate the appeal of modestly counterintuitive, religious representations to human minds. Second, they underrate the ease with which such religious representations are acquired and deployed. Finally and most remarkably, given their admiration and respect for science, they underestimate the incredible difficulties and expense that are attached to learning and doing science. As Wendy Kaminer comments: "Popular understanding of science is quite limited, and, in practice, we are much more at home with religious faith. Sunday school is, after all, a lot less taxing intellectually than science class."[48] It is not just intellectually that religion is less taxing. Science poses no threat to the persistence of popular religion, because, with respect to both cognitive and social arrangements, science is costly, difficult, and rare whereas religion is cheap, easy, and inevitable.

Near the end of his book, *Origins of the Modern Mind*, Donald asserts that "long after the role of writing in the government and control of human affairs was established, the uses of writing (and visuographic skill in general) remained subordinate to mythic thought and narrative skills."[49] Donald errs, if anything, on the side of caution. The maturationally natural predilections of mind that undergird not only mythic thought and narrative skills but also the entire array of representations and processes that inform everyday religious cognition are no less prominent now than they were in the ancient world. Literacy, the systematic reflection it affords, and the science that very occasionally arises are, respectively, increasingly recent additions to the toolkit of *Homo sapiens. They displace nothing.* The contributions of maturationally natural mental capacities to the human cognitive economy and to the shape of human cultures remain undiminished. But for a few exceptional minds, humans continue to be as thoroughly susceptible to popular religious forms as they ever have been.

Relevant Disabilities Will Render Religion Baffling

Cognitive readiness is all. Armed with their maturationally natural cognitive proclivities, human beings are equipped to manage not only the common problems of the everyday world but the common problems that the world's religions present too. It is not the failure to acquire new, esoteric cognitive tools but, rather, the failure of standard cognitive equipment that will prevent religion from proving catchy to a human mind. Narrative skills, mythic thought, and the representations that are pivotal to religious understandings will be obscure, at best, to minds that lack a maturationally natural theory of mind and the capacity for its automatic engagement. A mind that does not readily recognize other minds will be ill equipped to appreciate the intentional states that stand behind agents' actions, the twists and turns of narratives, or the most common currency of religious representations, namely, the mental states and actions of agents possessing counterintuitive properties.

The eighth feature in Fodor's list of criteria for mental modules is that modular systems will manifest characteristic patterns of breakdown. As the result of injury or stroke, individuals do not suffer a general diminishment of their perceptual, cognitive, or action capacities. Instead, they usually show quite specific deficits, pertaining to such things as language processing (aphasias) or face recognition (prosopagnosia) or visual processing and voluntary motor control (hemineglect). In each case the presumption is that domain-specific modules have, so to speak, become damaged or dislodged.

The problems on which I wish to focus here, however, are not about systems that stop working due to injury or stroke but about systems that fail to coalesce adequately in the course of normal maturation, due to congenital or developmental problems.[50] The analogy here would be not so much with modules that are unplugged but, rather, with mechanisms that are not wired right, whenever the relevant circuits happen to be laid down. The difference here is like the difference between a television that failed to work very well after someone bumped it especially hard (and loosened one of its circuits) as opposed to a television that never worked satisfactorily from the beginning because of a factory wiring defect or because it was not set up properly or both.

In the last decade, psychological researchers have discovered developmental versions of both prosopagnosia and phonagnosia.[51] The first disability concerns persons who, for their entire lives, seem never to have been able to recognize individuals' faces, including the faces of persons with whom they are familiar, even though they have experienced neither an accident nor a stroke precipitating such a deficit. The second condition concerns persons who exhibit a similar pattern with respect to (even what should be familiar) voices. They, for example, do not recognize the voices of family members or old friends on the telephone.

Religious representations ride on the backs of a collection of maturationally natural cognitive systems that are entrenched in human minds. I also argued that among those systems, theory of mind stands out. Facility with representations of agents possessing counterintuitive properties, of their intentional states, and of their actions is a prerequisite for dealing with all sorts of religious matters—whether understanding myths and stories, appreciating the import of rituals, motivating moral and religious admonitions, or explaining events.

Is there a disability pertaining to theory of mind that is analogous to the *developmental* forms of prosopagnosia and phonagnosia? Or, to put it other ways, are there people who, throughout their lives, lack a maturationally natural theory of mind? Are there people who possess no maturationally natural basis for understanding others' actions and psychological states? Does some people's conduct exhibit a considerably lesser ability to appreciate others' mental lives? Are there people whose knowledge of such matters is, so to speak, only skin-deep? If so, then a further question concerns what sorts of understandings such persons can have about distinctively religious beliefs, attitudes, utterances, and actions and what inferences they can draw from them. If there are people who lack maturationally natural theory of mind capacities, then, at least initially, they would find religion largely inscrutable and be unlikely to manage it spontaneously and, even in the long run, may well find much about it cognitively challenging.

Apparently, such persons exist. Many scientists argue that such "mindblindness" is one of the most prominent disabilities of children who are diagnosed with autism (or any autistic spectrum condition including Asperger's syndrome).[52] The mindblindness hypothesis holds that "the intuitive ability to understand that other people have minds is missing in autism."[53] People with autistic spectrum conditions are either substantially delayed in taking or unable to take some of the developmental steps that contribute to attaining a maturationally natural theory of mind. Not only do autistic people recall buildings and landscapes better than they recall human faces, autistic children seem indifferent to whether something is animate.[54] If autistic children do not distinguish between the things in their environments that possess minds and the things that do not, then they will treat all of these things the same way. If they are unable to recognize the minds of other human beings and know nothing about their operations, autistic people have no bases for identifying with other people on anything more than superficial physical grounds.[55] In fact, left (quite literally) to their own devices autistic children treat people no differently from the way that they treat objects. This failure to recognize other minds leads to a striking sense of "aloneness" in persons with autism and to a thoroughgoing lack of concern both for other people and with other people's opinions.[56]

Autistic children begin life, at least by all outward measures, like everyone else.[57] But by their first birthdays these children typically fail to make eye contact when their caregivers attempt to engage them face to face. Such interactions provide infants with experience at social exchange that includes taking turns with utterances and opportunities for focusing on others' eyes and, later, on the direction of another's gaze and their pointing as well. Not only do autistic children not attend to others' pointing, they fail to use pointing themselves for the communicative purpose of establishing joint attention with someone else to some third thing. Children on the autistic spectrum neither point (early on) nor speak (later) for the purposes of simply *showing* something or sharing attention. Empirical research indicates that establishing joint attention plays a crucial role in the normal acquisition of natural language.[58] (That people who are blind from birth acquire natural language demonstrates that more than just visual mechanisms can support joint attention.[59]) Failure to point and share attention leads to delayed language acquisition, at best, and constitutes a basis for diagnosing autism in toddlers.[60]

Classic autism, which involves not only difficulties with social communication, but also repetitive actions, highly focused interests, and the delayed onset of language comprehension and production (if linguistic competence develops at all), anchors one end of a spectrum, which moving in from that end includes Asperger's syndrome before shading into segments of the population with unspecified but pervasive developmental disorders that manifest less extreme versions of some of the traits that autistic people display. From there the spectrum shades into the "normal" population.[61]

Asperger's syndrome differs from classic autism in that it does not involve any significant delay in language acquisition and arises only in persons with average or above average general intelligence. People with Asperger's syndrome, however, share the narrow interests, the repetitive behaviors, and, especially, the incomprehension and awkwardness with social relations that characterize classic autism. Persons with either classic autism or Asperger's syndrome exhibit many traits in common that can also variously arise at subclinical levels among the rest of humanity. These include: (a) social difficulties such as lack of self-awareness, not anticipating others' emotional responses to actions, rigidity with respect to social rules, no interest in pretend play, difficulties in taking turns, and a predilection for monologues; (b) problems with language and communication such as literalness, problems deciphering figurative language and jokes, and echolalia (repeating what others say); (c) finding repetition appealing, such as wearing the same clothes, eating the same foods, maintaining rigid routines, and feeling upset by change; (d) motor traits such as walking on tip-toes and hand flapping; and (e) a variety of cognitive characteristics such as problems with shifting attention and multitasking, heightened memory for details, predilections for classifying, collecting, and listing, and sensory hypersensitivity.[62]

Not all of these characteristics are liabilities all of the time. In some circumstances expertise about the fine details of some part of the environment can be advantageous. Although the mindblindness theory makes good sense of the social deficits of persons with autism and Asperger's syndrome, it does not deal with this and many of their other symptoms. Consequently, researchers who found the analysis of autistic spectrum conditions in terms of mindblindness suggestive sought a more encompassing psychological theory that would both preserve the mindblindness theory's strengths and explain the other features of the autistic spectrum that it neglects.

Toward that end Simon Baron-Cohen has advanced a two-factor theory that looks to the comparative development of human minds' capacities for empathizing and for systemizing. Most people develop skill on both fronts, but Baron-Cohen holds that people with autistic spectrum conditions manifest delays and deficits in tasks requiring empathizing while possessing normal or even enhanced abilities to systemize. What distinguishes the minds of people with autism or Asperger's syndrome is the large discrepancy between their substandard abilities to empathize and what are often their superior abilities to systemize.[63]

The inability of people with autistic spectrum disorders to empathize spontaneously is a direct consequence of their mindblindness. They are unable to "mentalize," that is, to recognize others' mental states and to reason about them automatically.[64] Since they do not recognize others' psychological transactions, they are less able to empathize with their feelings or states of mind.[65] Nor do people with autistic spectrum conditions spontaneously respond empathetically to others' emotion-expressing behaviors, such as crying. The clearest measure of their substantial deficiencies at empathizing is their delay, if not their outright inability, to develop theory of mind. Their sometimes extraordinary general intelligence notwithstanding, even the highest functioning autistic people do not typically pass the standard false belief task until their teenage years.[66]

By contrast, their intact or even superior abilities at systemizing underlie their penchant for repetitive behaviors and what often seems to be their preoccupation with the fine details of things. The objects of their systemizing interests often range over items that easily evoke mathematical relationships such as calendars, telephone books, train schedules, car license plates, and sports statistics.

Adept at systemizing, high-functioning autistic people are not utterly bereft of resources for making sense of social affairs. Many people with autistic spectrum conditions learn after considerable experience to employ their systemizing powers to organize aspects of their social worlds and thereby obtain some ability to manage socially. Autistic children are capable, for example, of recalling the order of events in social routines so long as that ordering does not depend upon psychological attributions to the agents involved. Of course, such attributions are exactly the factors that enable people possessing theory of mind to manage and recall such things easily. The social knowledge that autistic people can acquire is all that can be understood by minds that are equipped with nothing more specialized for this task than the general capacities underlying conditioning. Autistic people learn what to do about human sociality on the basis of detecting regularities in peoples' overt behaviors. So, although an individual with Asperger's syndrome conceded to Baron-Cohen that another's tears elicited no emotional response in him, he had learned when and how to "fake it."[67]

This involves compiling a vast list of behavioral rules "the slow way,"[68] that is, without the benefit of intuitive mentalizing from an early age. After years of interactions, many high-functioning autistic people and people with Asperger's syndrome have constructed what is, in effect, an ersatz theory of mind, which amounts to a look-up table with instructions for comments and conduct in myriad social circumstances. Baron-Cohen suggests that we "imagine . . . Victorian books on etiquette . . . but writ long, to cover every eventuality in social discourse. Of course, it is impossible to be fully prepared, and while some of these individuals do a brilliant job in getting close to the goal, they find it physically exhausting."[69] Such a manual may suffice for the most conventionalized social interactions, but it still offers little guidance about other people's feelings and states of mind. At great cost, the conscious construction of this unwieldy list of behavioral rules provides some guidance for navigating in the social minefield that is everyday life.

Therapeutic practice and a body of therapeutic literature and learning aids have grown up around the task of aiding these people in their conscious, piecemeal construction of this ersatz theory of mind.[70] Baron-Cohen reports that this approach enables people with autistic spectrum conditions to learn generalizations connecting psychological states and overt behaviors (for example, "seeing leads to knowing") and what probably even counts as obtaining some psychological understanding (for instance, knowing that "people feel happy if they *think* they are getting what they want").[71] The crucial point, however, is that any facility with such a system that persons who have an autistic spectrum condition acquire is a thoroughly practiced naturalness. It is not that autistic people procure a maturationally natural theory of mind late; instead, they slowly, arduously assemble some empirical generalizations about social behavior piecemeal.

How prepared are people who lack a maturationally natural theory of mind to deal with religion? They will find much about religion cognitively challenging in ways that people who possess a maturationally natural theory of mind do not. Even with a hard-won, consciously acquired theory-of-mind-replacement, persons with autistic spectrum disorders are unlikely to possess familiarity with the ways of the gods, when they are construed as engaging, intentional agents.

I noted in chapter four that by early school age normal human minds are well prepared to acquire religion. Infants distinguish agents from other things in the world. Young children construe the world around them teleologically. Early school-age children not only understand false beliefs; they can talk about them cogently. Armed with a maturationally natural theory of mind, they have little problem carrying out inferences about agents' intentional states, even if those agents possess a counterintuitive property, such as invisibility.

By contrast, children who have been diagnosed with an autistic spectrum condition do not differentiate agents from other things in the world, do not pass the false belief task, and do not possess and, thus, do not apply a maturationally natural theory of mind. Therefore, at least throughout their childhoods, they draw few, if any, inferences about agents' intentional states. My suggestion, in short, is that there is every reason to suspect that these children find religious representations, beliefs, and actions largely baffling. To the extent that religious under-standings turn on the normal functioning of the peculiar sensitivities that are attached to a maturationally natural theory of mind, children who do not possess such will be lost, at least until they laboriously con-struct some theory-of-mind-stand-in as adults. Even then the evidence indicates that any spontaneous (as opposed to memorized) inferences they draw in these domains will require considerable effort.

I am not claiming that people with autistic spectrum conditions are perpetually condemned to absolute incomprehension with regard to religious materials. As I said, many high-functioning individuals can use their superior systemizing abilities to construct a fragmentary, piecemeal, ersatz theory of mind on their own. Still, Baron-Cohen reports that these individuals find using these consciously constructed, cognitive tools exhausting. That is true for them in the course of nego-tiating normal social situations, and religious cognition makes compa-rable cognitive demands. Still, they are not identical. With most gods there are no observable behaviors to systemize. Often no empirically available actions or interlocutors anchor the other half of participants' religious transactions. Our knowledge of the gods' deeds is nearly always acquired either by description or by inference, that is, by observation of the consequences of their putative action (or inaction) only. If autistic people face formidable barriers to understanding the agents whom they see, whose behaviors they can observe, and with whom they interact on a daily basis, it seems probable that they will be even more deeply puz-zled by the putative mental states and conduct of agents like those that religions presume, whom they often do not see and whose alleged inter-actions with them are not empirically detectable. The point is not that autistic people have failed to build special cognitive capacities for manag-ing information about invisible, supernatural agents, but rather that they do not develop the ordinary cognitive machinery for managing informa-tion about the visible agents of their everyday world. According to Oliver Sacks, autistic persons' efforts to understand the social world are like what the efforts of an anthropologist on another planet would be. He notes that even a high-functioning, intelligent, and accomplished autistic professor, Temple Grandin, finds myths, jokes, and theater thoroughly bewildering.[72] The subtleties of such forms are mostly beyond her.

Even if they are totally bewildered, it does not follow that everything about religion would be unmanageable for the mindblind. Autistic people find comfort in repetition and routines. They are also perfectly adept at tracking sequences of events and causal relations between agents, just so long as the accounts of those sequences and relations do not turn on those agents' intentional states. On these fronts, at least, religious rituals, at one level of description, seem tailor-made for autistic minds. Even here, though, things may not be as easy as they seem. At least some religious rituals might be activities that autistic people might be perfectly happy to repeat in exactly the right forms, but the more difficult part may be getting them to undertake those rituals in the first place.[73] Furthermore, nothing follows from their performances of religious rituals about what these people understand about those rituals or about what they take the rituals to mean. (Admittedly, though, the latter consideration should not count as a particularly telling point; since it is not much clearer what most nonautistic religious participants think their religious rituals mean.)

Some people with autism who are raised within a religious system will be able to acquire and employ familiar, standardized religious scripts when describing their religious lives and understandings. Their reliance on available cultural scripts is consonant with studies showing that autistic people may have nearly as much difficulty with self-understanding and episodic memory as they have with relating to others.[74] People who have problems keeping the boundaries between self and other clear may welcome having conventional religious formulae available for self-description. Rachel Brezis advances this view in her study of the religious lives and understandings of sixteen young people with autism in Israel.[75] Brezis repeatedly stresses her participants' penchant for relying on well-worn scripts to characterize their religious lives and religious understandings.

In the same way that they can gain some familiarity with everyday interactions at school, autistic people may come to feel some familiarity with their community's religious beliefs and practices, but they will probably show little creativity (or variation) in their use of conventional accounts, say, to make sense of some out-of-the-ordinary events or particularly complex problems. No one questions the ability of linguistically competent autistic people to recite or replay memorized scripts. The issue here concerns their abilities to carry out novel, unscripted inferences about CI-agents' mental states and likely actions.

The impaired appreciation of most religious materials that mind-blindness involves will be unaffected by any of the emotional and cognitive arousal that special agent religious rituals can elicit in those rituals' patients. No doubt, undergoing painful initiations or full immersion baptisms will grab the attention of people with autistic spectrum conditions and stimulate their emotions too. Given their hypersensitivity to sensory stimulation, autistic people, if anything, will likely have more extreme responses to such treatments than others. Such salient ritual experiences, however, will not enhance their mentalizing powers nor bring greater clarity about religious beliefs, utterances, or behaviors. It is not coincidental that Brezis reports that none of her participants showed any greater religious zealousness than was the norm in their religious communities. It is also clear from her study that at least some demonstrated noticeably less zealousness than those around them.

That religious rituals or special religious experiences are unlikely to increase the depth of autistic people's religious understandings has not prevented various religious groups from seizing upon autistic people as persons worthy of peculiar religious treatment or possessing some special religious status. The valences that various religious publics have attributed to autism, however, vary from one religious group to the next. Uta Frith recounts the positive regard for the early Franciscan monk Brother Juniper and for the Holy Fools of Old Russia, who in the various stories about them, she argues, exhibited all of the conspicuous symptoms of autism. By contrast, Scott Atran notes that some Muslims in Saudi Arabia and Pakistan think that persons with autism are possessed by spirits who should be exorcised.[76]

Crucially, the kinds of difficulties that religious materials will present for autistic people will arise regardless of their levels of intelligence. The population with autistic spectrum disorders varies in general intelligence as much as the overall population does. People with autistic spectrum disorders are not impaired on all cognitive and intellectual fronts, and with some cognitive and perceptual tasks, they perform better on average than nonautistic control groups do.[77] "The difficulty in autism is not one of making inferences in general, but is very specifically to do with thinking about mental states."[78] The point I am making about how people with autistic spectrum disorders manage religious materials only concerns the problems, with which they all grapple, about understanding others' minds and, as a consequence, with understanding their social environment. At five years of age, autistic children with above average intelligence overall fail the false belief task, which normal children and even children with Down Syndrome find simple.[79] What matters, from the standpoint of the question about how well they manage religious materials, is their bewilderment with social and psychological matters.

In sum, a subset of people of normal or above average intelligence is simply not built to acquire or mentally maneuver with religion as effortlessly as everyone else is. Though people with autistic spectrum disorders may have religion thrust upon them, they will be no clearer about its import and no more creative with its peculiarly religious contents than what they can commit to memory.

This analysis, of course, has plenty of implications that are empirically, indeed experimentally, testable. With an increasing rate of diagnoses of autism spectrum disorders over the past fifteen years or so, clinically and therapeutically oriented writings understandably abound, and some religious people have produced what are, in effect, sectarian discussions about addressing the special challenges that religious participants with autistic spectrum disorders present. Experimental research on autistic people's religious beliefs and understandings, however, is, it is safe to say, scarce at best.

Ara Norenzayan, an experimental psychologist at the University of British Columbia,[80] and his colleagues have commenced studies on the connections between mentalizing, that is, using theory of mind, and religious belief. I should stress at the outset that these experiments and analyses are still under way as I write and the findings are preliminary and, as yet, unpublished.

Norenzayan and his colleagues have conducted several studies. In one, they compared a sample of autistic adolescents with a matched control group and found significantly lower belief in God in the autistic group. In another study they found an inverse link between the autism spectrum and belief in God in a broad national sample of American adults, as the analysis that I have offered here would predict. They have also obtained evidence that individual differences in mentalizing capacity seem to mediate this relationship. So far, this has proven true even after controlling for a variety of other correlates of autism and of religious belief, including age, interests in science and mathematics, educational level, religious attendance, and gender.[81]

That list of Norenzayan and his colleagues' controls touches on a final, related matter. I have developed a case for suspecting that, virtually from the outset, some minds will find standard religious ideas and practices perplexing. I have also suggested that such a problem with respect to theory of mind may be roughly parallel to the problems that developmental prosopagnosics have with respect to the recognition of faces. That analogy makes some recent findings about some humans' face recognition abilities particularly intriguing.

Richard Russell, Bradley Duchaine, and Ken Nakayama have tested four self-selected participants, who approached them claiming to have superior face recognition ability.[82] On the short and long forms of the Cambridge Facial Memory Test, all four of these experimental participants outperformed all of the twenty-five control participants, and, as a group, they substantially outperformed controls on the Before They Were Famous (BTWF) test, which investigated participants' abilities to recognize the faces of well-known people at earlier stages in their lives. By virtue of their clearly superior performance on these tests of facial memory, the four were categorized by the researchers as "super-recognizers." Further experimentation with the super-recognizers, controls, and developmental prosopagnosics indicated that the super-recognizers were about the same amount better than controls than the developmental prosopagnosics were worse (that is, between two and three standard deviations). This was true with both face recognition and face perception tasks. These groups look like they constitute samples from what may well be a normal distribution of abilities for face processing, concerning which these people only differ in degree. Super-recognizers stand at the opposite end of the spectrum of face recognition abilities from where the prosopagnosics stand.

By analogy, this would imply that just as people with autistic spectrum disorders are the analogues of developmental prosopagnosics, we should expect to find persons who stand with respect to the theory of mind spectrum just as these super-recognizers stand with respect to the spectrum of face processing abilities. As some people possess heightened abilities to perceive and recognize faces, might there also be people who possess heightened abilities to detect and draw inferences about minds? These people would be in the opposite tail of the normal distribution for theory of mind capacities from the tail that people with autism populate.

On the two-factor theory that Baron-Cohen advances, such people would, presumably, be hyper-empathizers who may also have substandard abilities as systemizers (if, in fact, there is a trade-off between the cognitive resources that can be devoted to these two capacities). Do such hyper-empathetic people exist, and if so, who are they?[83]

Baron-Cohen certainly countenances this possibility and in approaching these questions deploys a framework originally offered by Hans Asperger himself in 1944.[84] Asperger describes autism as "an extreme variant of male intelligence."[85] The notion is that people with autistic spectrum disorders have *hyper-male* minds (which pair extremely increased systemizing abilities with extremely decreased empathizing abilities). That researchers have ascertained that autism is partly heritable, that classic autism occurs in four times as many males as females, and that Asperger's syndrome occurs in nine times as many males as females lends credence to this proposal.[86] The theory aims, however, to supply an account of a good deal more than these well-known ratios.

The theory holds that characteristic features of people with autistic spectrum disorders are instances of exaggerated versions of various traits that, *on average*, males reveal more often and more prominently than do females, *on average*. The phrase "on average" appears in italics twice in the previous sentence to underscore the fact that Baron-Cohen is talking about averages across populations. It can be unhelpful to take up ready talk of male and female minds, brains, or behaviors.[87] Although he employs such shorthand, Baron-Cohen is clear that he is talking about the differences between averages across populations of the two sexes on a variety of behavioral, cognitive, and neural measures.[88] One of the consequences of using this shorthand is that, in fact, many females display the ratio of empathizing and systemizing abilities that Baron-Cohen associates with what he calls a "male" brain and that many males show the ratio of those abilities that Baron-Cohen associates with what he calls a "female" brain. (Baron-Cohen hypothesizes that the causal mechanism that stands behind this distinction has to do with variability in the timing of fetal androgen levels across the first four months of gestation, *regardless of the individual's sex*.[89])

It is also worthwhile to note that Baron-Cohen is not making a point about individuals' sexual orientations. That is because, first, he is not even talking about sexual orientations (and has no evidence that the patterns he discusses have any bearing on them), and second and more important, he is, ultimately, not making a point about individuals. His talk about "male" and "female" brains is about the differences between the averages of two populations on various features of cognitive processing pertaining to people's systemizing and empathizing abilities.[90]

Autistic spectrum disorders might be described as involving a hyper-male mind, because males, on average, give evidence of higher levels of systemizing than females on everything from differences between infants' comparative looking times at videos of faces as opposed to looking times at videos of cars, to differences in adults' performances on standardized tests of systemizing.[91] On such tests males, on average, appear to be better systemizers than females, and persons who have been diagnosed with autistic spectrum disorders appear, on average, to be even better systemizers than males. (See figure 5-3.) But for my purposes here, it is not the hyper-male profile of persons with autistic spectrum disorders that is of interest, but the possibility of what Baron-Cohen would call the "hyper-female" profile, that is, the *hyper-empathizing* mind.[92]

A variety of measures, including standardized tests of empathizing, indicate that females, on average, show higher levels of empathy than males. Baron-Cohen notes results from a swarm of relevant tests, including theory of mind tests, a Friendship and Relationship Questionnaire, various tests of language and reading facility, and tests of persons' abilities to ascertain mental states from facial expressions

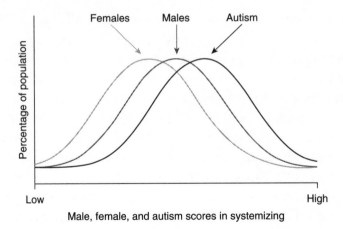

Figure 5-3. Distributions of systemizing abilities (after Baron-Cohen 2003)

generally and from the eyes only. On all of these measures, females, on average, outperform males, who, in turn, on average, outperform persons diagnosed with autistic spectrum disorders.[93] (See figure 5-4.)

Baron-Cohen's analyses suggest both that we should find persons with hyper-empathetic capacities (analogous to the "super-recognizers" of faces) and that a sizable majority of these hyper-empathetic persons will be females, since a decided majority of "female minds," in fact, come in female bodies.

These proposals suggest a partial explanation, which, in turn, occasions a prediction.

Overall, women appear to be more religious than men. Regardless of the stage of life in question and, in nearly all cases, regardless of the kind of religious system and accordant beliefs at stake, women express interest in religion, affirm personal religious commitment, attend religious services, read religious materials, and pray more frequently than men.[94] Sociological studies have turned up such results for nearly a century, and such outcomes arise so regularly that virtually every quantitative study of religiosity controls for sex.[95]

Sociologists have advanced various hypotheses to explain these phenomena. For example, women's elevated religiosity may turn on the fact that, traditionally at least, fewer women than men have been

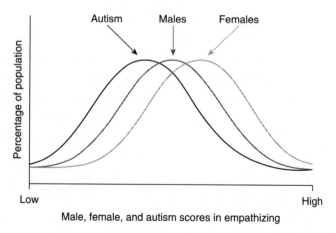

Figure 5-4. Distributions of empathizing abilities (after Baron-Cohen 2003)

involved with wage labor and, thus, are less likely to have their values shaped by the sensibilities of the marketplace. Traditionally, women are far more likely than men to have been assigned social roles as nurturers, which instills sensibilities that readily cohere with conceptions of caring gods, at least. Sociological research has found that religiosity correlates with a constellation of personality traits associated with femininity (whether in females or in males).[96] Others have pointed to the decreased likelihood, compared with males, of females engaging in risky behaviors.[97] None of these explanatory hypotheses, however, has proven fully satisfactory.[98]

We can add to that list the verdict that, on average, females are more empathetic than males, since it also goes some way toward explaining sociologists' findings about females' religiosity. The analysis here is not complicated. Women, on average, have superior empathetic abilities, indicating an enhanced facility with theory of mind, which plays an especially prominent role in religion. Thus, women, on average, will demonstrate an enhanced facility with religion, and women will (again on average) find religion more psychologically and cognitively appealing than men find it.[99]

Finally, a prediction. Without many well-calibrated measures of theory-of-mind capacities specially tailored for testing adults and with little research on the topic, finding those hyper-empathetic minds awaits further investigation. If the hyper-empathetic are attracted to religion, though, as the explanatory hypothesis that I have just entertained proposes, then it seems reasonable to begin the search for such minds among the feminine faithful. It is only half a joke to suggest that researchers might be well advised to get themselves to a nunnery. This is not to say that religious orders are either the only or the richest repositories of hyper-empathetic minds, but only that they constitute settings where, on this hypothesis, the probabilities would appear to be better than chance of finding some of those minds.

Koko, the feckless but scheming Lord High Executioner of Gilbert and Sullivan's *Mikado*, identifies another type where hyper-empathetic minds might occur at rates greater than chance. Unfortunately, it constitutes an entry on his famous "little list" of putative undesirables, who, he thinks, are good candidates for execution, since, as Koko avows, "they'd none of 'em be missed—they'd none of 'em be missed." The type in question is, of course, "the lady novelist," about whom Koko may at least be on the right track when he declares her "a singular anomaly."[100] Although not exactly singular or anomalous, hyper-empathetic minds, at three standard deviations above the mean, assuredly, will not be plentiful.

Science Is Inherently Social

Among our knowledge-seeking activities, science stands, as I commented earlier, second to none in its dependability and in its explanatory and predictive accomplishments, yet experimental research discloses all sorts of cognitive biases and flawed reasoning in the thinking of individual scientists. How can science be so successful, when the people who practice it so often look to be as susceptible as everyone else to the limitations, foibles, and fallacies that plague human thought? How can so many progressive investigations spring from the work of these all-too-human individuals, who are no less self-interested and, most of the time, no more dispassionate about their projects than the rest of us? The fact that science is an inherently social undertaking points to a path that circumvents these paradoxes, even if it does not solve all of these problems completely.

I do not pretend that an account of science that puts special emphasis on its social dimensions originates with me. Many philosophers have advanced social conceptions of science, especially in the past three decades.[101] The influence of *The Structure of Scientific Revolutions*, in which Kuhn proposed that models of scientific rationality ought to accord with the history of science, gave birth to that general trend. Psychological and cognitive scientists' scrutiny of individual scientists' thinking has only accelerated it. As Miriam Solomon has aptly remarked, "What matters is not how individual scientists reason—*it's* not *the thought that counts*— but what the aggregate community of scientists does."[102] In laying out what such a conception of science amounts to, I will mostly traverse the via *negativa*, canvassing some things that such a conception is not.

A social understanding of science flies in the face of both the dominant philosophical conception of human reasoning for the past three centuries as well as the popular conception that I mentioned at the outset of this section. That dominant philosophical conception takes its inspiration from the work of René Descartes, whose account focuses on the operations of an isolated, individual mind, considered independently of its connections with a body. (Of course, a disembodied mind is also a dis-embedded mind.) That mind carefully carries out deductive inferences from theoretical principles, the most fundamental of whose truth reveals itself clearly and distinctly by "the light of nature."[103] Descartes strives to provide a philosophical clarification of our everyday views of the human mind and of human reasoning, which are themselves rooted in our maturationally natural theory of mind.[104]

A social account of science, by contrast, maintains that the principal locus of scientific rationality does *not* reside between matched pairs of human ears. Although they typically manage problems adeptly within their areas of expertise, individual scientists still forget things, operate with cognitively natural (but biased) heuristics, make errors in reasoning, prefer their own theories to those of others (pursuing evidence accordingly), and, of course, can prove susceptible to the intrusions of maturationally natural dispositions of mind. This is not to deny that individual scientists regularly make valuable contributions to their fields, but rather that histories of science may sometimes overplay the roles of prominent individuals in the service of producing gripping narratives.[105]

In the early stages of many sciences' development, some individuals, no doubt, qualified as the giants on whose shoulders subsequent researchers stood, but these days the scientific enterprise is mostly carried along by small armies of researchers dispersed in research groups that continuously interact, often in collectively regulated public forums at professional meetings and in scientific journals.[106] Our penchant for lionizing important contributors in the history of science is easy enough to understand. We are, after all, animals with the kinds of minds that look for the actions of individual agents to explain human achievements and who readily follow narratives about the heroes and heroines who contributed prominently to those achievements. As historians of science have emphasized for at least a generation now though, the resulting Great Man conceptions of the history of science (until the last half dozen decades few of these stories' protagonists have been female) are probably as misleading as they are helpful.

Ultimately, science must be characterized in terms of distinctive social arrangements.[107] The issue is not whether alternative social circumstances, for example, amongst the Chinese or the Arabs in the ancient or medieval worlds, yielded impressive technical developments. The question, instead, is whether societies eventually undergo a transformation that simultaneously (1) permits freer inquiry and, especially, freer criticism of proposals about how the world works, which includes community-regulated, public settings for displaying and carrying out such inquiries by credentialed researchers; and (2) a public, self-conscious recognition, especially among the political leadership, of the importance of just such practices and of their preservation.

From ancient times until the emergence of modern science in Europe, the Chinese enjoyed parity, at least, and usually superiority technologically over the cultures to their west. Recall, however, that I argued on a variety of grounds for making a clear distinction between science and technology. On that view it does not follow that a culture's advanced technology is a sure sign of its scientific accomplishments.

At least some historians of technology see no close tie between science and technology until the nineteenth century in Europe and America. China's many technological breakthroughs did not signal the transformation of the relevant social and political conditions. No formally recognized social space was opened up for freer inquiry about the world. Throughout the Middle Ages, literate civil servants during the Sung and Ming dynasties were chosen, in part, on the basis of their performance on examinations, but those examinations focused on knowledge of literary and poetic traditions and contained virtually nothing scientific.[108] Without open forums for discussing proposals about the world's workings and without institutionalized settings that encouraged theoretical reflection, the Chinese enjoyed no theoretical advantages over their contemporaries in Europe and western Asia, their technological superiority notwithstanding.

The primary barriers to the requisite social and political conditions necessary for persisting, progressive science in the medieval Islamic world had nothing to do with any lack of theoretical sophistication or want of technological or theoretical ingenuity. Not only had medieval Arab scholars inherited many of the great philosophical, mathematical, and scientific works of the ancient Greeks, they had discovered many places where ancient theories failed to capture the empirical facts.

Hospitals and observatories were founded on the basis of religious endowments in the medieval Islamic world. This meant that they were, ultimately, religious institutions that fell within the framework of Islamic law, which imposed substantial constraints on their activities. The possibility of establishing independent scientific institutions or of incorporating science (beyond mathematics and astronomy) into any form of religiously approved education was rarely, if ever, seriously considered.

Pedagogy in Islamic madrassas was and is no more hospitable to the knowledge production science pursues. From its beginnings Islam has granted orality an epistemic prominence that is unlikely to promote scientific creativity. The focus of Islamic education is the memorization of the *Qur'an*, first and foremost, but, until the widespread acceptance of printing, it involved the memorization of other texts as well. This stems from a long tradition of personal testimony in support of the authenticity of a text, on the basis of the fact that the authority in question had previously memorized it. The time and effort devoted to memorizing texts, whether religious or scientific, does not leave much time, energy, or motivation to explore criticisms of the positions advanced in those texts. People who have invested thousands of hours of their lives memorizing various texts are not likely to prove the most receptive audience for criticisms of those texts.

As so much about the philosophical and scientific theories of the ancient Greeks proved contrary to the metaphysical and empirical assumptions embedded in Islamic belief and practice, science in the medieval Islamic world vitally depended on the support and protection of local political leaders. Some scholars and teachers associated with Islamic educational and legal institutions pursued extracurricular scientific investigations just so long as their local patrons gave them cover from less curious, less tolerant guardians of Islamic orthodoxy. Sometimes, leaders' support of scientific inquiries was lasting and conspicuous, but those inquiries were always contingent upon such assistance.[109] On multiple occasions in one locale or another, conditions approximated those necessary for a continuing pursuit of science, but they always proved temporary only. Toby Huff summarizes the consequence, commenting that "the development of natural sciences finally aborted after the thirteenth and fourteenth centuries in the Islamic world."[110]

I would be remiss if I failed to note that until European Christians discovered and translated the works of the ancient Greeks (acquired by way of the Arab Muslims) and until European universities emerged as independent institutions,[111] the conditions in medieval Europe had been considerably less likely than those prevailing in China or Islamic civilization to have fostered a rebirth of science. Throughout human history the sort of systematic empirical investigation of theories about how worldly things work that stands at the core of scientific activity has popped up here and there, but other than the tradition of empirical research that took form in European culture in the seventeenth and eighteenth centuries, only the ancient Greeks came at all close to establishing an ongoing tradition of scientific research across a variety of fields of empirical inquiry.[112] It was the birth of modern science that transformed Europe from an utter backwater into the leading center of intellectual life on the planet.

The crucial point here, though, is that all of this contrasts starkly with the default assumptions that inform the interactions of modern scientific communities. Members of those communities collaborate and compete, conjecture and refute, and routinely work in teams. Lisa Jardine opens her treatment of the progressive institutionalization of science during the late seventeenth and the early eighteenth centuries, in England and France especially, by stressing "the fundamentally collaborative nature of the scientific project." On this count, things have changed little since the founding of the Royal Society and the Académie Royale des Sciences. "Anyone who has watched a team of scientists at work in a modern laboratory will know that there is more to scientific inquiry than the lonely, rational pursuit of truth. From the designing of experiments to the writing up of results, science is conducted by vigorous group discussion and debate."[113] It is not just that scientific knowledge and criticism are distributed across those dispersed research teams, so is scientific decision making.[114]

The level of collaboration and international cooperation among scientists from England, France, and the Dutch Republic throughout the second half of the seventeenth and the early eighteenth centuries, involving "joint initiatives, and the free exchange of information," was remarkable.[115] This held true even with regard to subjects of strategic military importance, such as astronomical findings bearing on navigation, during a period of virtually constant cold war, punctuated periodically by outright hostilities. Among scientists, however, cooperation was the rule. For example, in the same year that he was appointed the first British Astronomer Royal, John Flamsteed along with Edmund Halley arranged with Gian Domenico Cassini (the French Astronomer Royal) to observe the lunar eclipse of 26 June 1675 jointly in London and Paris, respectively. On the basis of the differences in the local times they recorded for the event, they "were able to obtain precise measurements for the relative longitudes of their two locations."[116] The prevailing conception of scientific activity was overtly international, as astronomers, in particular (but biologists too), sought observations (specimens) from locations all over the globe. Of a piece with that conception, John Wilkins, a member of the Royal Society, proposed and developed a universal written language to assist international scientific communication.[117]

Still, as noted earlier, scientists both cooperate and *compete*. Scientists learned long ago what it seems capitalists and their bankers, in particular, have never been able to learn, namely, that competition must be carefully regulated to ensure transparency and fairness in the marketplace, whether commercial or scientific. The scientific communities' insistence on a variety of constraints on those competitions helps to ensure that they are comparatively fair over the long haul, no matter how much they might be manipulated by less scrupulous individuals in the short run. The most important of these measures is the demand for the replicability of experimental results, but they also include peer review, blind refereeing, and the public availability through publication (sooner or later) of theoretical principles, experimental apparatus, and empirical findings. When they are publicly accessible, such materials become the objects of extended scrutiny by qualified experts and, sometimes, by the public at large.

Alas, fraud does occur. Reports in the popular press of breakdowns in scientific integrity pop up periodically. The crucial point, though, is that it is virtually always other members of the scientific community who smoke out and expose the malefactors.[118] As Solomon's quip stresses, "*It's* not *the thought that counts*—but what the aggregate community of scientists does."[119] Not only are individual scientists fallible, the scientific community does not do a flawless job of policing itself. No institution, however, not even the law, is any more committed to the integrity of that self-policing. All the evidence suggests that science does a better job of this self-monitoring than any other public institution in human history.

It is, then, the social institutions of science that guarantee that, sooner or later, qualified, credentialed practitioners scrutinize all scientific proposals. The breadth, depth, detail, publicity, and integrity of that scrutiny and of the scrutiny of that scrutiny enable the scientific community to compensate for the irrationalities, limitations, biases, prejudices, weaknesses, and self-interest of the community's individual members.

Science Depends More Fundamentally on Institutional Support Than Religion Does

Science is expensive. Sustaining worldwide communities of teams of scientific researchers and all of the institutional arrangements necessary for disseminating information and for policing malfeasance requires dedication, honesty, and lots of hard work by lots of highly educated people. These things do not come cheaply. And this tally does not include the resources it takes to produce suitable conditions for experimentation. Modern science is such a complicated and costly undertaking that it is now universally pursued within the frameworks of sponsorship by the very largest institutions with the very largest budgets—governments, corporations, militaries, universities, research centers, and hospitals. Whatever the appearances to the contrary, both the inherently social character of science and the demand for the public availability of scientific materials, including experimental results, show the respect in which its persistence depends fundamentally upon institutional support in a way that is not at all true about religion.

I have argued how integral institutional support is to the continuing pursuit of science. If my account of the interest, excitement, shape, content, and appeal of religions for human minds is sound, then it follows that religion may turn far less on institutional support than the appearances suggest.

Recall the arguments from natural history in chapter four about the origins of religion. There I emphasized that religion, unlike science, but quite like technology, has prehistoric origins. Considerable controversy whirls around exactly what sort of archaeological evidence justifies attributing religiosity to our prehistoric forebears, but no one contests that the evidence for it is substantial at hundreds of archaeological sites around the world. In prehistoric hunter-gatherer groups and small-scale societies, religion existed with considerably less institutional support than, say, the Southern Baptist Convention.

"Religions of the book" certainly appear to depend upon literacy, printing, and educational institutions in a way that is not true of prehistoric religion. Remember, however, that religions of the book do not exhaust the manifestations of human religiosity, and, historically, they are comparative late-comers, having arisen only in the last thirty-five hundred years. Things like ecclesiastical hierarchies, cathedrals, monasteries, codified doctrines, and religious schools aside, scholars are in danger of overestimating the importance of literacy for the perpetuation of religion. As I noted, Donald seriously underestimates the natural predilections of mind when he suggests that even after the invention of literacy and its recruitment in government and public affairs it remained "subordinate" to mythic and narrative skills in the ancient world.[120] It *still* remains subordinate! Along with ethnographers' findings about abundant religiosity among groups that do not even know that literacy exists, the archaeological records suggest that most of the institutional frameworks associated with the religions with which most of us are most familiar are thoroughly unnecessary to the outbreak and persistence of both religiosity and religion. Recent trends point to a time in what is, perhaps, the not-too-distant future when scholars may also ask about whether these institutions are sufficient for religion. For example, according to friends and foes alike, the Church of England comprises copious institutional structures with steadily dwindling amounts of both participation and religiosity.

That religiosity and religions emerge and persist even when the institutions most readily identified with them are suppressed also suggests that the institutional support of religions is less essential than we might expect. Whether it is the early Christian groups in ancient Rome, the Jehovah's Witnesses in the former Soviet Union, or the Falun Gong in contemporary China, religious movements erupt and spread in human populations and, sometimes, even thrive when they are actively and vigorously persecuted.

That religion predates both literacy and the dawn of human history, that it arises in every human culture, and that it reappears and persists even when it is forcefully hampered, all indicate that it relies on institutional support far less than appearances suggest. The contrast with science could not be much starker.

First, science is rare. Few people in the history of our species have carried out scientific investigations. Even more obviously, the kind of social and political conditions for the enduring pursuit of science, which I sketched in the previous section, have been scarce historically and remain uncommon to this day. If its continuing pursuit began with the ancient Greeks, science still counts as a relative newcomer in our species' history.[121] Few people have carried out scientific investigations because few societies have established the social arrangements necessary for its persistence.

If science is inherently social, then it follows that it is inherently institutional as well. For example, science does not merely require literacy; it depends upon the widespread mastery of advanced forms of linguistic and mathematical literacy. Preserving and transmitting such proficiencies turn on ample investments in an extensive educational infrastructure. Participating in science at its highest levels routinely requires more than twenty years of formal education. But all such edifices and efforts are for naught unless accompanied by a set of institutional arrangements that secure the openness, publicity, and integrity of scientific research. Jardine argues that formally enshrining scientific standards was critical to the rise of modern science:

> at the heart of the Royal Society's institutionalized procedures lay the "witnessing" or "attesting" to experimental outcomes. This was established early on as an absolute requirement for validating results . . . Confirmation of any remarkable finding by a select group of scientifically qualified members was required before an experimental outcome could be officially recorded as fact in the *Philosophical Transactions*. It had also to be shown that the result could be reproduced on more than one occasion.[122]

As these early practices of the Royal Society indicate, maintaining scientific institutions demands the articulation and strict enforcement of rigorous standards. It also relies on the production of educated practitioners and the expenditure of vast resources.

The historian of science Edward Grant argues that the gradual development of (comparatively) independent universities in Europe proved to be a critical variable buttressing the long-term success of science in the West. The universities have made at least two significant contributions. First, they have offered education in the sciences. Universities in

the late Middle Ages deemed natural philosophy a legitimate component of advanced education, and they developed the notion of a standardized curriculum that included it. Eventually, in the modern period,
those curricula served as a prerequisite for credentialing scientific practitioners, but even in the Middle Ages they served to exclude from
formally sanctioned study pseudo-sciences and occult practices such
as astrology, magic, and alchemy.[123] Second, the universities have supported scientific research. Although medieval natural philosophy oper-
ated with conceptions of both nature and natures and of natural law,
methods of inquiry, and the character of intellectual progress that differed appreciably from the conceptions that led to the onset of modern
science in the seventeenth century, as early as the thirteenth century
the universities had grouped Aristotle's threefold division of theoretical knowledge, namely, metaphysics, physics, and mathematics, all
within the purview of natural philosophy. The medieval universities
safeguarded the legitimacy of inquiries into natural philosophy, and
they positioned it in such a way intellectually that it would be open to
upheavals when new theories and methods of inquiry began to change
that terrain three centuries later.

No methodological achievements were more pivotal in the transition from medieval natural philosophy to the emergence of modern
science than William Gilbert and Galileo's invention of scientific experimentation and the pursuit of systematic observational research in the
seventeenth and eighteenth centuries.[124] I wish to focus here, however,
not on their intellectual import but, rather, on their implications for
the social and economic arrangements that sustaining modern science
would require.

In less than a hundred years experimentation and systematic observation substantially increased the price of doing science. Modern science
requires institutional support in the form of an exotic infrastructure.
This involves the construction of specialized apparatus for probing
environments to which scientists would not, otherwise, have either
ready access or, in some cases, any access. The proliferation of technologies over the last twenty-five years to view processing in normal
human brains is an example of the first situation. The construction of
complex apparatus and facilities—from the Greenwich Observatory

(constructed in 1675–1676) to the Hubble telescope—nicely illustrates the second. Modern science has required that scientists must travel to new environments too. By the early eighteenth century, some European governments and companies were investing in expeditions to the earth's far reaches to gain strategic advantages and to initiate profitable ventures, certainly, but to gather data and specimens and, later, to test scientific hypotheses as well. Science in the modern era also involves the construction of rare environments, like those made possible by such things as particle accelerators. In such settings and with such apparatus hypotheses that readily account for phenomena in our normal environments can be tested experimentally in unusual environments about which we know much less. Scientists construct these contrived environments in such a way as to gain control over variables that would, under normal circumstances, influence the causal processes under scrutiny. The huge expenses connected with all of this guarantees that modern science is overwhelmingly dependent on major institutions with access to heaps of funds.

Science's Continued Existence Is Fragile

Perhaps the most important consequence of the comparison of the cognitive foundations of science and religion is that, contemporary appearances to the contrary notwithstanding, the persistence of science is startlingly vulnerable on some crucial fronts. For a variety of reasons, science's continued existence, at least in the long run, is fragile—certainly in comparison to the continued existence of religion.

One of the reasons science is so vulnerable is that the relative openness of scientific inquiry means that it will likely conflict with powerful interests. Huff comments that "science is . . . the natural enemy of all vested interests—social, political, and religious."[125] The Catholic Church's response to Galileo's discoveries is the most famous example, but the more science has expanded in the modern era, the more such tensions arise. As scientists have invented innovative means for studying more and more of the ways that the world works, their researches inevitably clash with an increasingly wider array of common practices (for example, eating meat from factory farms that spawn antibiotic-resistant pathogens and despoil water supplies), deeply rooted beliefs (for example, that species are fixed), and profitable business interests (for example, when scientific studies disclose how burning fossil fuels adds to greenhouse gases, which, in turn, produces climate change). The requisite institutional arrangements of modern science promote conditions that reliably yield knowledge that is uncongenial to the interests of powerful institutions, be they religious, political, or commercial.

This inevitable conflict between science and other influential institutions less concerned with the pursuit of truth is one of the reasons that Popper argued that science is one of the major forces in history that has made for human freedom.[126] It would be misleading, though, to pretend that these relationships are always or inevitably adversarial—even the relationships between science and Rome. Copernicus, after all, was a central contributor to the Church's efforts at calendar reform. Today governments and corporations supply most scientific funding. Their influences on the character and direction of scientific research are less ungainly than the Church's measures in Galileo's time. What governments and corporations are willing to finance has a profound effect on what scientists study. Corporate funding initiatives are nearly always targeted at problems whose solutions will likely contribute to those corporations' increased profits. Grant applications must appeal to these corporate sponsors, and sometimes the results of such corporately funded research are deemed proprietary. This is why it is so critical that government funding agencies largely turn their funding decisions over to panels of scientists, whom they mostly recruit from university faculties. Those panels make collective judgments about the value of research proposals primarily on the basis of what they take to be their scientific merits. The system is not perfect, but it is better than the alternatives.

The history of science is a story of unexpected outcomes and periodic surprises. The directions that scientific research takes and the findings it produces are not thoroughly predictable. Science does not work by merely tolerating unregimented skepticism. On the contrary, its institutional structures foster a *disciplined* skepticism that is rooted in a command of the prevailing methods, theories, and findings as well as in a familiarity with the major theoretical challengers. Sooner or later, such educated skepticism unearths problems not just for dominant views among the public and the powerful but often for dominant views among the scientists themselves.[127] Huff's comment quoted earlier continues: "Science is ... the natural enemy of all vested interests—social, political, and religious, including those of the scientific establishment itself." Unearthing such problems can uncover the seeds of scientific revolutions. Kuhn showed how sciences can shelve the occasional anomaly. Repeated failures, important failures, or widespread failures, however, will stir up a theoretical crisis. Such crises call for the formulation and exploration of new theoretical options, whose successes in the face of empirical tests can bring about an upheaval within science itself. Even established science is vulnerable to its own standards of practice.

The failure of scientists, educators, and journalists to convey these dimensions of scientific pursuits to the general public is unfortunate. Too often science is taught as truths-to-be-memorized instead of as our tentative, best-available answers (given the current state of the inquiry) in a never-ending investigation of how we might improve upon what we know. The public's failure to appreciate these features of scientific inquiry breeds its dismay and impatience with the reversals in expert scientific judgment from one stage of the research to the next.

Although science is as well established in America as it has been anywhere or at any time, circumstances in the United States over the past few decades may prove instructive here. They offer a glimpse of science's vulnerability, even in the short run. The activities of America's universities, foundations, corporations, and government had collectively rendered the United States the world's leading center of scientific activity. Over the past few decades, though, public dismay and impatience with science have been the least of it. Corporate, government, and religious misuse of science in the United States since the Reagan administration has been particularly egregious. That misuse has taken a variety of forms—from neglect and inattention to resistance to out-right interference and misrepresentation. Chris Mooney's book *The Republican War on Science*[128] documents dozens of attempts by government, corporations, and political and religious groups in America to ignore, obscure, or subvert scientific findings and evidence, to defy and prevent the dissemination of prevailing scientific theories, and to disrupt and misrepresent scientific positions, the state of scientific debate, and the standards of scientific practice.

In America, various groups' rejection of and interference with the teaching of Darwin's theory of biological evolution by natural selection has a long history that stretches at least from the Scopes trial in Dayton, Tennessee, in 1925 to George W. Bush's exhortations to teach the (putative) controversy. Controversies abound in contemporary biological science—even controversies about aspects of biological evolution,[129] but none of those controversies concern creationism or design or the role of the divine.

Evolution, however, has largely given way during the last decade to the issue of climate change as the prime target of political and religious obfuscation of science.[130] In addition to these two, the list of targeted topics by these groups has included (but is certainly not exhausted by):

(1) *environmental issues* such as acid rain, ozone depletion, mercury contamination, the effects of atrazine and dozens of other chemicals on the environment, and the designation of endangered species,

(2) *public health issues* such as secondhand smoke, an epidemic of obesity, the availability of the vaccine for the human papillomavirus, and the effects of dozens of additives in foods and drinks (sugar and salt, in particular),

(3) *issues of reproductive health* such as the physical and psychological impact of abortion, the availability of the "morning after" pill, and the effectiveness of condom distribution for limiting unwanted pregnancies and the spread of HIV without increasing sexual activity,[131]

(4) *other biomedical research issues* concerning such things as embryonic stem cells and measures of brain death, and

(5) *technological issues* concerning the Strategic Defense Initiative, automobile categorization and mileage standards, and the limits of New Orleans's levees.

The long list of topics about which recent scientific research has been targeted for one or another form of abuse is but one indication of a growing trend by these groups to downplay, if not undermine, scientific knowledge, scientific practice, scientific integrity, and scientific influence.[132] That trend makes it all the more difficult for liberal democratic governments in general and the United States, in particular, to challenge the antiscientific stances of fundamentalist religion in other places, for example, in 2005 when some Muslim clerics in Nigeria characterized international efforts to immunize the population against measles as an anti-Islamic plot and encouraged their followers not to get the vaccine.[133]

Such worries about science in a society where it still plays such a prominent role may engender suspicions about overstatement and alarmism on my part. If so, then consider the testimony of persons much closer to the day-to-day conflicts. Paul Nurse, the president of Rockefeller University and the winner of the 2001 Nobel Prize in physiology and medicine, has stated that "present policies are set to damage a whole generation of young research workers, and the negative impact on recruitment of the next generation of scientists will be seen for years to come."[134] Alan Leshner, the chief executive officer of the American Association for the Advancement of Science, sees even greater dangers. Leshner comments:

> What we are seeing is the empowerment of ideologues who have the ability to influence the course of science far more than ever before. They say, "I don't like the science, I don't like what it is showing," and therefore they ignore it. And we are at a place in this country today where that can work. *The basic integrity of science is under siege.*[135]

These abuses of science by government, corporate, and religious groups have not created a perfect storm. They have, however, created storm enough, especially in the face of

- American students' generally not-so-great performances on international science and mathematics examinations (relative to the performances of students in the rest of the developed world),[136]
- the declining percentages of American college students majoring in science, technology, engineering, and mathematics,[137]
- a decline in the percentages of publications by American scientists and of citations to those publications in leading scientific journals over the past few years (admittedly, largely a function of the increasing number of such publications by scientists from the countries of the European Union),[138] and
- the declining levels of government and corporate support for most areas of scientific research.

I have already underscored the costliness of science. It makes the defense and support of science even more problematic during economic downturns. As scientific researchers, universities, philanthropic institutions, and the governments of the wealthiest open societies around the world all recognize, the infrastructure and institutions of science are frightfully expensive to create and maintain. Science's continued existence, thus, depends upon the collective success of those very same political and commercial institutions from which it must maintain its independence.

One counterargument to my claims about the vulnerability of science looks to its intimate connections with technology over the past century. The success of capitalist enterprises has largely depended upon technological advances, and those advances have regularly emerged from research in the basic sciences, so capitalism relies on basic science and will not permit its demise. This argument makes sense, so far as it goes. The argument's soundness, though, depends upon at least three unstated assumptions: (1) that liberal, democratic governments will continue to be the principal source of support for scientific research, (2) that the priorities of liberal, democratic governments will not be held hostage by corporate interests, and (3) that executives will both recognize their corporations' long-term interests and rank those interests among their top priorities. The first and second assumptions describe conditions that ensure that neither an entrenched political class (for example, the Communist party in China) nor particular corporations (either individually or in concert) will dominate the character and direction of that research in any scientific field. The third assumption aims to guard against the possibility that the people who run corporations do not run them into the ground. Fortunately, current circumstances satisfy these conditions fairly well in many liberal democracies around the world, but nothing guarantees any of this.[139] The cultural and political arrangements, the legal measures, and the sheer effort necessary to sustain such conditions quickly uncover the close connections between modern science and open, democratic societies in a world where, simultaneously, the ties between science and technology have become so intimate and the pursuit of science has become so esoteric.

Even under the best of conditions, this involves a difficult balancing act that depends upon the scientific community steadfastly protecting its integrity and politicians, business leaders, and, ultimately, all citizens simultaneously knowing enough to give scientists' substantive quarrels a very wide berth while continuing to learn enough about science and its projects to make intelligent, responsible decisions about the allocation of limited resources in a world of competing demands—a difficult balance, indeed, in which the continued health of science hangs. Generally, the *quality* of humans' decision making on these fronts is at least roughly proportional to the *quantity* of their understanding. This is one of the reasons that a scientifically educated citizenry is so critical, and, thus, why the support of science education is so vital. Unfortunately, from the standpoint that I have defended in this book, science bears two inescapable cognitive burdens.

First, even in a time when the connections between technology and science are as intimate as they have ever been, the technological payoffs are neither obvious nor immediate outcomes of basic scientific research. Failures to recognize this loom ever more prominently when a public appears to be increasingly less literate scientifically, as time passes.

This is a fundamental challenge to science educators. It is also one of the costs of increasingly effective but increasingly sophisticated sciences, which is to say that it is one of the costs of science's radical counterintuitiveness.

Second, science's radical counterintuitiveness makes it cognitively unnatural in the extreme. Humans have produced science so infrequently in their history because not only does it not come to them naturally but because it is incredibly difficult to do and the doing of it is incredibly difficult to sustain.[140] Some ideas have natural disadvantages cognitively; science's esoteric interests, radically counterintuitive claims, and specialized forms of thinking are perfect examples. Such ideas are not easy to acquire, nor easy to retain, nor easy to communicate. Acquiring and engaging the cognitive tools necessary to make use of these ideas cuts directly against the grain of our maturationally natural cognitive dispositions. Any cognitive naturalness that their use may take on is a decidedly *practiced* naturalness that requires a couple of decades of education and implementation to achieve.

Historians and philosophers of science,[141] who point to *two* critical episodes in the history of Western thought, namely, the science of the ancient Greeks and modern science born at the turn of the seventeenth century, hold, in effect, that science was once lost and had to be reinvented. One consequence of the position that I have been defending is that nothing about human nature would ever prevent the loss of science again.

NOTES

Prelims

1. For the relevant passages, see Smith (2009, 131–32).
2. Smith (2009, 135, 137, 139, 148).

Introduction

1. Evans and Frankish (2009).
2. See, for example, Barnes (2000, 9).
3. Fodor (1983).
4. Mercier and Sperber (2009).
5. For example, Boyer (2001).
6. See especially Gopnik, Meltzoff, and Kuhl (1999).

Chapter 1

1. Psalms 127:5 (New Oxford Annotated Bible with the Apocrypha [Revised Standard Version]).
2. Trollope (1963/1857, 233).
3. I will return to this matter in chapter five.
4. Dijksterhuis et al. (2006).
5. Ekman (1984).
6. Haidt (2001, 2006); Thagard (2010).
7. McCloskey (1983a).
8. Popper (1992 , chap. 10, secs. XIII–XXII).
9. P. S. Churchland (1986, 13–14).
10. Johnson (1987).
11. Lakoff and Johnson (1980); D. L. McCauley (1986).
12. Damasio (1999); Barsalou (1999, 2003, 2005).
13. Donald (1991); Clark (1997, 2008).
14. Day (2004); Bechtel (1996).
15. McCauley and Lawson (2007).

16. Hutchins (1994).
17. Clark (1997).
18. McMillan (2002).
19. Tomasello (1999).
20. Gergely, Egyed, and Király (2006).
21. Rochat (2001, chap. 4).
22. Haith, Bergman, and Moore (1977); Maurer and Salapatek (1976).
23. Tomasello (1999); Rochat (2001, 134).
24. Rochat (2001, 134).
25. Gilbert and Sullivan (1976/1895, 308).
26. Callaghan et al. (2005, 382).
27. Tomasello (1999, 51–52).
28. Tooby and Cosmides (1992, 96).
29. Chase and Simon (1973).

Chapter 2

1. Gilbert and Sullivan (1976/1895).
2. Gibson (1966; 1979).
3. Kennedy and Portal (1990).
4. Rochat (2001, 86).
5. P. M. Churchland (1995).
6. Dennett (1991).
7. P. M. Churchland (1988).
8. Kottenhoff (1957).
9. P. M. Churchland (1988).
10. P. M. Churchland (1979).
11. Papineau (2000); Tremlin (2006, 177); Sloman (2002).
12. Fodor (1983).
13. Fodor (1983, 73).
14. Fodor (1990, 249).
15. See, however, McCauley and Henrich (2006).
16. Richerson and Boyd (2005).
17. Barrett and Kurzban (2006); Karmiloff-Smith (1992); and Tomasello (1999), respectively.
18. Fodor (1983, 47–101).
19. Fodor (1983, 37).
20. Mercier and Sperber (2009) show that they need not be.
21. Fodor (1983, 53).
22. Fodor (1983, 64).
23. Rosch et al. (1976).
24. Fodor (1983, 98).
25. Farah (1990); Duchaine and Nakayama (2006); Pinker (1994, 46–48, 299–302, 307–10).
26. Fodor (1983, 100).
27. Pinker (1994, 262–96) vs. Tomasello (2003, 7).

28. Fodor (2000, 63).
29. Fodor (1983, 65).
30. Such as the process of filling in the blind spot. Dennett (1991, chap. 11); McCauley (1993).
31. Fodor (1983, 76–77).
32. Fodor (1983, 66).
33. Examples include Karmiloff-Smith (1992) and Mithen (1996).
34. Barrett and Kurzban (2006).
35. Barrett and Kurzban (2006, 628).
36. Barrett and Kurzban (2006, 629); see Sperber (1994).
37. Barrett and Kurzban (2006, 634).
38. Barrett and Kurzban (2006, 638).
39. Barrett and Kurzban (2006, 638).
40. For more modules, see Hirschfeld and Gelman (1994) and Carruthers, Laurence, and Stich (2005). Evolutionary psychologists include Tooby and Cosmides (1992); Pinker (1997, 2002); Plotkin (1998).
41. Fodor (2000) regards massive modularity as modularity run amok.
42. Lieberman, Tooby, and Cosmides (2007).
43. "Fat-Related Woes Spread Far and Wide" (2006).
44. Cosmides and Tooby (1994, 108–10).
45. Cosmides (1989); Cosmides and Tooby (1992; 2005).
46. Wason (1966; 1968).
47. For example, Yachanin and Tweney (1982).
48. Cosmides and Tooby (1992, 191); Stone et al. (2002).
49. Critics include Fodor (2000, 101–4) and Buller (2005, 163–90). Sperber, Cara, and Girotto (1995) and Holyoak and Cheng (1995) propose alternative explanations. On connections to mainstream psychology, see McCauley (2009).
50. See Tooby and Cosmides (1992, 39, 40, 70–72, 89, 97–99, 113).
51. Pinker (1997, 28).
52. On other animals' brains, see Lettvin et al. (1959) and Dawkins (2006, 173). On humans having more instincts than other animals, see Pinker (1994, 20).
53. Richardson (2007).
54. Barrett and Kurzban (2006, 634, 638).
55. For example, Piaget (1955).
56. For example, Spelke (1994).
57. Tomasello (1999, 48–51).
58. See Bushnell (2001) and Rochat (2001, 136–39).
59. Spelke et al. (1992); much of the discussion in the remainder of this section follows Annette Karmiloff-Smith's (1992) organization and treatment of these materials.
60. Spelke et al. (1992).
61. Spelke et al. (1992); Carey and Spelke (1994).
62. Streri and Spelke (1988) and Spelke (1990); see Karmiloff-Smith (1992, 67–74).
63. On gestures, see Namy and Waxman (1998); on irregular past tenses see Rumelhart and McClelland (1986) and Bechtel and Abrahamsen (2002, 130–52), and on block balancing, see Karmiloff-Smith (1992, 84–87).

64. Sperber (1996; 2000).
65. Karmiloff-Smith (1992, 86).
66. Karmiloff-Smith (1992, 88).
67. Karmiloff-Smith (1992, 78–79).
68. Shaw (1960, 438).
69. Meltzoff and Moore (1977; 1983).
70. See, however, Bechtel and Abrahamsen (2002, 141–52) and Elman et al. (1996, chap. 4).
71. For Fodor's criticisms of this view, see Fodor (1998a, chaps. 11 and 12).
72. See Vygotsky (1978) and Tomasello (1999, 51).
73. Dennett (2006, 107).
74. Tomasello (1999; 2003, 108–9); Thiessen, Hill, and Saffran (2005).
75. Or at least nearly so; see Pinker (1994, 40).
76. Fernald et al. (1989); Gopnik, Meltzoff, and Kuhl (1999, 128–32).
77. A possible exception is children with Williams Syndrome (Karmiloff-Smith 2005).
78. Tomasello (2003, 21).
79. Tomasello (2003, 25–28).
80. See Segall, Campbell, and Herskovits (1966), de Fockert et al. (2007), and Miyamoto, Yoshikawa, and Kitayama (2011).
81. Karmiloff-Smith (1992, chap. 4); Gelman and Brenneman (1994).
82. Karmiloff-Smith (1992, 108); also see Barth (1975).
83. As examples, see Tomasello (1999, 165, 198), Rochat (2001, chap. 5), and Callaghan et al. (2005).
84. Rochat (2001, 83).
85. Rozin, Haidt, and McCauley. (2000).
86. Dunbar (1996, 87).
87. See, for example, Leslie (1994).
88. Rochat (2001, 26–27); Pinker (1994, 264).
89. Rochat (2001, 27).
90. See Meltzoff and Moore (1977; 1983); Bushnell (2001); Legerstee (1991); Rochat (2001, 139–41).
91. Massey and Gelman (1988).
92. Rochat, Morgan, and Carpenter (1997).
93. Rochat (2001, 154).
94. Baldwin and Baird (1999); Baldwin et al. (2001).
95. Zacks and Tversky (2001); Zacks, Tversky, and Iyer (2001); Boyer and Lienard (2006).
96. Rochat (2001, 154–55).
97. Gergely et al. (1995).
98. Wellman (1990, 254–68).
99. Wimmer and Perner (1983).
100. Avis and Harris (1991).
101. Callaghan et al. (2005).
102. Onishi and Baillargeon (2005); also see Surian, Caldi, and Sperber (2007).
103. Tomasello (1999, 176–77).

104. Dennett (1987; 2006, 109–11); Tomasello (1999, 53, 174).
105. Kelemen (1999a; 1999b).
106. Mithen (1996, 55).
107. See, for example, Dennett (2006, 116–17).
108. Atran (2002); by contrast, see Harris (1994, 308).
109. See Barrett (2000; 2004).
110. Compare Tomasello (1999, 22–25).

Chapter 3

1. Lay et al. (2005).
2. British Geological Survey (2005).
3. Han et al. (2006).
4. West, Sánchez, and McNutt (2005).
5. Geist et al. (2005).
6. Lay et al. (2005).
7. Geist et al. (2006).
8. Cummins (2004).
9. Cummins and Leonard (2005).
10. Cummins (2004, 6).
11. Before charging into an account of science's cognitive unnaturalness in later sections, I must first clarify two matters. I will discuss the first, pertaining to the distinction between science and technology, in this section and the second, which concerns two cognitively *natural* dimensions of science, in the next. I make no claim for the originality of much of what follows in this chapter. The renowned British biologist Lewis Wolpert offered a similar, book-length analysis of science in 1992. My differences with Wolpert's account are minor and few. Although I came to my views about the cognitive unnaturalness of science before I discovered Wolpert's *The Unnatural Nature of Science*, I benefited from reading it in numerous ways. There is no place in what follows that I owe more of a debt to Wolpert's work than I do in beginning this discussion as he begins his, namely, by examining the distinction between science and technology.
12. Smith (2009, 137).
13. Gribbin (2003, p. xx).
14. Smith (2009, 132, 135).
15. See, for example, Popper (1992, chap. 5); Cunningham and Williams (1993); Huff (1993); and Grant (1996).
16. Donald (1991, 311).
17. Gould (1999, 64).
18. Mithen (1996, 56–60).
19. Mithen (1996, 142–46).
20. If Mithen's hypothesis is true that the modules underlying our basic technical intelligence arose as the result of natural selection and, hence, are adaptive, then, according to the case that I will lay out, the cognitive foundations of technology will prove even more cognitively natural than are those of religion. See McCauley (2003).

21. Mithen (1996, 215).
22. Compare Fodor (1983, pt. IV; 1990, 202).
23. Hunt (1996); Weir, Chappell, and Kacelnik (2002); Kenward et al. (2005).
24. Donald (1991, 340).
25. Wrangham et al. (1994); van Schaik et al. (2003).
26. Goody (1987).
27. Popper (1972).
28. Donald (1991, 342).
29. Donald (1991, 341).
30. As quoted in Wolpert (1992, 41).
31. See Popper (1992, 101–2).
32. Toulmin (1961).
33. Klahr (2000, 4).
34. Gopnik, Meltzoff, and Kuhl (1999).
35. P. M. Churchland (1989, chap. 9); I too am a member of this dissenting group.
36. See Brewer and Samarapungavan (1991).
37. Pinker (2002, 221).
38. Compare Donald (1991, 215).
39. Tweney (2011).
40. Popper (1992, 127, 126, and 216, respectively).
41. Legare (2010).
42. Galilei (1967, 328); see Popper (1992, 102).
43. P. M. Churchland (1989, 259).
44. Sellars (1963).
45. Pinker (2002, 219).
46. Barrett (2004, 9).
47. Dawkins (2006, 364).
48. Klahr (2000, 3).
49. Barry (200, 72, 154).
50. Dawkins (2006, 117).
51. Brumby (1984); Greene (1990).
52. Shtulman (2006).
53. Sellars (1963); Husserl (1970).
54. Pinker (2002, 239); compare Slingerland (2008, 237).
55. Gratzer (2000, 264).
56. Gratzer (2000, chap. 8).
57. Gratzer (2000, 247–49).
58. Popper (1992, 102); also see Gribbin (2003, xxi).
59. Slingerland (2008, 234–36).
60. See McCauley (2007a); for examination of a particularly controversial contemporary case, see McCauley (1987) and Iten, Stainton, and Wearing (2007).
61. Dawkins (2006, 183–84).
62. Dennett (1987).
63. Bechtel and Abrahamsen (2002); Thagard (1988, 1992); Holyoak and Thagard (1995).
64. Wolpert (1992, 6).

65. See Chomsky (1975, 124); Fodor (1998b, 169); Geary (2002); and Pinker (1997, 222).
66. Reif and Allen (1992).
67. Jardine (2000, 18).
68. Legare (2010).
69. See Johnson (2009). One of my all-time favorites in psychology (and a terrific paper as well) is Neely (1977).
70. Stone et al. (2002).
71. Kuhn (2007).
72. See, especially, Kahneman, Slovic, and Tversky (1982); Gilovich, Griffin, and Kahneman (2002).
73. Tversky and Kahneman (1982a).
74. Gilovich (1991, 136); also see Tversky and Kahneman (2002, 22).
75. Although they do not take up that question at much length, it is fair to say that to address it Tversky and Kahneman, in effect, look, first, to the maturationally natural dispositions that inform human perception and judgment. See Tversky and Kahneman (2002, 20); also see Tversky and Kahneman (1982b, 163); Gilovich and Griffin (2002, 10).
76. Gilovich (1991, 136).
77. Poses and Anthony (1991).
78. On images and memory, see Paivio (1986). On ease with performing a task, see Sherman et al. (2002).
79. Others include anchoring, perceptual fluency, affect, causal prominence, (intuitive) similarity, abnormality, and surprise (Gilovich and Griffin 2002, 17).
80. Tversky and Kahneman (2002, 20, emphasis added).
81. Some advocates advance an even stronger view, arguing, not implausibly, that this research contributes directly to an account of the evolution of the human mind. See Gilovich and Griffin (2002, 10).
82. Gilovich and Griffin (2002, 3–5); Gigerenzer and Selten (2001).
83. Dawkins (2006, 220).
84. Piattelli-Palmarini (1994).
85. Camerer and Hogarth (1999).
86. Chase and Simon (1973).
87. Tversky and Kahneman (2002, 26).
88. As examples, see Piattelli-Palmarini (1994, 66); Koehler, Brenner, and Griffin (2002, 692).
89. Piattelli-Palmarini (1994, 142, 159).
90. McCloskey, Caramazza, and Green (1980); Caramazza, McCloskey, and Green (1981); McCloskey (1983a, 1983b); McCloskey, Washburn, and Felch (1983); McCloskey and Kohl (1983); Kaiser, McCloskey, and Proffitt (1986).
91. McCloskey (1983a); also see Anderson et al. (1992); Liu and MacIsaac (2005).
92. McCloskey and Kohl (1983, 153).
93. McCloskey, Washburn, and Felch (1983).
94. McCloskey (1983a, 125); McCloskey, Washburn, and Felch (1983).
95. Liu and MacIsaac (2005).

96. Peters (1982).
97. Kim and Pak (2002).
98. See, for example, Tuminaro and Redish (2007).
99. Proffitt and Gilden (1989).
100. Gratzer (2000, 309).
101. See Fodor (1990, 251); Gopnik, Meltzoff, and Kuhl (1999, 161).
102. Popper (1972, chap. 1; 1992, chap. 1).
103. Bechtel (2008, chap. 4).
104. See Wason and Johnson-Laird (1972, chap. 16); Wason (1977); Mynatt, Doherty, and Tweney (1977); Piattelli-Palmarini (1994, 122–23); Gratzer (2000).
105. Tweney, Doherty, and Mynatt (1981, 115–28).
106. Gilovich (1991, 33–37); for a historical illustration, see Jardine (2000, 27).
107. Mynatt, Doherty, and Tweney (1977); Tweney, Doherty, and Mynatt (1981, 145–57); also see Barrett (2004, 28).
108. See, for example, Kitcher (2002).
109. Mahoney (1977); see Gilovich (1991, 56, 201).
110. Kuhn (1970, esp. chap. 10).
111. Kuhn (1970, 150–51, 204).
112. See Kuhn (1970, 115–17).
113. Kuhn (1970, 115).
114. Jardine (2000, 169–71).
115. Donald (1991, 272; also see 273–74).
116. Postman (1982, 46; also see 12–13).
117. Donald (1991, 279).
118. Clark (1997, 220).
119. Gilovich (1991, 57).
120. See, for example, Barry (2004, 263).
121. Jardine (2000, 316).
122. Gratzer (2000) surveys a dozen or so prominent cases over the past 130 years.
123. See Solomon (2001, 12, 135); Dennett (2006, 372). This is precisely where the plausibility of Gopnik, Meltzoff, and Kuhl's suggestion that the underlying dynamics of children's cognitive development are the same as those that inform theoretical change in science comes to an abrupt halt. See Harris (1994). They acknowledge this limitation but underestimate its import.

Chapter 4

1. Horan (2000).
2. Wilde (1996, 351).
3. See McCauley and Lawson (2002, 42–44, 183–201); McCauley (forthcoming).
4. See Vogt (2006), reporting on the findings of Sheila Coulson.
5. Burkert (1996, 19).
6. McBrearty and Brooks (2000).

7. See, for example, Huff (1993, 179–80).
8. Actually, *rediscovery* is, perhaps, the better term here. See Mercader et al. (2007).
9. Staal (1979a); Hinde (1972).
10. Staal (1979b; 1984; 1990).
11. Lawson and McCauley (1990, chap. 6); Whitehouse (2004).
12. See Lawson and McCauley (1990, chap. 6).
13. See Solecki (1971); Gargett (1989); Mithen (1996).
14. Boyer (2001, chap. 1).
15. Tremlin (2006, 72).
16. See, especially, Boyer (1994; 2001). Also see McCauley (2000b); Barrett (2000; 2004); Pyysiäinen (2001); Atran (2002); Tremlin (2006).
17. Pinker (1997, 557, emphasis added).
18. Wiebe (1991).
19. Whitehouse (2000; 2004).
20. Thagard (2005); Humphrey (1996, 58).
21. Whitehouse (2004) is skeptical about the last of these possibilities.
22. For an example of the apparent absence of theological reflection, see Barth (1975). For an example of the virtual absence of ecclesiastical hierarchy, see Barth (1987).
23. Even among cognitively oriented theorists, this by-product view is by no means the only game in town (Sosis 2009; Pyysiäinen and Hauser 2009). Some theorists have either appealed to natural selection to propose that various religious sensibilities are adaptive (Bering 2006; Bering and Johnson 2005), to either group selection or cultural selection to propose that religious systems overall are adaptive (Wilson 2002; Alacorta and Sosis 2005), or to natural selection, cultural selection, and cognitive by-products in an integrated account of religions and many of their features (Henrich 2009; Atran and Henrich 2010). As the very possibility of an integrated account suggests, the by-product view is neither inconsistent with proposals about religions resulting from cultural evolution nor is it even necessarily at odds with an account that looks to natural selection, so long as such an account does not take *every* feature of human religiosity as adaptive. At one point later I will, in fact, appeal to processes of cultural selection as well. The theoretical proposal I advance here is not intended to provide either a comprehensive theory of religion or even a comprehensive theory of religious cognition. What it does capture, though, is a substantial portion of the cognitive proclivities that inform a wide variety of recurrent religious forms.
24. Cosmides and Tooby (1994, 87).
25. Burkert (1996, 22–23).
26. Boyer (2001).
27. Sperber (1994, 66–67, 50–53).
28. Lienard and Boyer (2006).
29. Tremlin (2006, 44).
30. For a more recent version of this line of thought, see Horton (1993).
31. Burkert (1996); Guthrie (1993); Barrett (2000; 2004).

32. Hinde (1999, 54–55).
33. Sperber (1996); Boyer (2001).
34. Ward (1994); Durmysheva and Kozbelt (2004); Ward, Patterson, and Sifonis (2004).
35. Bateson, Nettle, and Roberts (2006); Hinde (1999, 115).
36. Wilson (2002).
37. See, for example, McGrath and McGrath (2007, 59–63, 77); however, also see Sloan (2006).
38. Stark (1997, esp. chaps. 4, 5, and 7).
39. Pinker (1997, 525); for a closely related account that does look to natural selection, see Bering (2006) and Bering and Johnson (2005).
40. For an interesting exception, see Whitehouse (1995).
41. For this and the discussion that follows, see Boyer (1994; 1996; 1998; 2001); Boyer and Ramble (2001); Boyer and Walker (2000).
42. Mithen (1996, 177, 195).
43. Mithen (1996, chap. 5).
44. Goodall (1992).
45. Boyer and Ramble (2001); also see Barrett (2004, chap. 2).
46. Barrett and Nyhof (2001); also see Gonce et al. (2006) and Norenzayan et al. (2006).
47. Tweney et al. (2006).
48. Barrett (2008).
49. Tremlin (2006, 112–13).
50. Whitehouse (2004, 31); Barrett (2004, 25–26).
51. Hinde (1999, 54–55).
52. Hinde (1999, 101).
53. Boyer (2001, 86).
54. Barrett (2004, 22–28); Dennett (2006, 309).
55. Stark and Bainbridge (1996, 82).
56. Samarin (1972, 104–9).
57. Horton (1969, 29); May (1956).
58. Samarin (1972, 112).
59. Goodman (1972); Cohen (2007).
60. Cohen and Barrett (2008a; 2008b).
61. Malony and Lovekin (1985, 32–33).
62. See Pinker (1994, 171, 264–65, respectively).
63. See Samarin (1972, 124, 83, receptively).
64. Samarin (1972, 74).
65. Samarin (1972, 83).
66. Goodman (1972, esp. 121–23, 150).
67. Samarin (1972, 85).
68. Also see Mahony and Lovekin (1985, 37).
69. Samarin (1972, 166).
70. Fodor (1983, 56).
71. Samarin (1972, 104–9).

72. Goodman (1972, 151).
73. Rozin and Nemeroff (1990); Rozin, Markwith, and Nemeroff (1992); Rozin, Haidt, and McCauley (2000); Nemeroff and Rozin (2000); Hejmadi, Rozin, and Siegal (2004).
74. Nemeroff and Rozin (2000, 29).
75. Rozin, Markwith, and Nemeroff (1992).
76. Boyer (2001, 120).
77. Hejmadi, Rozin, and Siegal, (2004, 468).
78. Boyer and Lienard (2006); by contrast, see Burkert (1996, 123).
79. Henrich and Gil-White (2001).
80. Rozin, Markwith, and Nemeroff (1992).
81. Tomasello (1999, 174).
82. Guthrie (1993); Rochat, Morgan, and Carpenter (1997); also see Tremlin (2006, chap. 3).
83. Dunbar (1996, 81); Hinde (1999, 54–55); Barrett (2004, 31, 36).
84. Mithen (1996, 55).
85. Tomasello (1999, 185).
86. Stark and Bainbridge (1996, 83).
87. Donald (1991, 268, 347).
88. Donald (1991, 214); Brewer and Nakamura (1984).
89. Stark and Bainbridge (1996, 113–14); Stark (1997, 80).
90. Popper (1992, 126–28).
91. Gregory (2009).
92. Piattelli-Palmarini (1994, 133–37).
93. Piattelli-Palmarini (1994, 136, 137).
94. Richert (2006).
95. Tomasello (1999, 74).
96. Lienard and Boyer (2006).
97. Lawson and McCauley (1990); McCauley and Lawson (2002).
98. Whitehouse (2004, 166).
99. Humphrey and Laidlaw (1994).
100. Whitehouse (2004, 166).
101. McCauley and Lawson (2002, 13–16).
102. Barrett (2002); Whitehouse (2004, chap. 3).
103. Malley and Barrett (2003).
104. Van Gennep (1960); Lawson and McCauley (1990); McCauley and Lawson (2002).
105. Boyer and Lienard (2006); Lienard and Boyer (2006).
106. Barrett and Lawson (2001); Sørensen, Lienard, and Feeny (2006).
107. Stark and Bainbridge (1996, 89–104).
108. McCauley and Lawson (2002, 26–33).
109. Lawson and McCauley (1990, 134, note 8).
110. For an example, see McCauley and Lawson (2002, 192–201).
111. For particularly intriguing possibilities, see Persinger and Healey (2002).
112. Whitehouse (1996); Atran (2002, 175).

113. McCauley (1999).
114. See Whitehouse (2004, 113–15).
115. Brown and Kulik (1977); Luminet and Curci (2009).
116. Neisser (2000).
117. Neisser and Harsch (2000).
118. Neisser et al. (1996); also see Er (2003).
119. McCauley and Lawson (2002, 59–64); also see Goodman and Paz-Alonso (2006, 236); Pillemer (2009, 128–31).
120. Talarico and Rubin (2003).
121. Bluck et al. (2005).
122. Barth (1975); Whitehouse (1996).
123. Diamond (1998, chap. 14).
124. Firth (1963).
125. For a discussion of exceptions to this pattern, see McCauley and Lawson (2002, 149–55).
126. Whitehouse (2004).
127. Hinde (1999, 110).
128. McCauley and Lawson (2007).
129. McCauley and Lawson (2002, 149–55).
130. Whitehouse (1995).
131. McCauley and Lawson (2002, 195–207).
132. McCauley and Lawson (2002, 157–78).
133. Slone (2004).
134. Guthrie (1993).
135. Guthrie even offers a few illustrations from the sciences (1993, 164–76).
136. Epley, Waytz, and Cacioppo (2007).
137. Guthrie (1993, 49–50).
138. Barth (1975).
139. Hinde (1999, 115).
140. Laufer (1965).
141. See Barrett (2004, chap. 7, esp. 101).
142. Epley et al. (2009).
143. Epley et al. (2004).
144. Barrett and Keil (1996).
145. Boyer (2001, chap. 8).
146. Stark and Bainbridge (1996).
147. McCauley (2000a).
148. Barth (1975; 1987).
149. Grant (1996).
150. Wiebe (1991).
151. Drees (1996).
152. Pullman (1996).
153. Bechtel and Richardson (1993); Bechtel (2007); Craver (2001); Glennan (2002); Machamer, Darden, and Craver (2000).
154. Tillich (1951, 12).
155. Diamond (1998).

156. Barrett (2004, 19); also see Barrett (2001).
157. Barrett (pers. comm.).
158. A sidebar: this concern for carrying out *cross-cultural experimentation* is one of the important contributions of the cognitive science of religion to the experimental cognitive and psychological sciences. All too often, experimental researchers in those fields have relied exclusively on pools of participants no broader than the undergraduate students of North American and European universities as the basis for making declarations about the character of human cognition (Henrich, Heine, and Norenzayan 2010). Developmental psychologists have forestalled presumptions about the applicability of many of these findings to the more junior members of the species, but the cognitive and psychological sciences have conducted far too few experiments investigating the roles that *cultural* variables may or may not play in human cognition. Exceptions to this generalization include Boyer and Ramble (2001); Henrich et al. (2005); Henrich et al. (2006); and Nisbett (2003). Prominent exceptions from an earlier era include Segall, Campbell, and Herskovits (1966); Cole and Scribner (1974).
159. See Tremlin (2006, 108); McGrath and McGrath (2007, 37).
160. Contrary, for example, to the speculations in Churchland (1989, chap. 1).
161. Hinde (1999, 229–30); Barrett (2004, 72).
162. Pyysiäinen (2001, 215–34).
163. Also see Faber (2004, 25).
164. See Barrett (2004, chap. 6); Barrett and Richert (2003).
165. Kelemen (2004).
166. See Bering, Hernández-Blasi, and Bjorklund (2005); Bering and Parker (2006). For some relevant findings with pre–school-age children, see Bering and Bjorklund (2004).

Chapter 5

1. Thagard (2010, chap. two).
2. Slingerland (2008, chap. six).
3. Stark and Bainbridge (1996).
4. Dennett (2006); Silk (2006).
5. See Lawson and McCauley (1990, chap. 1) for illustrations of the latter. Drees (1996) is a welcome corrective to such special pleading.
6. Gould (1999, 6).
7. This is one of those areas where it is easy to underestimate the influence that culture exerts on conviction, even if we are inclined to overestimate its influence on contents. See Hinde (1999, chaps. 12–14); Boyer (2001, chap. 5).
8. Sullivan (2001).
9. Gould (1999, 148).
10. That is why *Die deutsche Physik* movement of the Third Reich, as *science*, was doomed. See Gratzer (2000, 244–67, esp. 251).
11. Gould (1999, 211).
12. Lanman (2007).
13. See Lawson and McCauley (1990, chap. 1).

14. In a recent volume (Harper 2005) featuring one hundred perspectives on science and religion that covered everything from quantum mechanics to the contemplation of the virtues cognitive approaches received no attention. That oversight is unfortunate.
15. McCauley (1988).
16. Bechtel (2008).
17. Frith (2003, for example, 109) argues that even many social accomplishments do not rely on theory of mind.
18. Piattelli-Palmarini (1994, 142, 159).
19. Boyer (2001, 283–85); also see Boyer (2010) and Slone (2004).
20. Whitehouse (1995); McCauley and Lawson (2002).
21. Cohen (2007, 49–50).
22. Cohen (2007, 48).
23. Cohen (2007, 53).
24. Cohen and Barrett (2008b).
25. Cohen and Barrett (2008a).
26. Whitehouse (2004, 129–30).
27. Tremlin (2006, 108).
28. Sperber (1996, 58).
29. This and the previous paragraph owe an obvious debt to Sperber (1996, chap. 5).
30. A classic presentation of dual processing models of cognition appears in the dual articles Schneider and Shiffrin (1977) and Shiffrin and Schneider (1977). For more recent work see Evans (2008) and Evans and Frankish (2009).
31. Tremlin (2006, 172–82).
32. See Harris (2004; 2006); Dawkins (2006); Hitchens (2007); Dennett (2006).
33. On values and facts, see Johnson (1993); on meanings and explanations, see Lawson and McCauley (1990, chap. 1) and Slingerland (2008).
34. See, for example, Mooney (2005, 181–82).
35. Barrett (2001).
36. I am grateful to Justin Barrett for discussions of these matters.
37. Burkert (1996, 128).
38. Association of Religion Data Archives.
39. www.harrisinteractive.comHarris Interactive (the Harris Poll).
40. See, for example, Wilbert (2004) and Stanley (2007).
41. Farha and Steward (2006).
42. Stark (2005).
43. Association of Religion Data Archives.
44. Yao and Badham (2007).
45. Barnes (2000) discusses this (see, for example, 216).
46. See, for example, Bowler (2007).
47. Dennett (2006, 335).
48. Kaminer (1999, 162–63).
49. Donald (1991, 347).
50. Compare Frith (2003, 95) with Baron-Cohen (2003, 159).
51. See Duchaine and Nakayama (2006) and Garrido et al. (2009), respectively.
52. See, for example, Baron-Cohen (1995).

53. Frith (2003, 15); compare Baron-Cohen (2008, 57–58).
54. Frith (2003, 104).
55. Gopnik, Meltzoff, and Kuhl (1999, 54); Tomasello (1999, 77).
56. Frith (2003, 43).
57. Frith (2003, 103).
58. For summary discussions and references, see Tomasello (2003, 21–28, 65–72).
59. Baron-Cohen (1995, 66–69).
60. Tomasello (1999, 63).
61. Baron-Cohen (2008, 25, fig. 2.11; see also 30–32).
62. See Baron-Cohen (2008, esp. 17–19, 77–83).
63. Baron-Cohen (2008, 62–63).
64. Frith (2003, 79).
65. See, however, Frith (2003, 112–14).
66. Baron-Cohen (2003, 141).
67. Baron-Cohen (2003, 143).
68. Frith (2003, 218–19).
69. Baron-Cohen (2003, 141).
70. See, for example, Howlin, Baron-Cohen, and Hadwin (1999) and Baron-Cohen (2008, 109–13).
71. Baron-Cohen (2008, 111–12).
72. Baron-Cohen (1995, 140).
73. See Atran (2002, 193–94) and Baron-Cohen (2003, 148–49).
74. On problems of self-understanding, see Frith and Happe (1999) and Hobson and Meyer (2005). On problems with episodic memory, see Millward et al. (2000).
75. Brezis (2008).
76. Frith (2003, 19–23); Atran (2002, 194).
77. Frith (2003, 88, 161–62).
78. Frith (2003, 89).
79. Karmiloff-Smith (1992, 168).
80. See Norenzayan et al. (2006); Shariff and Norenzayan (2007); Norenzayan and Shariff (2008); and Norenzayan et al. (2009).
81. Norenzayan, personal comm. (18 Dec. 2010 and 22 Dec. 2010). See Norenzayan, Gervais, and Trzesniewski (forthcoming).
82. Russell, Duchaine, and Nakayama (2009).
83. Also see Ridley (2003, 62).
84. Baron-Cohen (2008, 71–76; 2003, 149).
85. Baron-Cohen (2003, 149).
86. Baron-Cohen (2008, 33).
87. Fine (2010) raises just such concerns about Baron-Cohen (and others') use of this distinction.
88. For example, Baron-Cohen (2003, 57, fig. 5; 83, fig. 7; 2008, 71–75).
89. Baron-Cohen (2003, chap. 8).
90. Baron-Cohen (2003, 107).
91. Baron-Cohen (2003, 71, 82–84).

92. See Crespi and Badcock (2008) for a related but different account of the psychological contrast case to autistic spectrum disorders.
93. Baron-Cohen (2003, 31, 57–59, 151–52).
94. Miller and Hoffmann (1995); Sullins (2006).
95. Stark (2002, 496).
96. Thompson (1991); Francis and Wilcox (1996; 1998); Saroglou (2002); Sherkat (2002).
97. Miller and Hoffman (1995); Miller and Stark (2002).
98. Sullins (2006).
99. See Barrett (2004, 42–43).
100. Gilbert and Sullivan (1976/1895, 305–6).
101. Examples include Longino (1990); Solomon (2001).
102. Solomon (2001, 135).
103. Descartes (1641/1993, 26–27).
104. Bloom (2004).
105. Waller (2002).
106. See, however, Jardine (1999, 40–41).
107. Huff (1993, 14).
108. Huff (1993, 308–9).
109. Huff (1993, 69, 182).
110. Huff (1993, 168).
111. Grant (1996, 34); Huff (1993, 11–12).
112. Grant (1996, 168); Sambursky (1963).
113. Jardine (2000, 5); also see Dunbar (1995; 1997).
114. Solomon (2001, 12).
115. Jardine (2000, 177).
116. Jardine (2000, 178).
117. Jardine (2000, 313, 321).
118. See Gratzer (2000); Mooney (2005).
119. Solomon (2001, 135).
120. Donald (1991, 347).
121. Donald (1991, 311); Gould (1999, 64).
122. Jardine (2000, 316).
123. Grant (1996, 137).
124. Gribbin (2003, 71).
125. Huff (1993, 1).
126. Popper (1992, 102).
127. See Humphrey (1996, 22).
128. Mooney (2005).
129. See Shapiro (2005); Jablonka and Lamb (2005, 9–45).
130. Kaufman (2010).
131. Specter (2006, 60).
132. Kennedy (2004); Revkin (2004); Tucker (2007).
133. Samuel (2005).
134. Cited in Specter (2006, 69).
135. Specter (2006, 68, emphasis added).

136. Murfin (2010); Specter (2006, 68).
137. Chen (2009).
138. Ware (2009, 9–10).
139. See Gratzer (2000, chaps. 9–11).
140. Wolpert (1992, 6, 11).
141. For example, Popper (1992, 121).

REFERENCES

Alacorta, C., and R. Sosis. 2005. "Ritual, Emotion, and Sacred Symbols: The Evolution of Religion as an Adaptive Complex." *Human Nature* 16:323–59.

Anderson, T., A. Tolmie, C. Howe, T. Mayes, and M. MacKenzie. 1992. "Mental Models of Motion." In *Models in Mind: Theory, Perspective, and Application*, edited by Y. Rogers, A. Rutherford, and P. A. Bibby, 57–71. London: Academic.

Association of Religion Data Archives, www.thearda.com.

Atran, S. 2002. *In Gods We Trust.* Oxford: Oxford University Press.

Atran, S., and J. Henrich. 2010. "The Evolution of Religion: How Cognitive By-Products, Adaptive Learning Heuristics, Ritual Displays, and Group Competition Generate Deep Commitments to Prosocial Religions." *Biological Theory* 5:18–30.

Avis, J., and P. L. Harris. 1991. "Belief-Desire Reasoning among Baka Children: Evidence for a Universal Conception of Mind." *Child Development* 62:460–67.

Baldwin, D. A., and J. A. Baird. 1999. "Action Analysis: A Gateway to Intentional Inference." In *Early Social Cognition: Understanding Others in the First Months of Life*, edited by P. Rochat, 215–40. Mahwah, NJ: Erlbaum.

Baldwin, D. A., J. A. Baird, M. M. Saylor, and M. A. Clark. 2001. "Infants Parse Dynamic Action." *Child Development* 72:708–717.

Barnes, M. H. 2000. *Stages of Thought: The Co-Evolution of Religious Thought and Science.* New York: Oxford University Press.

Baron-Cohen, S. 1995. *Mindblindness: An Essay on Autism and Theory of Mind.* Cambridge: MIT Press.

———. 2003. *The Essential Difference: Male and Female Brains and the Truth about Autism.* New York: Basic.

———. 2008. *Autism and Asperger Syndrome: The Facts.* Oxford: Oxford University Press.

Barrett, H. C., and R. Kurzban. 2006. "Modularity in Cognition: Framing the Debate." *Psychological Review* 113:628–47.

Barrett, J. L. 2000. "Exploring the Natural Foundations of Religion." *Trends in Cognitive Science* 4:29–34.

———. 2001. "How Ordinary Cognition Informs Petitionary Prayer." *Journal of Cognition and Culture* 1:259–69.

———. 2002. "Smart Gods, Dumb Gods, and the Role of Social Cognition in Structuring Ritual Intuitions." *Journal of Cognition and Culture* 2:183–93.

———. 2004. *Why Would Anyone Believe in God?* Walnut Creek, CA: Alta Mira Press.

———. 2008. "Coding and Quantifying Counterintuitiveness in Religious Concepts: Theoretical and Methodological Reflections." *Method and Theory in the Study of Religion* 20:308–38.

Barrett, J. L., and F. Keil. 1996. "Conceptualizing a Non-Natural Entity: Anthropomorphism in God Concepts." *Cognitive Psychology* 31:219–47.

Barrett, J. L., and E. T. Lawson. 2001. "Ritual Intuitions: Cognitive Contributions to Judgements of Ritual Efficacy." *Journal of Cognition and Culture* 1: 183–201.

Barrett, J. L., and M. A. Nyhof. 2001. "Spreading Non-Natural Concepts: The Role of Intuitive Conceptual Structures in Memory and Transmission of Cultural Materials." *Journal of Cognition and Culture* 1:69–100.

Barrett, J. L., and R. A. Richert. 2003. "Anthropomorphism or Preparedness? Exploring Children's Concept of God." *Review of Religious Research* 44:300–312.

Barry, J. 2004. *The Great Influenza: The Epic Story of the Deadliest Plague in History.* New York: Penguin.

Barsalou, L. 1999. "Perceptual Symbol Systems." *Behavioral and Brain Sciences* 22:577–660.

———. 2003. "Abstraction in Perceptual Symbol Systems." *Philosophical Transactions of the Royal Society London: Biological Sciences* 358:1177–87.

———. 2005. "Abstraction as Dynamical Interpretation in Perceptual Symbol Systems." In *Building Object Categories*, edited by L. Gershkoff-Stowe and D. Rakison, 389–431. Majwah, NJ: Erlbaum.

Barth, F. 1975. *Ritual and Knowledge among the Baktaman of New Guinea.* New Haven, CT: Yale University Press.

———. 1987. *Cosmologies in the Making: A Generative Approach to Cultural Variation in Inner New Guinea.* Cambridge: Cambridge University Press.

Bateson, M., D. Nettle, and G. Roberts. 2006. "Cues of Being Watched Enhance Cooperation in a Real-World Setting." *Biology Letters* 2:412–14.

Bechtel, W. 1996. "What Should a Connectionist Philosophy of Science Look Like?" In *The Churchlands and Their Critics*, edited by R. McCauley, 121–44. Oxford: Blackwell.

———. 2007. "Reducing Psychology while Maintaining Its Autonomy via Mechanistic Explanations." In *The Matter of Mind: Philosophical Essays on Psychology, Neuroscience, and Reduction*, edited by M. Schouten and H. Looren de Jong, 172–98. Oxford: Blackwell.

———. 2008. *Mental Mechanisms: Philosophical Perspectives on Cognitive Neuroscience.* New York: Routledge.

Bechtel, W., and A. Abrahamsen. 2002. *Connectionism and the Mind: An Introduction to Parallel Processing in Networks.* 2nd ed. Oxford: Basil Blackwell.

Bechtel, W., and R. C. Richardson. 1993. *Discovering Complexity: Decomposition and Localization as Strategies in Scientific Research*. Princeton: Princeton University Press.

Bering, J. M. 2006. "The Cognitive Psychology of Belief in the Supernatural." *American Scientist* 94:142–49.

Bering, J. M., and D. F. Bjorklund. 2004. "The Natural Emergence of Reasoning about the Afterlife: As a Developmental Regularity." *Developmental Psychology* 40:217–33.

Bering, J. M., C. Hernández-Blasi, and D. F. Bjorklund. 2005. "The Development of 'Afterlife' Beliefs in Religiously and Secularly Schooled Children." *British Journal of Developmental Psychology* 23:587–607.

Bering, J. M., and D. D. P. Johnson. 2005. "O Lord . . . You Perceive My Thoughts from Afar: Recursiveness and the Evolution of Supernatural Agency." *Journal of Cognition and Culture* 5:118–42.

Bering, J. M., and B. D. Parker. 2006. "Children's Attributions of Intentions to an Invisible Agent." *Developmental Psychology* 42:253–62.

Bloom, P. 2004. *Descartes' Baby: How the Science of Child Development Explains What Makes Us Human*. New York: Basic.

Bluck, S., N. Alea, T. Habermas, and D. C. Rubin. 2005. "A Tale of Three Functions: The Self-Reported Uses of Autobiographical Memory." *Social Cognition* 23: 91–117.

Bowler, P. 2007. *Monkey Trials and Gorilla Sermons: Evolution and Christianity from Darwin to Intelligent Design*. Cambridge, MA: Harvard University Press.

Boyer, P. 1994. *The Naturalness of Religious Ideas: A Cognitive Theory of Religion*. Berkeley: University of California Press.

———. 1996. "What Makes Anthropomorphism Natural: Intuitive Ontology and Cultural Representations." *Journal of the Royal Anthropological Institute*, n.s., 2:83–97.

———. 1998. "Cognitive Tracks of Cultural Inheritance: How Evolved Intuitive Ontology Governs Cultural Transmission." *American Anthropologist* 100: 876–89.

———. 2001. *Religion Explained: The Evolutionary Origins of Religious Thought*. New York: Basic.

———. 2010. *The Fracture of an Illusion: Science and the Dissolution of Religion*. Göttingen: Vendenhoek & Ruprecht.

Boyer, P., and P. Lienard. 2006. "Why Ritualized Behavior? Precaution Systems and Action Parsing in Developmental, Pathological, and Cultural Rituals." *Behavioral and Brain Sciences* 29:595–612.

Boyer, P., and C. Ramble. 2001. "Cognitive Templates for Religious Concepts: Cross-Cultural Evidence for Recall of Counter-Intuitive Representations." *Cognitive Science* 25 (4): 535–64.

Boyer, P., and S. Walker. 2000. "Intuitive Ontology and Cultural Input in the Acquisition of Religious Concepts." In *Imagining the Impossible: Magical, Scientific, and Religious Thinking in Children*, edited by K. S. Rosengren, C. N. Johnson, and P. L. Harris, 130–56. Cambridge: Cambridge University Press.

Brewer, W. F., and G. V. Nakamura. 1984. "The Nature and Function of Schemas." *Handbook of Social Cognition*, vol. 1, edited by R. S. Wyer and T. K. Srull, 119–60. Hillsdale, NJ: Erlbaum.

Brewer, W. F., and A. Samarapungavan. 1991. "Childrens' Theories vs. Scientific Theories: Differences in Reasoning or Differences in Knowledge?" In *Cognition and the Symbolic Processes: Applied and Ecological Perspectives*, edited by R. R. Hoffman and D. S. Palermo, 209–32. Hillsdale, NJ: Erlbaum.

Brezis, R. 2008. "Autism and Religious Development: A Window onto the Intricate Alignment of Self, Culture, and Cosmos." Unpublished manuscript, Department of Comparative Human Development, University of Chicago.

British Geological Survey. 2005. "The 2004 Sumatra-Andaman Earthquake and Tsunami, One Year On." Available at http://www.bgs.ac.uk/esissues/sumatraupdate.html (accessed August 2006).

Brown, R., and J. Kulik. 1977. "Flashbulb Memories." *Cognition* 5:73–99.

Brumby, M. N. 1984. "Misconceptions about the Concept of Natural Selection by Medical Biology Students." *Science Education* 68:493–503.

Buller, D. J. 2005. *Adapting Minds: Evolutionary Psychology and the Persistent Quest for Human Nature*. Cambridge, MA: MIT Press.

Burkert, W. 1996. *Creation of the Sacred: Tracks of Biology in Early Religions*. Cambridge, MA: Harvard University Press.

Bushnell, I. W. R. 2001. "Mother's Face Recognition in Newborn Infants: Learning and Memory." *Infant and Child Development* 10:67–74.

Callaghan, T., P. Rochat, A. Lillard, M. L. Claux, H. Odden, S. Itakura, S. Tapanya, and S. Singh. 2005. "Synchrony in the Onset of Mental-State Reasoning." *Psychological Science* 16:378–84.

Camerer, C. F., and R. M. Hogarth. 1999. "The Effects of Financial Incentives in Experiments: A Review and Capital-Labor Production Framework." *Journal of Risk and Uncertainty* 19:7–42.

Caramazza, A., M. McCloskey, and B. Green. 1981. "Naive Beliefs in 'Sophisticated' Subjects: Misconceptions about Trajectories of Objects." *Cognition* 9:117–24.

Carey, S., and E. Spelke. 1994. "Domain-Specific Knowledge and Conceptual Change." In *Mapping the Mind*, edited by L. Hirschfeld and S. A. Gelman, 169–200. New York: Cambridge University Press.

Carruthers, P., S. Laurence, and S. Stich, eds. 2005. *The Innate Mind: Structure and Contents*. New York: Oxford University Press.

Chase, W. G., and H. A. Simon. 1973. "Perception in Chess." *Cognitive Psychology* 4:55–81.

Chen, X. 2009. "Students Who Study Science, Technology, Engineering, and Mathematics (STEM) in Postsecondary Education." National Center for Education Statistics. U.S. Department of Education. Available at nces.ed.gov/pubs2009/2009161.pdf.

Chomsky, N. 1975. *Reflections on Language*. New York: Pantheon.

Churchland, P. M. 1979. *Scientific Realism and the Plasticity of Mind*. Cambridge: Cambridge University Press.

———. 1988. "A Perceptual Plasticity and Theoretical Neutrality: A Reply to Jerry Fodor." *Philosophy of Science* 55:167–87.

————. 1989. *A Neurocomputational Perspective: The Nature of Mind and the Structure of Science.* Cambridge, MA: MIT Press.

————. 1995. *The Engine of Reason, the Seat of the Soul: A Philosophical Journey into the Brain.* Cambridge, MA: MIT Press.

Churchland, P. S. 1986. *Neurophilosophy.* Cambridge, MA: MIT Press.

Clark, A. 1997. *Being There: Putting Brain, Body, and World Together Again.* Cambridge, MA: MIT Press.

Clark, A. 2008. *Supersizing the Mind: Embodiment, Action, and Cognitive Extension.* New York: Oxford University Press.

Cohen, E. 2007. *The Mind Possessed: The Cognition of Spirit Possession in an Afro-Brazilian Religious Tradition.* Oxford: Oxford University Press.

Cohen, E., and J. L. Barrett. 2008a. "When Minds Migrate: Conceptualizing Spirit Possession." *Journal of Cognition and Culture* 8:23–48.

————. 2008b. "Conceptualising Spirit Possession: Ethnographic and Experimental Evidence." *Ethos* 36:245–66.

Cole, M. and S. Scribner. 1974. *Culture and Thought: A Psychological Introduction.* New York: Wiley.

Cosmides, L. 1989. "The Logic of Social Exchange: Has Natural Selection Shaped How Humans Reason? Studies of the Wason Selection Task." *Cognition* 31: 187–276.

Cosmides, L., and J. Tooby. 1992. "Cognitive Adaptations for Social Exchange." In *The Adapted Mind*, edited by J. Barkow, L. Cosmides, and J. Tooby, 163–228. New York: Oxford University Press.

————. 1994. "Origins of Doman Specificity: The Evolution of Functional Organization." In *Mapping the Mind: Domain Specificity in Cognition and Culture*, edited by L. Hirschfeld and S. Gelman, 85–116. Cambridge: Cambridge University Press.

————. 2005. "Neurocognitive Adaptations Designed for Social Exchange." In *Evolutionary Psychology Handbook*, edited by D. Buss, 584–627. New York: Wiley.

Craver, C. F. 2001. "Role Functions, Mechanisms, and Hierarchy." *Philosophy of Science* 68:53–74.

Crespi, B., and C. Badcock. 2008. "Psychosis and Autism as Diametrical Disorders of the Social Brian." *Behavioral and Brain Sciences* 31:241–320.

Cummins, P. 2004. "Small Threat, but Warning Sounded for Tsunami Research." *AusGeo News* 75:4–7.

Cummins, P., and M. Leonard. 2005. "The Boxing Day 2004 Tsunami—A Repeat of the 1833 Tsunami?" *AusGeo News* 77:4–7. Available at http://www.ga.gov.au/ausgeonews/ausgeonews200503/tsunami.jsp.

Cunningham, A., and P. Williams. 1993. "De-centering the 'Big' Picture: The Origins of Modern Science and the Modern Origins of Science." *British Journal of the History of Science* 26:407–32.

Damasio, A. R. 1999. *The Feeling of What Happens: Body and Emotion in the Making of Consciousness.* New York: Harcourt Brace & Company.

Dawkins, R. 2006. *The God Delusion.* Boston: Houghton Mifflin.

Day, M. 2004. "Religion, Off-Line Cognition and the Extended Mind." *Journal of Cognition and Culture* 4:101–21.

de Fockert, J., J. Davidoff, J. Fagot, C. Parron, and J. Goldstein. 2007. "More Accurate Size Contrast Judgments in the Ebbinghaus Illusion by a Remote Culture." *Journal of Experimental Psychology: Human Perception and Performance* 33: 738–42.

Dennett, D. C. 1987. *The Intentional Stance*. Cambridge, MA: MIT Press.

———. 1991. *Consciousness Explained*. Boston: Little, Brown and Company.

———. 2006. *Breaking the Spell: Religion as a Natural Phenomenon*. New York: Viking.

Descartes, R. 1641/1993. *Meditations on First Philosophy in Which the Existence of God and the Distinction of the Soul from the Body Are Demonstrated*. Translated by D. A. Cress. Indianapolis: Hackett.

Diamond, J. 1998. *Guns, Germs, and Steel: The Fates of Human Societies*. New York: Norton.

Dijksterhuis, A., M. W. Bos, L. F. Nordgren, and R. B. van Baaren. 2006. "On Making the Right Choice: The Deliberation-without-Attention Effect." *Science* 311:1005–7.

Donald, M. 1991. *Origins of the Modern Mind: Three Stages in the Evolution of Culture and Cognition*. Cambridge, MA: Harvard University Press.

Drees, W. 1996. *Religion, Science and Naturalism*. Cambridge: Cambridge University Press.

Duchaine, B., and K. Nakayama. 2006. "Developmental Prosopagnosia: A Window to Content-Specific Face Processing. *Current Opinion in Neurobiology* 16 (2): 166–73.

Dunbar, K. 1995. "How Scientists Really Reason: Scientific Reasoning in Real-World Laboratories." In *The Nature of Insight*, edited by R. J. Sternberg and J. Davidson, 365–95. Cambridge, MA: MIT Press.

———. 1997. "How Scientists Think: On-Line Creativity and Conceptual Change in Science." In *Creative Thought: An Investigation of Conceptual Structures and Processes*, edited by T. Ward, S. Smith, and S. Vaid, 461–93. Washington, DC: APA Press.

Dunbar, R. 1996. *Grooming, Gossip, and the Evolution of Language*. Cambridge, MA: Harvard University Press.

Durmysheva, Y., and A. Kozbelt. 2004. "The Creativity of Invented Alien Creatures: The Role of Invariants." In *Proceedings of the 26th Annual Conference of the Cognitive Science Society*, edited by K. Forbus, D. Gentner, and T. Regier, 1554. Mahwah, NJ: Erlbaum.

Ekman, P. 1984. "Expression and the Nature of Emotion." In *Approaches to Emotion*, edited by K. Scherer and P. Ekman, 319–43. Hillsdale, NJ: Erlbaum.

Elman, J. L., E. A. Bates, M. H. Johnson, A. Karmiloff-Smith, D. Parisi, and K. Plunkett. 1996. *Rethinking Innateness: A Connectionist Perspective on Development*. Cambridge, MA: MIT Press.

Epley, N., B. A. Converse, A. Delbosc, G. Monteleone, and J. Cacioppo. 2009. "Believers' Estimates of God's Beliefs Are More Egocentric Than Estimates of Other People's Beliefs." *Proceedings of the National Academy of Sciences* 106:21533–38.

Epley, N., B. Keysar, L. Van Boven, and T. Gilovich. 2004. "Perspective Taking as Egocentric Anchoring and Adjustment." *Journal of Personality and Social Psychology* 87:327–39.

Epley, N., A. Waytz, and J. T. Cacioppo. 2007. "On Seeing Human: A Three Factor Theory of Anthropomorphism." *Psychological Review* 114:864–86.

Er, N. 2003. "A New Flashbulb Memory Model Applied to the Marmara Earthquake." *Applied Cognitive Psychology* 17:503–17.

Evans, J. St. B. T. 2008. Dual-Processing Accounts of Reasoning, Judgment and Social Cognition. *Annual Review of Psychology* 59:255–78.

Evans, J. St. B. T., and K. Frankish, eds. 2009. *In Two Minds: Dual Process and Beyond.* New York: Oxford University Press.

Faber, M. D. 2004. *The Psychological Roots of Religious Belief: Searching for Angels and the Parent-God.* Amherst, NY: Prometheus.

Farah, M. J. 1990. *Visual Agnosia: Disorders of Object Recognition and What They Tell Us about Normal Vision.* Cambridge, MA: MIT Press.

Farha, B., and G. Steward. 2006. "Paranormal Beliefs: An Analysis of College Students." *Skeptical Inquirer* 30:37–40.

"Fat-Related Woes Spread Far and Wide." 2006. *Atlanta Journal and Constitution,* September 4, A4.

Fernald, A., T. Taeschner, J. Dunn, M. Papousek, B. de Boysson-Bardies, and I. Fukui. 1989. "A Cross-Language Study of Prosodic Modification in Mothers' and Fathers' Speech to Preverbal Infants." *Journal of Child Language* 16:477–501.

Fine, C. 2010. *Delusions of Gender: How Our Minds, Society, and Neurosexism Create Difference.* New York: Norton.

Firth, R. 1963. "Offering and Sacrifice: Problems of Organization." *Journal of the Royal Anthropological Institute* 93:12–24.

Fodor, J. 2000. *The Mind Doesn't Work That Way: The Scope and Limits of Computational Psychology.* Cambridge, MA: MIT Press.

Fodor, J. A. 1983. *The Modularity of Mind.* Cambridge, MA: MIT Press.

———. 1990. *A Theory of Content and Other Essays.* Cambridge, MA: MIT Press.

———. 1998a. *Concepts: Where Cognitive Science Went Wrong.* Oxford: Oxford University Press.

———. 1998b. *In Critical Condition: Polemical Essays on Cognitive Science and the Philosophy of Mind.* Cambridge, MA: MIT Press.

Francis, L. J., and C. Wilcox. 1996. "Religion and Gender Orientation." *Personality and Individual Differences* 20:119–21.

———. 1998. "Religiosity and Femininity: Do Women Really Hold a More Positive Attitude toward Christianity?" *Journal for the Scientific Study of Religion* 37: 462–69.

Frith, U. 2003. *Autism: Explaining the Enigma.* 2nd ed. Oxford: Blackwell.

Frith, U., and F. Happe. 1999. "Theory of Mind and Self-Consciousness: What Is It Like to Be Autistic?" *Mind and Language* 14:1–22.

Galilei, G. 1967. *Dialogues Concerning the Two Chief World Systems—Ptolemaic and Copernican.* 2nd ed. Translated by S. Drake. Berkeley: University of California Press.

Gargett, R. H. 1989. "Grave Shortcomings: The Evidence for Neandertal Burial" (with "Comments" and "Reply"). *Current Anthropology* 30:157–90 (157–77, 177–84, 184–88, respectively).

Garrido, L, F. Eisner, C. McGettigan, L. Stewart, D. Sauter, J. R. Hanley, S. R. Schweinberger, J. D. Warren, and B. Duchaine. 2009. "Developmental Phonagnosia: A Selective Deficit of Vocal Identity Recognition." *Neuropsychologia* 47:123–31.

Geary, D. C. 2002. "Principles of Evolutionary Educational Psychology." *Learning and Individual Differences* 12:317–45.

Geist, E. L., V. V. Titov, and C. E. Synolakis. 2006. "Tsunami: Wave of Change." *Scientific American* 294 (1, January): 56–63.

Gelman, R., and K. Brenneman. 1994. "First Principles Can Support Both Universal and Culture-Specific Learning about Number and Music." In *Mapping the Mind: Domain Specificity in Cognition and Culture*, edited by L. A. Hirschfeld and S. A. Gelman, 369–90. Cambridge: Cambridge University Press.

Gergely, G., K. Egyed, and I. Király. 2006. "On Pedagogy." *Developmental Science* 10:139–46.

Gergely, G., Z. Nádasdy, G. Csibra, and S. Bíró. 1995. "Taking the Intentional Stance at 12 Months of Age." *Cognition* 56:1654–193.

Gibson, J. J. 1966. *The Senses Considered as Perceptual Systems*. Boston: Houghton-Mifflin.
———. 1979. *The Ecological Approach to Visual Perception*. Boston: Houghton Mifflin.

Gigerenzer, G., and R. Selten. 2001. *Bounded Rationality: The Adaptive Toolbox*. Cambridge, MA: MIT Press.

Gilbert, W. S., and A. Sullivan. 1976/1895. *The Complete Plays of Gilbert and Sullivan*. New York: Norton.

Gilovich, T. 1991. *How We Know What Isn't So: The Fallibility of Human Reason in Everyday Life*. New York: Free Press.

Gilovich, T., and D. Griffin. 2002. "Introduction—Heuristics and Biases: Then and Now." In *Heuristics and Biases: The Psychology of Intuitive Judgment*, edited by T. Gilovich, D. Griffin, and D. Kahneman, 1–18. Cambridge: Cambridge University Press.

Gilovich, T., D. Griffin, and D. Kahneman. 2002. *Heuristics and Biases: The Psychology of Intuitive Judgment*. Cambridge: Cambridge University Press.

Glennan, S. 2002. "Rethinking Mechanistic Explanation." *Philosophy of Science* 69 (supplement): S342–353.

Gonce, L. O., M. A. Upal, D. J. Slone, and R. D. Tweney. 2006. "Role of Context in the Recall of Counterintuitive Concepts." *Journal of Cognition and Culture* 6:521–47.

Goodall, J. 1992. *In the Shadow of Man*. Boston: Houghton Mifflin.

Goodman, F. D. 1972. *Speaking in Tongues: A Cross-Cultural Study of Glossolalia*. Chicago: University of Chicago Press.

Goodman, G. S., and P. M. Paz-Alonso. 2006. "Trauma and Memory: Normal versus Special Memory Mechanisms." In *Memory and Emotion: Interdisciplinary Perspectives*, edited by B. Uttl, N. Ohta, and A. L. Siegenthaler, 233–57. Oxford: Blackwell.

Goody, J. 1987. *The Interface between the Written and the Oral*. Cambridge: Cambridge University Press.

Gopnik, A., A. Meltzoff, and P. Kuhl. 1999. *The Scientist in the Crib: Minds, Brains, and How Children Learn*. New York: William Morrow.

Gould, S. 1999. *Rocks of Ages: Science and Religion in the Fullness of Life*. New York: Ballantine.

Grant, E. 1996. *The Foundations of Modern Science in the Middle Ages: Their Religious, Institutional, and Intellectual Contexts*. Cambridge: Cambridge University Press.

Gratzer, W. 2000. *The Undergrowth of Science: Delusion, Self-Deception and Human Frailty*. Oxford: Oxford University Press.

Greene, E. D. 1990. "The Logic of University Students' Misunderstanding of Natural Selection." *Journal of Research in Science Teaching* 27:875–85.

Gregory, M. W. 2009. *Shaped by Stories: The Ethical Power of Narratives*. Notre Dame: University of Notre Dame Press.

Gribbin, J. 2003. *Science: A History*. London: Penguin.

Guthrie, S. 1993. *Faces in the Clouds*. Oxford: Oxford University Press.

Haidt, J. 2001. "The Emotional Dog and Its Rational Tail: A Social Intuitionist Approach to Moral Judgment." *Psychological Review* 108:814–34.

———. 2006. *The Happiness Hypothesis*. New York: Basic.

Haith, M. M., T. Bergman, and M. J. Moore. 1977. "Eye Contact and Face Scanning in Early Infancy." *Science* 198:853–55.

Hammond World Atlas. 2008. 5th ed. Springfield, NJ: Hammond World Atlas Corporation.

Han, S., C. K. Shum, M. Bevis, C. Ji, and C. Kuo. 2006. "Crustal Dilatation Observed by GRACE after the 2004 Sumatra-Andaman Earthquake." *Science* 313:658–62.

Harper, C. L. 2005. *Spiritual Information: 100 Perspectives on Science and Religion*. Philadelphia: Templeton Foundation Press.

Harris, P. L. 1994. "Thinking by Children and Scientists: False Analogies and Neglected Similarities." In *Mapping the Mind: Domain Specificity in Cognition and Culture*, edited by L. A. Hirschfeld and S. A. Gelman, 294–315. Cambridge: Cambridge University Press.

Harris, S. 2004. *The End of Faith: Religion, Terror, and the Future of Reason*. New York: Norton.

———. 2006. *Letter to a Christian Nation*. New York: Knopf.

Harris Interactive (The Harris Poll). www.harrisinteractive.com.

Hejmadi, A., P. Rozin, and M. Siegal. 2004. "Once in Contact, Always in Contact: Contagious Essence and Conceptions of Purification in American and Hindu Indian Children." *Developmental Psychology* 40:467–76.

Henrich, J. 2009. "The Evolution of Costly Displays, Cooperation, and Religion: Credibility Enhancing Displays and Their Implications for Cultural Evolution." *Evolution and Human Behavior* 30:244–60.

Henrich, J., R. Boyd, S. Bowles, H. Gintis, E. Fehr, C. Camerer, R. McElreath, M. Gurven, K. Hill, A. Barr, J. Ensminger, D. Tracer, F. Marlow, J. Patton, M. Alvard, F. Gil-White, and N. Henrich. 2005. "'Economic Man' in Cross-Cultural Perspective: Ethnography and Experiments from 15 Small-Scale Societies." *Behavioral and Brain Sciences* 28:795–855.

Henrich, J., and F. Gil-White. 2001. "The Evolution of Prestige: Freely Conferred Status as a Mechanism for Enhancing the Benefits of Cultural Transmission." *Evolution and Human Behavior* 22:1–32.

Henrich, J., S. J. Heine, and A. Norenzayan. 2010. "The Weirdest People in the World?" *Behavioral and Brain Sciences* 33:1–75.

Henrich, J., R. McElreath, A. Barr, J. Ensimger, C. Barrett, A. Bolyanatz, J. C. Cardenas, M. Gurven, E. Gwako, N. Henrich, C. Lesorogol, F. Marlowe, D. Tracer, and J. Ziker. 2006. "Costly Punishment across Human Societies." *Science* 312: 1767–70.

Hinde, R., ed. 1972. *Non-Verbal Communication*. Cambridge: Cambridge University Press.

———. 1999. *Why Gods Persist*. New York: Routledge.

Hirschfeld, L. A., and S. A. Gelman, eds. 1994. *Mapping the Mind: Domain Specificity in Cognition and Culture*. Cambridge: Cambridge University Press.

Hitchens, C. 2007. God Is Not Great: How Religion Poisons Everything. New York: Twelve.

Hobson, R. P., and J. A. Meyer. 2005. "Foundations for Self and Other: A Study in Autism." *Developmental Science* 8:481–91.

Holyoak, K. J., and P. W. Cheng. 1995. "Pragmatic Reasoning about Human Voluntary Action: Evidence from Wason's Selection Task." In *Perspectives on Thinking and Reasoning: Essays in Honor of Peter Wason*, edited by S. Newstead and J. St. B. T, 67–89. Evans East Essex, UK: Erlbaum.

Holyoak, K. J., and P. Thagard. 1995. *Mental Leaps: Analogy in Creative Thought*. Cambridge, MA: MIT Press.

Horan, D. 2000. *Oxford*. New York: Interlink.

Horton, R. 1969. "Types of Spirit Possession in Kalabari Religion." In *Spirit Mediumship and Society in Africa*, edited by J. Beattie and J. Middleton, 14–49. London: Routledge and Kegan Paul.

Horton, R. 1993. *Patterns of Thought in Africa and the West: Essays on Magic, Religion, and Science*. Cambridge: Cambridge University Press.

Howlin, P., S. Baron-Cohen, and J. Hadwin. 1999. *Teaching Children with Autism to Mind-Read: A Practical Guide for Teachers and Parents*. San Francisco: Wiley.

Huff, T. 1993. *The Rise of Early Modern Science: Islam, China, and the West*. Cambridge: Cambridge University Press.

Humphrey, C., and J. Laidlaw. 1994. *The Archetypal Actions of Ritual: A Theory of Ritual Illustrated by the Jain Rite of Worship*. Oxford: Oxford University Press.

Humphrey, N. 1996. *Leaps of Faith: Science, Miracles, and the Search for Supernatural Consolation*. New York: Copernicus.

Hunt, G. R. 1996. "Manufacture and Use of Hook-Tools by New Caledonian Crows." *Nature* 379:249–51.

Husserl, E. 1970. *The Crisis of European Sciences and Transcendental Phenomenology: An Introduction to Phenomenological Philosophy*. Translated by D. Carr. Evanston: Northwestern University Press.

Hutchins, E. 1994. *Cognition in the Wild*. Cambridge, MA: MIT Press.

Iten, C., R. Stainton, and C. Wearing. 2007. "On Restricting the Evidence Base for Linguistics." In *Handbook of Philosophy of Science: Philosophy of Psychology and Cognitive Science*, edited by P. Thagard, 219–46. Amsterdam: Elsevier.

Jablonka, E., and M. J. Lamb. 2005. *Evolution in Four Dimensions: Genetic, Epigenetic, Behavioral, and Symbolic Variation in the History of Life*. Cambridge, MA: MIT Press.

Jardine, L. 1999. *Ingenious Pursuits: Building the Scientific Revolution*. London: Abacus.

Johnson, G. 2009. *The Ten Most Beautiful Experiments*. New York: Vintage.

Johnson, M. 1987. *The Body in the Mind*. Chicago: University of Chicago Press.

———. 1993. *Moral Imagination: Implications of Cognitive Science for Ethics*. Chicago: University of Chicago Press.

Kahneman, D., P. Slovic, and A. Tversky, eds. 1982. *Judgement under Uncertainty: Heuristics and Biases*. Cambridge: Cambridge University Press.

Kaiser, M. K., M. McCloskey, and D. Proffitt. 1986. "Development of Intuitive Theories of Motion: Curvilinear Motion in the Absence of External Forces." *Developmental Psychology* 22:67–71.

Kaminer, W. 1999. *Sleeping with Extra-Terrestrials: The Rise of Irrationalism and Perils of Piety*. New York: Vintage.

Karmiloff-Smith, A. 1992. *Beyond Modularity: A Developmental Perspective on Cognitive Science*. Cambridge, MA: MIT Press.

Karmiloff-Smith, A. 2005. "Modules, Genes and Evolution: What Has the Study of Atypical Language Acquisition Taught Us?" Emory Cognition Project Conference on Developmental Cognitive Neuroscience, Emory University, Atlanta, GA (April 4).

Kaufman, L. 2010. "Darwin Foes Add Warming to Target List." *New York Times*, March 4, A1 and A4.

Kelemen, D. 1999a. "The Scope of Teleological Thinking in Pre-School Children." *Cognition* 70:241–72.

———. 1999b. "Why Are Rocks Pointy? Children's Preference for Teleological Explanations of the Natural World." *Developmental Psychology* 33:1440–52.

———. 2004. "Are Children 'Intuitive Theists'? Reasoning about Purpose and Design in Nature." *Psychological Science* 15:295–301.

Kennedy, J. M., and A. Portal. 1990. "Illusions: Can Change of Vantage Point and Invariant Impressions Remove Deception?" *Ecological Psychology* 2:37–53.

Kennedy, R. F. 2004. "The Junk Science of George W. Bush." *The Nation*, March 8, 11–18.

Kenward, B., A. A. S. Weir, C. Rutz, and A. Kacelnik. 2005. "Tool Use by Naive Juvenile Crows." *Nature* 433:121.

Kim, E., and S. Pak. 2002. "Students Do Not Overcome Conceptual Difficulties after Solving 1000 Traditional Problems." *American Journal of Physics* 70:759–65.

Kitcher, P. S. 2002. "Social Psychology and the Theory of Science." In *The Cognitive Basis of Science*, edited by P. Carruthers, S. Stich, and M. Siegal, 263–81. Cambridge: Cambridge University Press.

Klahr, D. 2000. *Exploring Science: The Cognition and Development of Discovery Processes*. Cambridge, MA: MIT Press.

Koehler, D. J., L. Brenner, and D. Griffin. 2002. "The Calibration of Expert Judgment: Heuristics and Biases beyond the Laboratory." In *Heuristics and Biases: The Psychology of Intuitive Judgment*, edited by T. Gilovich, D. Griffin, and D. Kahneman, 686–715. Cambridge: Cambridge University Press.

Kottenhoff, H. 1957. "Situational and Personal Influences on Space Perception with Experimental Spectacles Part One: Prolonged Experiments with Inverting Glasses." *Acta Psychologica* 13:79–97.

Kuhn, D. 2007. "Jumping to Conclusions: Can People Be Counted on to Make Sound Judgments?" *Scientific American Mind* 18 (1): 44–51.

Kuhn, T. 1970. *The Structure of Scientific Revolutions*. 2nd ed. Chicago: University of Chicago Press.

Lakoff, G., and M. Johnson. 1980. *Metaphors We Live By*. Chicago: University of Chicago Press.

Lanman, J. A. 2007. "How 'Natives' Don't Think: The Apotheosis of Overinterpretation." In *Religion, Anthropology, and Cognitive Science*, edited by H. Whitehouse and J. Laidlaw, 105–32. Durham: Carolina Academic Press.

Laufer, B. 1965. "The Development of Ancestral Images in China." In *Reader in Comparative Religion: An Anthropological Approach*, edited by W. Lessa and E. Vogt, 445–52. New York: Harper and Row.

Lawson, E. T., and R. N. McCauley. 1990. *Rethinking Religion: Connecting Cognition and Culture*. Cambridge: Cambridge University Press.

Lay, T., H. Kanamori, C. J. Ammon, M. Nettles, S. N. Ward, R. C. Aster, S. L. Beck, S. L. Bilek, M. R. Brudzinski, R. Butler, H. R. DeShon, G. Ekström, K. Satake, and S. Sipkin. 2005. "The Great Sumatra-Andaman Earthquake of 26 December 2004." *Science* 308:1127–33.

Legare, C. H. Forthcoming. "Exploring Explanation: Explaining Inconsistent Evidence Informs Exploratory, Hypothesis-Testing Behavior in Young Children." *Child Development*.

Legerstee, M. 1991. "The Role of Person and Object in Eliciting Early Imitation." *Journal of Experimental Child Psychology* 51:423–33.

Leslie, A. 1994. "ToMM, ToBY, and Agency: Core Architecture and Domain Specificity." In *Mapping the Mind*, edited by L. Hirschfeld and S. A. Gelman, 119–48. New York: Cambridge University Press.

Lettvin, J. Y., H. R. Maturana, W. S. McCulloch, and W. H. Pitts. 1959. "What the Frog's Eye Tells the Frog's Brain." *Proceedings of the Institute of Radio Engineers* 47:1940–51.

Lieberman, D., J. Tooby, and L. Cosmides. 2007. "The Architecture of Human Kin Detection." *Nature* 445:727–31.

Lienard, P., and P. Boyer. 2006. "Whence Collective Rituals? A Cultural Selection Model of Ritualized Behavior." *American Anthropologist* 108:814–28.

Liu, X., and D. MacIsaac. 2005. "An Investigation of Factors Affecting the Degree of Naïve Impetus Theory Application." *Journal of Science Education and Technology* 14:101–16.

Longino, H. E. 1990. *Science as Social Knowledge: Values and Objectivity in Scientific Inquiry*. Princeton, NJ: Princeton University Press.

Luminet, O., and A. Curci, eds. 2009. *Flashbulb Memories: New Issues and New Perspectives*. New York: Psychology Press.

Machamer, P., L. Darden, and C. F. Craver. 2000. "Thinking about Mechanisms." *Philosophy of Science* 67:1–25.

Mahoney, M. J. 1977. "Publication Prejudice: An Experimental Study of Confirmatory Bias in the Peer Review System." *Cognitive Therapy and Research* 1:161–75.

Malley, B., and J. Barrett. 2003. "Can Ritual Form Be Predicted from Religious Belief? A Test of the Lawson-McCauley Hypotheses." *Journal of Ritual Studies* 17: 1–14.

Malony, H. N., and A. A. Lovekin. 1985. *Glossolalia: Behavioral Science Perspectives on Speaking in Tongues*. New York: Oxford University Press.

Massey, C., and R. Gelman. 1988. "Preschoolers' Ability to Decide Whether Pictured or Unfamiliar Objects Can Move Themselves." *Developmental Psychology* 24:307–17.

Maurer, D., and P. Salapatek. 1976. "Developmental Changes in the Scanning of Faces by Young Infants." *Child Development* 47:523–27.

May, H. G., and B. M. Metzger. 1977. *The New Oxford Annotated Bible with the Apocrypha* (Revised Standard Version). New York: Oxford University Press.

May, L. C. 1956. "A Survey of Glossolalia and Related Phenomena in Non-Christian Religions." *American Anthropologist* 58:75–96.

McBrearty, S., and A. S. Brooks. 2000. "The Revolution That Wasn't: A New Interpretation of the Origin of Modern Human Behavior." *Journal of Human Evolution* 39:453–563.

McCauley, D. L. 1986. *An Exploration of Metaphor in Therapy*. Ph.D. dissertation. Purdue University.

McCauley, R. N. 1987. "The Not So Happy Story of the Marriage of Linguistics and Psychology or How Linguistics Has Discouraged Psychology's Recent Advances." *Synthese* 72:341–53.

———. 1988. "Epistemology in an Age of Cognitive Science." *Philosophical Psychology* 1:143–52.

———. 1993. "Why the Blind Can't Lead the Blind: Dennett on the Blind Spot, Blindsight, and Sensory Qualia." *Consciousness and Cognition* 2:155–64.

———. 1999. "Bringing Ritual to Mind." In *Ecological Approaches to Cognition: Essays in Honor of Ulric Neisser*, edited by E. Winograd, R. Fivush, and W. Hirst, 285–312. Hillsdale, NJ: Erlbaum.

———. 2000a. "Overcoming Barriers to a Cognitive Psychology of Religion." In "Perspectives on Method and Theory in the Study of Religion Method and Theory in the Study of Religion," edited by A. Geertz and R. McCutcheon, 12:141–61. Special issue of *Method and Theory in the Study of Religion*.

———. 2000b. "The Naturalness of Religion and the Unnaturalness of Science." In *Explanation and Cognition*, edited by F. Keil and R. Wilson, 61–85. Cambridge, MA: MIT Press.

———. 2003. "Is Religion a Rube Goldberg Device? Or, Oh, What a Difference a Theory Makes!" In *Religion as a Human Capacity: A Festschrift in Honor of E. Thomas Lawson*, edited by B. Wilson and T. Light, 45–64. Leiden: Brill.

———. 2007a. "Reduction: Models of Cross-Scientific Relations and Their Implications for the Psychology-Neuroscience Interface." In *Handbook of the Philosophy of Science: Philosophy of Psychology and Cognitive Science*, edited by P. Thagard, 105–58. Amsterdam: Elsevier.

———. 2007b. "Enriching Philosophical Models of Cross-Scientific Relations: Incorporating Diachronic Theories." In *The Matter of the Mind: Philosophical Essays on Psychology, Neuroscience and Reduction*, edited by M. Schouten and H. Looren de Jong, 199–223. Oxford: Blackwell.

———. 2009. "Time Is of the Essence: Explanatory Pluralism and Accommodating Theories about Long Term Processes." *Philosophical Psychology* 22:611–35.

———. Forthcoming. "The Importance of Being 'Ernest.'" In *Integrating the Sciences and Humanities: Interdisciplinary Approaches*, edited by E. Slingerland and M. Collard. New York: Oxford University Press.

McCauley, R. N., and J. Henrich. 2006. "Susceptibility to the Muller-Lyer Illusion, Theory Neutral Observation, and the Diachronic Cognitive Penetrability of the Visual Input System." *Philosophical Psychology* 19:79–101.

McCauley, R. N., and E. T. Lawson. 2002. *Bringing Ritual to Mind: Psychological Foundations of Cultural Forms*. Cambridge: Cambridge University Press.

———. 2007. "Cognition, Religious Ritual, and Archaeology." In *The Archaeology of Ritual*, edited by E. Kyriakidis, 209–54. Los Angeles: Cotsen Institute of Archaeology Publications.

McCloskey, M. 1983a. "Intuitive Physics." *Scientific American* 248:122–30.

———. 1983b. "Naïve Theories of Motion." In *Mental Models*, edited by D. Gentner and A. L. Stevens, 299–324. Hillsdale, NJ: Erlbaum.

McCloskey, M., A. Caramazza, and B. Green. 1980. "Curvalinear Motion in the Absence of External Forces: Naive Beliefs about the Motion of Objects." *Science* 210:1139–41.

McCloskey, M., and D. Kohl. 1983. "Naive Physics: The Curvilinear Impetus Principle and Its Role in Interactions with Moving Objects." *Journal of Experimental Psychology: Learning, Memory, & Cognition* 9:146–56.

McCloskey, M., A. Washburn, and L. Felch. 1983. "Intuitive Physics: The Straightdown Belief and Its Origin," *Journal of Experimental Psychology: Learning, Memory & Cognition* 9:636–49.

McGrath, A., and J. C. McGrath. 2007. *The Dawkins Delusion: Atheist Fundamentalism and the Denial of the Divine*. London: SPCK.

McMillan, J. 2002. *Reinventing the Bazaar: A Natural History of Markets*. New York: Norton.

Meltzoff, A. N., and M. K. Moore. 1977. "Imitation of Facial and Manual Gestures by Human Neonates." *Science* 198:75–78.

———. 1983. "Newborn Infants Imitate Adult Facial Gestures." *Child Development* 54:702–9.

Mercader, J., H. Barton, J. Gillespie, J. Harris, S. Kuhn, R. Tyler, and C. Boesch. 2007. "4,300-Year-Old Chimpanzee Sites and the Origins of Percussive Stone Technology." *Proceedings of the National Academy of Sciences* 104:3043–48.

Mercier, H., and D. Sperber. 2009. "Intuitive and Reflective Inferences." In *In Two Minds: Dual Processes and Beyond*, edited by J. St. B. T. Evans and K. Frankish, 149–70. New York: Oxford University Press.

Miller, A. S., and J. P. Hoffmann. 1995. "Risk and Religion: An Explanation of Gender Differences in Religiosity." *Journal for the Scientific Study of Religion* 34:63–75.

Miller, A. S., and R. Stark. 2002. "Gender and Religiousness: Can Socialization Explanations Be Saved?" *American Journal of Sociology* 107:1399–423.

Millward, C., S. Powell, D. Messer, and R. Jordan. 2000. "Recall for Self and Other in Autism: Children's Memory for Events Experienced by Themselves and Their Peers." *Journal of Autism and Developmental Disorders* 30:15–28.

Mithen, S. 1996. *The Prehistory of the Mind*. London: Thames and Hudson.

Miyamoto, Y., S. Yoshikawa, and S. Kitayama, S. 2011. "Feature and Configuration in Face Processing: Japanese Are More Configural Than Americans." *Cognitive Science* 35:563–74.

Mooney, C. 2005. *The Republican War on Science*. Revised and updated. New York: Basic.

Murfin, W. 2010. "United States Student Performance on International Tests." Coalition for Excellence in Science and Math Education. Available at www.cesame-nm.org/index.php/wikula/main/tag/USSStudentPerformance (accessed July 2010).

Mynatt, C. R., M. E. Doherty, and R. D. Tweney. 1977. "Confirmation Bias in a Simulated Research Environment: An Experimental Study of Scientific Inference." *Quarterly Journal of Experimental Psychology* 29:85–95.

Namy, L. L., and S. R. Waxman. 1998. "Words and Gestures: Infants' Interpretations of Different Forms of Symbolic Reference." *Child Development* 69:295–308.

Neely, J. 1977. "Semantic Priming and Retrieval from Lexical Memory: Roles of Inhibitionless Spreading Activation and Limited-Capacity Attention." *Journal of Experimental Psychology: General* 106:226–54.

Neisser, U. 2000. "Snapshots or Benchmarks?" In *Memory Observed*, edited by U. Neisser and I. E. Hyman Jr., 68–74. 2nd ed. New York: Worth.

Neisser, U., and N. Harsch. 1992. "Phantom Flashbulbs: False Recollections of Hearing the News about *Challenger*." In *Memory Observed*, edited by U. Neisser and I. E. Hyman Jr., 75–89. 2nd ed. New York: Worth.

Neisser, U., E. Winograd, E. T. Bergman, C. A. Schreiber, S. E. Palmer, and M. S. Weldon. 1996. "Remembering the Earthquake: Direct Experience vs. Hearing the News." *Memory* 4:337–57.

Nemeroff, C., and P. Rozin. 2000. "The Makings of the Magical Mind: The Nature and Function of Sympathetic Magical Thinking." In *Imagining the Impossible: Magical, Scientific, and Religious Thinking in Children*, edited by K. S. Rosengren, C. N. Johnson, and P. L. Harris, 1–34. Cambridge: Cambridge University Press.

Nisbett, R. 2003. *The Geography of Thought: How Asians and Westerners Think Differently . . . and Why*. New York: Free Press.

Norenzayan, A., S. Atran, J. Faulkner, and M. Schaller. 2006. "Memory and Mystery: The Cultural Selection of Minimally Counterintuitive Narratives." *Cognitive Science* 30:531–53.

Norenzayan, A., I. Dar-Nimrod, I. G. Hansen, and T. Proulx. 2009. "Mortality Salience and Religion: Divergent Effects on the Defense of Cultural Values for the Religious and the Non-Religious." *European Journal of Social Psychology* 39:101–13.

Norenzayan, A., W. M. Gervais, and K. Trzesniewski. Forthcoming. "Reading the Mind of God: Associations between Mentalizing and Believing.".

Norenzayan, A., and A. F. Shariff. 2008. "The Origin and Evolution of Religious Prosociality." *Science* 322:58–62.

Onishi, K., and R. Baillargeon. 2005. "Do 15-Month-Old Infants Understand False Beliefs?" *Science* 308:255–58.

Paivio, A. 1986. *Mental Representations: A Dual Coding Approach*. New York: Oxford University Press.

Papineau, D. 2000. "The Evolution of Knowledge." In *Evolution and the Human Mind: Modularity, Language, and Meta-Cognition*, edited by P. Carruthers and A. Chamberlain, 170–206. Cambridge: Cambridge University Press.

Persinger, M. A., and F. Healey. 2002. "Experimental Facilitation of the Sensed Presences: Possible Intercalation between the Hemispheres Induced by Complex Magnetic Fields." *Journal of Nervous and Mental Disease* 190:533–41.

Peters, P. C. 1982. "Even Honors Students Have Conceptual Difficulties with Physics." *American Journal of Physics* 50:501.

Piaget, J. 1955. *The Child's Construction of Reality*. London: Routledge and Kegan Paul.

Piattelli-Palmarini, M., ed. 1994. *Inevitable Illusions: How Mistakes of Reason Rule Our Minds*. Translated by K. Botsford. New York: Wiley.

Pillemer, D. B. 2009. "'Hearing the News' versus 'Being There.'" In *Flashbulb Memories: New Issues and New Perspectives*, edited by O. Luminet and A. Curci, 125–40. New York: Psychology Press.

Pinker, S. 1994. *The Language Instinct: How the Mind Creates Language*. New York: HarperCollins.

———. 1997. *How the Mind Works*. New York: Norton.

———. 2002. *The Blank Slate: The Modern Denial of Human Nature*. New York: Penguin.

Plotkin, H. 1998. *Evolution in Mind: An Introduction to Evolutionary Psychology*. Cambridge, MA: Harvard University Press.

Popper, K. 1972. *Objective Knowledge: An Evolutionary Approach*. Oxford: Oxford University Press.

———. 1992. *Conjectures and Refutations: The Growth of Scientific Knowledge*. London: Routledge.

Poses, R. M., and M. Anthony. 1991. "Availability, Wishful Thinking, and Physicians; Diagnostic Judgments for Patients with Suspected Bacteremia." *Medical Decision Making* 11:159–68.

Postman, N. 1982. *The Disappearance of Childhood*. New York: Vintage.

Proffitt, D. R., and D. L. Gilden. 1989. "Understanding Natural Dynamics." *Journal of Experimental Psychology: Human Perception and Performance* 15:384–93.

Pullman, P. 1996. *The Golden Compass*. New York: Knopf.

Pyysiäinen, I. 2001. *How Religion Works*. Leiden: Brill.

Reif, F., and S. Allen. 1992. "Cognition for Interpreting Scientific Concepts: A Study of Acceleration." *Cognition and Instruction* 9:1–44.

Revkin, A. C. 2004. "Bush vs. the Laureates: How Science Became a Partisan Issue." *New York Times*, October 19, D1, D9.

Richardson, R. 2007. *Evolutionary Psychology as Maladapted Psychology*. Cambridge, MA: MIT Press.

Richerson, P. J., and R. Boyd. 2005. *Not by Genes Alone: How Culture Transformed Human Evolution*. Chicago: University of Chicago Press.

Richert, R. A. 2006. "The Ability to Distinguish Ritual Actions in Children." *Method and Theory in the Study of Religion* 18:144–65.

Ridley, M. 2003. *Nature via Nurture: Genes, Experience, and What Makes Us Human*. New York: Harper Collins.

Rochat, P. 2001. *The Infant's World*. Cambridge, MA: Harvard University Press.

Rochat, P., R. Morgan, and M. Carpenter. 1997. "Young Infants' Sensitivity to Movement Information Specifying Social Causality." *Cognitive Development* 12:441–65.

Rosch, E., C. Mervis, W. Gray, D. Johnson, and P. Boyes-Braem. 1976. "Basic Objects in Natural Categories." *Cognitive Psychology* 8:382–439.

Rozin, P., J. Haidt, and C. R. McCauley. 2000. "Disgust." In *Handbook of Emotions*, edited by M. Lewis and J. M. Haviland-Jones, 637–53. 2nd ed. New York: Guilford.

Rozin, P., M. Markwith, and C. Nemeroff. 1992. "Magical Contagion Beliefs and Fear of AIDS." *Journal of Personality and Social Psychology* 50:703–12.

Rozin, P., and C. Nemeroff. 1990. "The Laws of Sympathetic Magic: A Psychological Analysis of Similarity and Contagion." In *Cultural Psychology*, edited by J. W. Stigler, R. A. Shweder, and G. Herdt, 205–32. Cambridge: Cambridge University Press.

Rumelhart, D. E., and J. L. McClelland. 1986. "On Learning the Past Tense of English Verbs." In *Parallel Distributed Processing*, 216–71. Vol. 2. Cambridge, MA: MIT Press.

Russell, R., B. Duchaine, and K. Nakayama. 2009. "Super-Recognizers: People with Extraordinary Face Recognition Ability." *Psychological Bulletin and Review* 16:252–57.

Samarin, W. J. 1972. *Tongues of Men and Angels: The Religious Language of Pentecostalism*. New York: Macmillan.

Sambursky, S. 1963. *The Physical World of the Greeks*. London: Routledge and Kegan Paul.

Samuel, O. 2005. "Measles Vaccine Anti-Islamic Plot." *San Francisco Chronicle*, March 28, A7.

Saroglou, V. 2002. "Religion and the Five Factors of Personality: A Meta-Analytic Review." *Personality and Individual Differences* 32:15–25.

Schneider, W., and R. M. Shiffrin. 1977. "Controlled and Automatic Human Information Processing." *Psychological Review* 84:1–66.

Segall, M., D. Campbell, and M. J. Herskovits. 1966. *The Influence of Culture on Visual Perception*. New York: Bobbs-Merrill.

Sellars, W. 1963. "Empiricism and the Philosophy of Mind." In *Science, Perception, and Reality*, 127–96. London: Routledge and Kegan Paul.

Shapiro, J. 2005. "A 21st Century View of Evolution: Genome System Architecture, Repetitive DNA, and Natural Genetic Engineering." *Gene* 345:91–100.

Shariff, A. F., and A. Norenzayan. 2007. "God Is Watching You: Priming God Concepts Increases Prosocial Behavior in an Anonymous Economic Game." *Psychological Science* 18:803–9.

Shaw, G. B. 1960. "The Revolutionist's Handbook and Pocket Companion." In *Plays by George Bernard Shaw*. New York: Penguin.

Sherkat, D. E. 2002. "Sexuality and Religious Commitment in the United States: An Empirical Examination." *Journal for the Scientific Study of Religion* 41:313–23.

Sherman, S. J., R. B. Cialdini, D. F. Schwartzman, and K. D. Reynolds. 2002. "Imagining Can Heighten or Lower the Perceived Likelihood of Contracting a Disease: The Mediating Effect of Ease of Imagery." In *Heuristics and Biases: The Psychology of Intuitive Judgment*, edited by T. Gilovich, D. Griffin, and D. Kahneman, 98–102. Cambridge: Cambridge University Press.

Shiffrin, R. M., and W. Schneider. 1977. "Controlled and Automatic Human Information Processing II: Perceptual Learning, Automatic Attending, and a General Theory." *Psychological Review* 84:127–90.

Shtulman, A. 2006. "Qualitative Differences between Naïve and Scientific Theories of Evolution." *Cognitive Psychology* 56:170–94.

Silk, M. 2006. "Hold the Prayers." *Religion in the News* 9:1.

Slingerland, E. 2008. *What Science Offers the Humanities: Integrating Body and Culture*. New York: Cambridge University Press.

Sloan, R. P. 2006. *Blind Faith: The Unholy Alliance of Religion and Medicine*. New York: St. Martin's.

Sloman, S. A. 2002. "Two Systems of Reasoning." In *Heuristics and Biases: The Psychology of Intuitive Judgment*, edited by T. Gilovich, D. Griffin, and D. Kahneman, 379–96. Cambridge: Cambridge University Press.

Slone, J. 2004. *Theological Incorrectness: Why Religious People Believe What They Shouldn't*. New York: Oxford University Press.

Smith, B. H. 2009. *Natural Reflections: Human Cognition at the Nexus of Science and Religion*. New Haven, CT: Yale University Press.

Solecki, R. 1971. *Shanidar: The First Flower People*. New York: Knopf.

Solomon, M. 2001. *Social Empiricism*. Cambridge, MA: MIT Press.

Sørensen, J., P. Lienard, and C. Feeny. 2006. "Agent and Instrument in Judgements of Ritual Efficacy." *Journal of Cognition and Culture* 6:463–82.

Sosis, R. 2009. "The Adaptationalist-Byproduct Debate on the Evolution of Religion: Five Misunderstandings of the Adaptationist Program." *Journal of Cognition and Culture* 9:339–56.

Specter, M. 2006. "Political Science: The Bush Administration's War on the Laboratory." *New Yorker*, March 13, 58–69.

Spelke, E. S. 1990. "Principles of Object Perception." *Cognitive Science* 14:29–56.

———. 1994. "Initial Knowledge: Six Suggestions." *Cognition* 50:432–45.

Spelke, E. S., K. Breinlinger, J. Macomber, and K. Jacobson. 1992. "Origins of Knowledge." *Psychological Review* 99:605–32.

Sperber, D. 1994. "The Modularity of Thought and the Epidemiology of Representations." In *Mapping the Mind: Domain Specificity in Cognition and Culture*, edited by L. B. Hirschfeld and S. A. Gelman, 39–67. New York: Cambridge University Press.

———. 1996. *Explaining Culture: A Naturalistic Approach.* Oxford: Blackwell.

———, ed. 2000. *Metarepresentations: A Multidisciplinary Perspective.* Oxford: Oxford University Press.

Sperber, D., F. Cara, and V. Girotto. 1995. "Relevance Theory Explains the Selection Task." *Cognition* 57:31–95.

Staal, F. 1979a. "Ritual Syntax." In *Sanskrit and Indian Studies: Essays in Honor of Daniel Ingalls,* edited by M. Nagatomi, B. Matilal, and J. Masson, 119–42. Dordrecht: Reidel.

———. 1979b. "The Meaningless of Ritual." *Numen* 26:2–22.

———. 1984. "The Search for Meaning: Mathematics, Music, and Ritual." *American Journal of Semiotics* 2:1–57.

———. 1990. *Rules without Meaning: Ritual, Mantras, and the Human Sciences.* New York: Lang.

Stanley, A. 2007. "A Person Could Develop Occult." *New York Times,* October 14, arts and leisure section, 1, 11.

Stark, R. 1997. *The Rise of Christianity: How the Obscure, Marginal Jesus Movement Became the Dominant Religious Force in the Western World in a Few Centuries.* San Francisco: HarperCollins.

———. 2002. "Physiology and Faith: Addressing the 'Universal' Gender Difference in Religious Commitment." *Journal for the Scientific Study of Religion* 41: 495–507.

———. 2005. *The Rise of Mormonism,* edited by R. Neilson. New York: Columbia University Press.

Stark, R., and W. S. Bainbridge. 1996. *A Theory of Religion.* New Brunswick, NJ: Rutgers University Press.

Stone, V. E., L. Cosmides, J. Tooby, N. Kroll, and R. T. Knight. 2002. "Selective Impairment of Reasoning about Social Exchange in a Patient with Bilateral Limbic System Damage." *Proceedings of the National Academy of Sciences* 99:11531–36.

Streri, A., and E. S. Spelke. 1988. "Haptic Perception of Objects in Infancy." *Cognitive Psychology* 20:1–23.

Sullins, D. P. 2006. "Gender and Religion: Deconstructing Universality, Constructing Complexity." *American Journal of Sociology* 112:838–80.

Sullivan, A. 2001. "This *Is* a Religious War." *New York Times Magazine,* October 7, 44–47, 52–53.

Surian, L., S. Caldi, and D. Sperber, D. 2007. "Attribution of Beliefs by 13-Month-Old Infants." *Psychological Science* 18:580–86.

Talarico, J. M., and D. C. Rubin. 2003. "Confidence, Not Consistency, Characterizes Flashbulb Memories." *Psychological Science* 14:455–61.

Thagard, P. 1988. *Computational Philosophy of Science.* Cambridge, MA: MIT Press.

———. 1992. *Conceptual Revolutions.* Princeton, NJ: Princeton University Press.

———. 2005. "The Emotional Coherence of Religion." *Journal of Cognition and Culture* 5:58–74.

———. 2010. *The Brain and the Meaning of Life.* Princeton, NJ: Princeton University Press.

Thiessen, E. D., E. A. Hill, and J. R. Saffran. 2005. "Infant Directed Speech Facilitates Word Segmentation." *Infancy* 7:53–71.

Thompson, E. H. 1991. "Beyond the Sex Difference: Gender Variations in Religiousness." *Journal for the Scientific Study of Religion* 30:381–94.

Tillich, P. 1951. *Systematic Theology*. Vol. 1. Chicago: University of Chicago Press.

Tomasello, M. 1999. *The Cultural Origins of Human Cognition*. Cambridge, MA: Harvard University Press.

———. 2003. *Constructing a Language: A Usage-Based Theory of Language Acquisition*. Cambridge, MA: Harvard University Press.

Tooby, J., and L. Cosmides. 1992. "The Psychological Foundations of Culture." In *The Adapted Mind*, edited by J. Barkow, L. Cosmides, and J. Tooby, 19–136. New York: Oxford University Press.

Toulmin, S. 1961. *Foresight and Understanding: An Enquiry into the Aims of Science*. New York: Harper and Row.

Tremlin, T. 2006. *Minds and Gods: The Cognitive Foundations of Religion*. New York: Oxford University Press.

Trollope, A. 1963/1857. *Barchester Towers*. New York: New American Library.

Tucker, C. 2007. "Even Top Doc Had to Bow to Bush Agenda." *Atlanta Journal and Constitution*, July 15, E6.

Tuminaro, J., and E. F. Redish. 2007. "Elements of a Cognitive Model of Physics Problem Solving: Epistemic Games." *Physical Review STPER* 3, 020101-1-22.

Tversky, A., and D. Kahneman. 1982a. "Judgments of and by Representativeness." In *Judgement under Uncertainty: Heuristics and Biases*, edited by D. Kahneman, P. Slovic, and A. Tversky, 84–98. Cambridge: Cambridge University Press.

———. 1982b. "Availability: A Heuristic for Judging Frequency and Probability." In *Judgement under Uncertainty: Heuristics and Biases*, edited by D. Kahneman, P. Slovic, and A. Tversky, 163–78. Cambridge: Cambridge University Press.

———. 2002. "Extensional versus Intuitive Reasoning: The Conjunction Fallacy in Probability Judgment." In *Heuristics and Biases: The Psychology of Intuitive Judgment*, edited by T. Gilovich, D. Griffin, and D. Kahneman, 19–48. Cambridge: Cambridge University Press.

Tweney, R. 2011. "Toward a Cognitive Understanding of Science and Religion." In *Epistemology and Science Education: Understanding the Evolution vs. Intelligent Design Controversy*, edited by R. Taylor and M. Ferrari, 197–212. New York: Routledge.

Tweney, R., M. Doherty, and C. Mynatt, eds. 1981. *On Scientific Thinking*. New York: Columbia University Press.

Tweney, R. D., M. A. Upal, L. O. Gonce, D. J. Slone, and K. Edwards. 2006. "The Creative Structuring of Counterintuitive Worlds." *Journal of Cognition and Culture* 6:483–98.

Van Gennep, A. 1960. *The Rites of Passage*. Chicago: University of Chicago Press.

van Schaik, C. P., M. Ancrenaz, G. Borgen, B. Galdikas, C. D. Knott, I. Singleton, A. Suzuki, S. S. Utami, and M. Merrill. 2003. "Orangutan Cultures and the Evolution of Material Culture." *Science* 299:102–5.

Vogt, Y. 2006. "World's Oldest Ritual Discovered: Worshipped the Python 70,000 Years Ago." Translated by A. L. Belardinelli. *Appollon*. Available at http://www.apollon.uio.no/vis/art/2006_4/Artikler/python_english (accessed September 2007).

Vygotsky, L. 1978. *Mind in Society: The Development of Higher Psychological Processes*, edited by M. Cole. Cambridge, MA: Harvard University Press.

Waller, J. 2002. *Fabulous Science: Fact and Fiction in the History of Scientific Discovery*. New York: Oxford University Press.

Ward, T. B. 1994. "Structured Imagination: The Role of Conceptual Structure in Exemplar Generation." *Cognitive Psychology* 27:1–40.

Ward, T. B., M. J. Patterson, and C. M. Sifonis. 2004. "The Role of Specificity and Abstraction in Creative Idea Generation." *Creativity Research Journal* 16:1–9.

Ware, M. 2009. "Scientific Publishing in Transition: An Overview of Current Developments." Available at http://mrkwr.files.wordpress.com/2009/01/scientific_journal_publishing_-_stm_alpsp_white_paper_140906.pdf (accessed July 2010).

Wason, P. C. 1966. "Reasoning." In *New Horizons in Psychology*, edited by B. M. Foss, 135–51. Harmondsworth, UK: Penguin.

———. 1968. "Reasoning about a Rule." *Quarterly Journal of Experimental Psychology* 20:273–81.

———. 1977. "On the Failure to Eliminate Hypotheses . . . A Second Look." In *Thinking: Readings in Cognitive Science*, edited by P. N. Johnson-Laird and P. C. Wason, 307–14. Cambridge: Cambridge University Press.

Wason, P. C., and P. N. Johnson-Laird. 1972. *Psychology of Reasoning: Structure and Content*. Cambridge, MA: Harvard University Press.

Weir, A. A. S., J. Chappell, and A. Kacelnik. 2002. "Shaping of Hooks in New Caledonian Crows." *Science* 297:981.

Wellman, H. 1990. *The Child's Theory of Mind*. Cambridge, MA: MIT Press.

West, M., J. J. Sánchez, and S. R. McNutt. 2005. "Periodically Triggered Seismicity at Mount Wrangell, Alaska, after the Sumatra Earthquake." *Science* 308:1144–46.

Whitehouse, H. 1995. *Inside the Cult: Religious Innovation and Transmission in Papua New Guinea*. Oxford: Clarendon.

———. 1996. "Rites of Terror: Emotion, Metaphor, and Memory in Melanesian Initiation Cults." *Journal of the Royal Anthropological Institute* 2 (4): 703–15.

———. 2000. *Arguments and Icons: The Cognitive, Social, and Historical Implications of Divergent Modes of Religiosity*. Oxford: Oxford University Press.

———. 2004. *Modes of Religiosity: A Cognitive Theory of Religious Transmission*. Walnut Creek, CA: AltaMira.

Wiebe, D. 1991. *The Irony of Theology and the Nature of Religious Thought*. Montreal: McGill-Queen's University Press.

Wilbert, C. 2004. "Religion Stories Multiply in Media." *Atlanta Journal Constitution*, April 9, D1 and D3.

Wilde, O. 1996. *The Complete Oscar Wilde*. New York: Quality Paperback Book Club.

Wilson, D. S. 2002. *Darwin's Cathedral: Evolution, Religion, and the Nature of Society*. Chicago: University of Chicago Press.

Wimmer, H., and J. Perner. 1983. "Beliefs about Beliefs: Representations and Constraining Function of Wrong Beliefs in Young Children's Understanding of Deception." *Cognition* 13:103–28.

Wolpert, L. 1992. *The Unnatural Nature of Science*. Cambridge, MA: Harvard University Press.

Wrangham, R. W., W. C. McGrew, F. de Waal, and P. G. Heltne, eds. 1994. *Chimpanzee Cultures*. Cambridge, MA: Harvard University Press.

Yachanin, S. A., and R. D. Tweney. 1982. "The Effect of Thematic Content on Cognitive Strategies in the Four-Card Selection Task." *Bulletin of the Psychonomic Society* 19:87–90.

Yao, X., and P. Badham. 2007. *Religious Experience in Contemporary China*. Cardiff: University of Wales Press.

Zacks, J. M., and B. Tversky. 2001. "Event Structure in Perception and Conception." *Psychological Bulletin* 127:3–21.

Zacks, J. M., B. Tversky, and G. Iyer. 2001. "Perceiving, Remembering, and Communicating Structure in Events." *Journal of Experimental Psychology: General* 130:29–58.

INDEX